THE UNITED STATES
LEGAL SYSTEM

THE UNITED STATES LEGAL SYSTEM

AN INTRODUCTION

THIRD EDITION

Margaret Z. Johns
Rex R. Perschbacher

CAROLINA ACADEMIC PRESS
Durham, North Carolina

Library of Congress Cataloging-in-Publication Data
Johns, Margaret Z.
The United States legal system : an introduction / Margaret Z. Johns and
Rex R. Perschbacher. -- 3rd ed.
　p. cm.
Includes bibliographical references and index.
ISBN 978-1-61163-010-7 (alk. paper)
1. Law--United States. I. Perschbacher, Rex R., 1946- II. Title.

KF385.J64 2012
349.73--dc23

2012021341

CAROLINA ACADEMIC PRESS
700 Kent Street
Durham, North Carolina 27701
Phone (919)489-7486
Fax (919) 493-5668
www.cap-press.com

Printed in the United States of America

CONTENTS

ACKNOWLEDGMENTS

This Third Edition is only possible thanks to the hard work of a team of research assistants here at King Hall—Kurt Oldenburg, Courtney O'Brien, and Michael Palzes, all class of 2012, and especially Daniel Hoer, class of 2013, who has worked since last summer to make this revision a reality. For the book itself, I wish to thank Margaret Johns, whose dedication to the students at King Hall always shows, and my wife and colleague, Debbie, for her help and support.

Rex R. Perschbacher

It has been my great pleasure to work with Rex in developing this course and these materials. I'm grateful to my colleagues, friends, and family for their support and encouragement. As always Tim Colton at Carolina Academic Press did an outstanding job on the manuscript and cover. Most of all, my thanks to the first-year students at King Hall who have made teaching Introduction to Law an altogether wonderful experience.

Margaret Z. Johns

THE UNITED STATES LEGAL SYSTEM

CHAPTER 1

Introduction to United States Legal Education

In the United States today, the path to becoming a lawyer leads, almost invariably, through a university-based or stand-alone law school and is part of postgraduate college education. It was not always this way. This chapter will trace the history of legal education and examine the nature of legal education today.

1.1 The History of Legal Education

To help you understand the current structure and content of legal education in the United States, we will trace two historical threads that are woven into the modern curriculum. The first is the apprenticeship system which provided practical legal training from colonial days until the 20th century. The second is the academic model that moved legal education from the law office to the university campus.

1.1.1 The Apprenticeship System

From colonial and post-Revolutionary War America until the early 20th century, legal education usually involved a college education followed by an apprenticeship in a lawyer's office.[1] A student paid an established lawyer a fee

---

1. . Mark Warren Bailey, *Early Legal Education in the United States: Natural Law Theory and Law as Moral Science*, 48 J. Legal Educ. 311, 311 (1998); Charles R. McManis, *A History of First Century American Legal Education: A Revisionist Perspective*, 59 Wash. U. L.Q. 597, 601–06 (1981), *construed in* MacCrate et al., *Legal Education and Professional Development—An Educational Continuum*, 1992 ABA Sec. Legal Educ. & Admission to the B. 103–04 (hereinafter *MacCrate Report*).

to study under his tutelage.[2] Many distinguished attorneys served as apprentices including Thomas Jefferson, Joseph Story, Daniel Webster, John Adams, John Marshall, and John Quincy Adams.[3] The lawyer received cheap labor and a steady income in exchange for the use of his library, but whether the lawyer provided meaningful legal training beyond the opportunity for observation depended strictly on his interest and inclination. There was no consensus as to what a lawyer's education and training should be, how one became a lawyer, how lawyers should be regulated, or what functions a lawyer should serve.[4] In the apprenticeship system, the student simply hung around the lawyer's office, acting as a "gopher," copying legal documents, watching the lawyer work, and maybe reading Blackstone, Coke, and some regional legal texts. The quality of legal training was a hit-or-miss matter depending upon the abilities and commitment of the lawyer.

Soon, however, some lawyers gained a reputation for conscientious efforts to develop their apprentices. Eventually, these lawyers became more teachers than practitioners. The first recognized law school in the United States, Judge Tapping Reeve's school in Litchfield, Connecticut, grew from this model. Founded in 1784, it gained a national following, attracting fifty-five students in 1813, before it closed in 1833.[5] An estimated 1,000 lawyers gained their education in Litchfield where they followed a fourteen-month course of lectures based on Blackstone's *Commentaries on the Laws of England*.[6] The *Commentaries* were the assembled lectures William Blackstone delivered at Oxford beginning in 1753. Judge Reeve was a gifted teacher; his lectures organized the law methodically and outlined its primary features to provide an overview of the substantive law of England.[7] Students took detailed notes which were then transcribed into permanent notebooks.[8] They also participated in moot court

---

2. Albert J. Harno, Legal Education in the United States 19 (1953),*construed in MacCrate Report, supra* note 1, at 103. The use of masculine pronouns in this passage is not accidental; it is historical. During this period, lawyers were men; women were generally excluded from both law school and the bar. Indeed, the first woman was not admitted to practice before the United States Supreme Court until 1879 after Congress passed special legislation overruling the Court's refusal to allow her to practice. *See* David F. Pike, *High Court Gears Up for Final Stretch*, Sacramento Daily Recorder, Apr. 16, 1999, at 4.

3. *MacCrate Report, supra* note 1, at 103.

4. *Id.* at 105.

5. Harno, *supra* note 2, at 29.

6. *Id.* at 29–30; Marian C. McKenna, Tapping Reeve and the Litchfield Law School 84 (1986).

7. Harno, *supra* note 2, at 30; McKenna,*supra* note 6, at 84.

8. Harno, *supra* note 2, at 30.

for practical experience.[9] For three hours every Saturday, students were orally examined on the week's work.[10]

Several remarkable features distinguish the Litchfield School. First, formal legal education began exclusively as the creation of practitioners for practical purposes.[11] Second, Judge Reeve continued to practice law and illustrated his lectures with cases he was handling, integrating actual cases into doctrinal lectures.[12] In this approach, Judge Reeve foreshadowed the case method later introduced by Christopher Columbus Langdell at Harvard Law School in the 1870s.[13] Finally, Litchfield graduates achieved remarkable success. From its ranks came twenty-eight United States senators, 101 members of Congress, thirty-four state supreme court justices, fourteen state governors, ten state lieutenant governors, three vice presidents of the United States, three United States Supreme Court Justices, and six members of the Cabinet.[14]

1.1.2 The Academic Model

At about the same time that Judge Reeve opened his Litchfield School, university-based legal education began at the College of William and Mary in Williamsburg, Virginia. In 1779, as Governor of Virginia, Thomas Jefferson appointed his mentor George Wythe professor of "Law and Police."[15] In Jefferson's view, the new nation needed lawyers to provide leadership and they needed education in political theory, history, and moral philosophy as well as law.[16] Chairs in law rapidly expanded at other colleges,[17] although just what was being taught to undergraduates and why is uncertain.[18] The most successful early effort was at the University of Virginia, founded by Thomas Jefferson in 1825. Law was an integral part of the undergraduate curriculum, de-

---

9. *Id.*; McKenna, *supra* note 6, at 84.

10. Harno, *supra* note 2, at 30; McKenna, *supra* note 6, at 85.

11. Harno, *supra* note 2, at 30.

12. McKenna, *supra* note 6, at 85.

13. *Id.*

14. Harno, *supra* note 2, at 31.

15. Paul D. Carrington, *The Revolutionary Idea of University Legal Education*, 31 Wm. & Mary L. Rev. 527, 527 (1990).

16. Davison M. Douglas, *The Jefferson Vision of Legal Education*, 51 J. Legal Educ. 185, 185(2001).

17. *Id.* at 186.

18. R. B. Stevens, Law School: Legal Education in America from the 1850s to the 1980s 4–5 (1983).

signed to prepare future statesmen and legislators.[19] In these early days, professors lectured the students on the substantive law, relying heavily on Blackstone's *Commentaries*.[20] To be sure, the *Commentaries* had their critics, including at times Jefferson himself who feared that these well-written surveys of the law would make students too lazy in their own research and instill conservative, anti-republican values.[21] But Blackstone's *Commentaries* exerted a powerful influence on early legal education in America.

While university-based legal education began in Virginia, the modern approach to university-based legal education began with the Harvard Law School. Harvard College established a chair in law in 1816. And a separate law faculty began with Joseph Story, already a justice on the United States Supreme Court, who was appointed in 1829. Justice Story's school became very popular, with 163 students in attendance by 1844. Students earned an LL.B. (Bachelor of Laws) degree. The program consisted primarily of lectures emphasizing the common law. The Harvard faculty began writing treatises on the law, including Story's famous commentaries, and Harvard began to build a law library.[22]

As these formal law schools were emerging to train a cadre of academic lawyers in the first half of the 19th century, political forces pushed in the opposite direction, and the apprenticeship model still dominated the profession. During the populist era of Andrew Jackson's presidency, lawyers were often disdained as a professional elite, and some legislatures abolished all educational and training requirements for lawyers and simply allowed any adult citizen to become a lawyer.[23] By the Civil War, the lawyer's place in society had greatly diminished from the respect enjoyed in the Revolutionary War era. The Civil War itself adversely affected legal education. For example, with the exception of the University of Virginia, all of the law schools in Virginia were closed during the Civil War.[24] And in 1868, in North Carolina, those admitted to practice were called "twenty dollar lawyers" because that was the selling price of a law license.[25]

Following the Civil War, lawyers launched a movement to raise professional standards.[26] During the 1870s, leaders of the bar began forming pro-

---

19. *Id.*

20. W. Hamilton Bryson, *Introduction* to Essays on Legal Education in 19th Century Virginia 10–12 (W. Hamilton Bryson, ed. 1998).

21. *Id.* at 28–32.

22. Lawrence M. Friedman, A History of American Law 318–22 (2d ed. 1985).

23. *MacCrate Report, supra* note 1, at 104.

24. Bryson, *supra* note 20, at 10.

25. Robert MacCrate, *Yesterday, Today and Tomorrow: Building the Continuum of Legal Education and Professional Development*, 10 Clinical L. Rev. 805, 816 (2004).

26. *MacCrate Report, supra* note 1, at 105.

fessional associations and urging regulation of the profession.[27] As part of this effort, they began studying legal education and its relationship to admission to the bar.[28]

At the same time, leading universities began founding law schools similar to those we know today. These schools began as one-year programs which did not require any previous college attendance; two years became the norm by 1900. Most schools lacked a full-time faculty. The institution of a three-year curriculum taught by a full-time faculty was one of the major contributions of a giant in legal education, Christopher Columbus Langdell, who became dean of the Harvard Law School in 1870. Langdell required a college degree or completion of an admission test to enter Harvard Law School. In other words, instead of one or two years of undergraduate school, the Harvard law student now had to complete three years of law school on top of four years of undergraduate school. Langdell's revolution in legal education did not end with the establishment of a three-year, post-graduate curriculum. More than anyone else, Langdell conceived of legal education as the study of a science.[29] During this period, the intellectual world was infatuated with the emergence of many "new sciences," and Langdell pushed law into this academic craze.[30] We'll return to Langdell's Harvard approach in the next section when we examine the nature of legal education.

In 1878, just as Langdell was transforming legal education at Harvard, the first national bar organization, the American Bar Association, was established.[31] The ABA was a voluntary association dedicated to raising standards of the profession and improving the administration of justice. The ABA became a strong supporter of university-based legal education.[32] In 1881, the ABA passed a resolution recommending that the states adopt a standard of three years of law school training and grant apprenticeship credit for law school education. The ABA also spearheaded the establishment of an organization of "reputable" law schools, and in 1900, the Association of American Law Schools was founded (AALS) with thirty-two charter-member schools.[33] As a result of this campaign, legal educators, supported by the organized bar, created a three-year course of graduate study entirely within the law school.[34]

---

27. *Id.*
28. *Id.* at 105–106.
29. *Id.* at 106.
30. *Id.*
31. *Id.* at 105–106.
32. *Id.* at 106.
33. *Id.* at 107.
34. *Id.* at 106–108.

In 1923, the ABA issued its first list of approved law schools. A few years later, the ABA appointed the secretary of the AALS as its first full-time advisor on legal education.[35] The two associations continued their coordinated efforts to raise the standards of law schools and bar admissions.[36] By the late 1920s, only about half of the country's law schools were ABA-approved, and only about one-third of the law students attended these approved schools.[37] In 1927, *no* state as yet required attendance at law school for bar admission.[38] However, by 1928, every state, except Indiana, had a compulsory bar examination and the tide was beginning to turn.[39] By 1938, the ABA had approved 101 law schools, and they were educating about two-thirds of the nation's law students.[40] At the start of World War II, ABA-approved law schools were becoming the principal gateway to the profession.[41]

In the immediate post-war years, ABA-approved schools consolidated their position.[42] With the financial aid of the GI Bill, veterans opted for the accredited law schools.[43] In 1947 and 1948, the percentage of law students attending ABA-approved schools climbed to more than 85% of all law students.[44] The combination of wartime attrition and the GI Bill proved fatal to many unapproved, marginal law schools around the country, with California and Georgia as notable exceptions where these schools continued to thrive.[45]

Today, all but seven states require all bar applicants to have graduated from a three-year law school. California, Vermont, Virginia, and Washington permit law office study to qualify as a substitute for law school graduation; and Maine, New York, and Wyoming permit a combination of law school and law

---

35. W.K. Hobson, The American Legal Profession and the Organization Society 1890–1930 108 (1986), *construed in MacCrate Report, supra* note 1, at 111.

36. *MacCrate Report, supra* note 1, at 112.

37. *Id.*

38. *Id.*

39. *Id.*

40. *Id.*

41. *Id.*

42. *Id.*

43. *Id.*

44. *Id.*

45. *See* Stevens, *supra* note 18, at 207–09 n.32, 220–21 n.33, 244–45, *construed in MacCrate Report, supra* note 1, at 112. California has continued to use the bar examination as the exclusive control on admissions to the bar, but recently it has flirted with taking quite a contrary approach under which law schools would be required to offer certain courses of study and applicants for admission to the bar would be required to show that they had completed these courses.

office study as a substitute for law school graduation.[46] Even today the California Committee of Bar Examiners has accredited nineteen law schools which are not accredited by the ABA; and California is also home to sixteen unaccredited law schools and seven correspondence law schools.[47] Students in the last two categories must take an additional examination at the end of their first year of law study in order to continue with their legal education.[48]

The growth of ABA-approved schools is reflected by annual statistics. In 1965, 136 ABA-approved law schools enrolled 56,510 students.[49] In 1980, 171 ABA-approved schools enrolled 119,502 students. Today, there are 201 ABA-approved law schools (including the Judge Advocate General's school).[50] In the summer of 2009–10, the ABA reported law school J.D. candidate attendance of 145,239 (including 68,502 women).[51] In other words, in 2009–10, 53% of J.D. candidates were men and 47% were women.[52] The number of minorities enrolled in J.D. programs in 2009–10 was 32,505, compared to 10,575 in 1980.[53]

In 1991, ABA-approved law school faculty included 5,585 full-time faculty (1,455 women and 586 minorities); 3,718 part-time faculty (902 women and 308 minorities); 1,365 deans and administrators (722 women and 17 minorities); and 1,182 librarians (792 women and 134 minorities).[54] By fall 2008 the ABA reported that law schools employed 8,095 full-time faculty (3,134 women and 1,359 minorities); 7,729 part-time faculty (2,455 women and 777 minorities); 4,122 deans and administrators (2,491 women and 888 minorities); and 1,800 librarians (1,174 women and 315 minorities).[55]

In short, during the twentieth century, legal education in the United States was transformed from practical, ad hoc apprenticeships in law offices to a regulated, academic program of post-graduate education. Yet, these two threads—practical and scholarly—weave the fabric of legal education today and will determine how legal education evolves in the 21st century.

---

46. *MacCrate Report, supra* note 1, at 108.
47. RULES REGULATING ADMISSION TO PRACTICE LAW IN CALIFORNIA, http://www.cal-bar. ca.gov (last visited Jan. 1, 2006).
48. *Id.*
49. *MacCrate Report, supra* note 1, at 112.
50. ABA Miscellaneous Statistics, http://www.americanbar.org/content/dam/aba/migrated/legaled/statistics/charts/stats_8.authcheckdam.pdf (last visited April 5, 2012).
51. *Id.*
52. *Id.*
53. *Id.*
54. *MacCrate Report, supra* note 1, at 113.
55. ABA Miscellaneous Statistics, *supra* note 50.

1.2 The Nature of Legal Education

We'll now consider how the history of legal education influences the structure and content of legal education today. As you'll see, the two threads—scholarly and practical—create a curriculum that strives to provide students with a solid academic base while developing the skills necessary to practice law. We'll also present two relatively recent developments in legal education: (1) instruction in professional responsibility; and (2) incorporation of transnational perspectives.

1.2.1 Langdell's Harvard Model

Christopher Columbus Langdell's many innovations at Harvard provide the basic structure for much of today's law school curriculum. In addition to increasing the legal education program to three years, Langdell also divided the curriculum into courses of set units arranged in an established progression. And, to the dismay of generations of law students, he instituted final examinations. Before Langdell, "legal education ... amounted to an undemanding, gentlemanly acculturation into the profession."[56] Langdell transformed it into a competitive model wherein academic achievement determined one's professional merit and career prospects.[57] Langdell's Harvard featured large classes and high student-teacher ratios, rising to 78:1 into the 1920s.[58] Obviously, this was an inexpensive way to package legal education and was thus attractive to university administrators. But by far the most significant innovation was Langdell's conception of legal education as the study of a "science."[59]

Langdell held that law "consists of certain principles or doctrines" and that those scientific principles "are contained in printed books."[60] Langdell believed that legal education should occur in the classroom, not the law office; he flatly rejected the traditional apprenticeship system.[61] According to Langdell, even

---

56. Bruce A. Kimball, *Students' Choices and Experience During the Transition to Competitive Academic Achievement at Harvard Law School, 1876–1882,* 55. J. Legal Educ. 163, 164 (2005).

57. *Id.* at 165.

58. *MacCrate Report, supra* note 1, at 113.

59. *Id.* at 106.

60. Steven H. Leleiko, *Legal Education—Some Crucial Frontiers,* 23 J. Legal Educ. 502, 504 (1971) (quoting Address by Dean Christopher Columbus Langdell, Harvard Law School Association, 1886).

61. *See* John J. Costonis, *The MacCrate Report: Of Loaves, Fishes, and the Future of American Legal Education,* 43 J. Legal Educ. 157, 160 (1993).

though legal education was professional education, it belonged in the academic university because its object was to teach "legal science" through the case method.[62] Some critics argued that law was simply a trade like plumbing and that legal education had no place on a university campus. The economist Thorsten Veblen is said to have remarked, "Law schools belong in the university no more than schools of dance."[63] Responding to this argument, Langdell explained:

> First, that law is a science; secondly, that all the available materials of that science are contained in printed books. If law be not a science, a university will best consult its own dignity in declining to teach it. If it be not a science, it is a species of handicraft, and may best be learned by serving an apprenticeship to one who practices it.[64]

In the case method, students read and discuss the appellate decisions of judges in individual disputes litigated in court. For example, to learn about assault and battery, students read a judge's decision resolving a dispute between two individuals who engaged in a fistfight and sued each other for the injuries they suffered. In contrast, Blackstone's *Commentaries,* which had previously served as the backbone of legal education, provided a generalized overview of the substantive law. Langdell's case method looked at law through the microscope of individual judicial decisions, rejecting sweeping summaries in favor of precise, individual analysis. The casebook (collecting these individual decisions) and the library were the law school's laboratory.[65] As Langdell explained, law was a science to be studied in the library which "is to us all that the laboratories of the university are to the chemists and physicists, the museum of natural history to the zoologist, the botanical garden to the botanists."[66]

In Langdell's view, by studying the cases on a subject, the student would learn the legal doctrines which they embody. Since, in this view, law was a sci-

---

62. *Id.*

63. Kenney Hegland, Introduction to the Study and Practice of Law in a Nutshell 344 (3d ed. 2000).

64. Charles Warren, History of the Harvard Law School 374 (1908); C.C. Langdell, *Address Delivered at the 250th Anniversary of Harvard College,* 3 L.Q. Rev. 123, 124 (1887) (hereinafter *Harvard Address*), *construed in* Edwin W. Patterson, *The Case Method in American Legal Education: Its Origins and Objectives,* 4 J. Legal Educ. 1, 3 (1951).

65. *See* Costonis, *supra* note 61, at 160.

66. *Harvard Address, supra* note 64, *construed in* Edwin W. Patterson, *The Case Method in American Legal Education: Its Origins and Objectives,* 4 J. Legal Educ. 1, 3 (1951).

ence to be studied by scholars, law teachers did not need any practical experience in the profession. Rather, they required only academic training. As Langdell explained: "What qualifies a person, therefore, to teach law is not experience in the work of a lawyer's office, not experience in dealing with men, not experience in the trial or argument of causes—not experience, in short, in using law, but experience in learning law."[67] This observation reflected Langdell's view that he was educating legal scientists, not training lawyers to practice law.

Initially, Langdell's innovations proved wildly unpopular with law students who deserted his classes in droves, fleeing to Boston University which opened across the river from Cambridge in 1872.[68] But Langdell's approach proved irresistible to university administrators who succumbed to the low-cost, high-return pedagogy.[69] Ultimately, Langdell's method triumphed and survives today in many ways. Much of your first-year curriculum is the direct descendant of Langdell's 19th-century Harvard curriculum.

The survival of Langdell's model has assured law schools a place in the modern university while providing the profession with an educational program that raises the standing and the standards of the bar.[70] Because this elevation of the profession coincided with its goals, the ABA embraced the Langdell model. By supporting this model, the ABA could both advance competence within the profession and control the number and, perhaps, the ethnic and religious derivation of new entrants to the bar.[71] If anything, law schools today are more than ever an academic arm of higher education, and have moved further from the profession. Langdell would be pleased.

1.2.2 Practical Professional Training

The Harvard model continues to dominate legal education, despite the rejection of Langdell's view that law is a "science." However, a countervailing strand in legal education has consistently emphasized a practical approach, an element that probably can be traced to the apprenticeship method and the Litchfield Law School. The legal realist movement of the first half of the 20th century supported this view.

---

67. J.W. HURST, GROWTH OF AMERICAN LAW 263 (1950) (quoting Langdell).
68. Kimball, *supra* note 56, at 166.
69. Costonis, *supra* note 61, at 160–61.
70. *MacCrate Report, supra* note 1, at 106.
71. Costonis, *supra* note 61, at 162.

The realists argued that law is not a science at all. In their view, law must be understood not as a set of rules and doctrines, but as an instrument for effecting social policy. Laws are not eternal, abstract principles residing in the library, said the realists, but the products of a rough-and-tumble political system with real-world consequences. Rosco Pound, who somewhat ironically later became dean of Harvard Law School himself, labeled Langdell's legal science "mechanical jurisprudence" and argued that common law judges should engage in social engineering to make law serve the good of society.[72] To the realists, law students must not only ask, "What is the rule?" (which Langdell would answer by locating an appellate case on the question in the law library), but also "What good is the rule for society?" and "What effects does it have in the real world?" We'll now briefly consider this reform movement.

The legal realists of the 1920s and 1930s examined law in the context of the Roaring Twenties, the Great Depression, and the New Deal. They believed that social progress would come through legislative reform.[73] They strived to make the curriculum more functional and to "make legal education more efficient and more policy-oriented by integrating law with the social sciences."[74] In emphasizing the need for an interdisciplinary approach, the realists echoed Thomas Jefferson's call for broadly educating lawyers not just in the law, but also in history, political theory, and moral philosophy.[75]

In the 1920s, Alfred Zantzinger Reed was a leader of the movement for more practical education. Pessimistic about the resources available for legal education, Reed believed that law schools should allocate their modest resources among three critical components:

1. Practical training (skills instruction);
2. Technical knowledge (doctrinal or substantive course coverage); and
3. General education (interdisciplinary, policy-oriented inquiry).[76]

---

72. Stephen M. Feldman, *The Transformation of an Academic Discipline: Law Professors in the Past and Future (or Toy Story Too)*, 54 J. LEGAL EDUC. 471, 483 (2004).

73. Laura G. Holland, *Invading the Ivory Tower: The History of Clinical Education at Yale Law School*, 49 J. LEGAL EDUC. 504, 507 (1999).

74. *Id.*(quoting Laura Kalman, LEGAL REALISM AT YALE 1927–1960 (Chapel Hill, 1986)).

75. Douglas, *supra* note 16, at 185.

76. Costonis, *supra* note 61, at 164.

Reed also believed that legal education's principal mission was to train practitioners of private law,[77] and he urged law schools to "reduce theoretical instruction to the smallest possible proportions."[78]

Echoing Reed's call for practical training, the legal realist Jerome Frank attacked the Harvard model and charged that by following Langdell, legal education had allowed itself to be "seduced by a brilliant neurotic."[79] To Frank, "the neurotic escapist character of Langdell stamped itself on the educational programs of our leading law schools … [to such an extent that] the Langdell spirit choked legal education."[80] Frank considered the case system to be "myopic."[81] Perhaps the different approaches of Langdell and Frank can be explained by their professional careers: Frank practiced law for nineteen years, some ten of which involved trial work,[82] and he accused Langdell of spending his career hidden in the library, "a cloistered, bookish man, and bookish, too, in the narrow sense."[83] In Frank's view, Langdell had a "snobbish disdain" for trial courts where legal battles are primarily fought.[84]

From his days in the trial-court trenches, Frank concluded that the real reasons for a particular legal outcome are not always reflected in the judge's decision. Indeed, the official version may, in fact, politely disguise political and social prerogatives. To Frank, the formal decision might be nothing but a dressed-up and rationalized version of the most blatant exercise of power and privilege. As he explained, the decision's sanitized language often masked the ugly truth behind it:

> On that score the history of zoning is illuminating. California was the first state to sustain a zoning ordinance. The ordinance in question prohibited the carrying on of certain kinds of businesses except within prescribed boundaries. The historians tell us that the secret of this first victory for zoning is to be found in the name of the case— *In re Hang Kie*—in the fact that the case was decided in California,

---

77. Alfred Z. Reed, *Training for the Public Profession of the Law* (Carnegie Found. Bull. No. 15, New York 1921), *construed in* Costonis, *supra* note 61, at 164.

78. *See* Costonis, *supra* note 61, at 164.

79. Jerome Frank, *A Plea for Lawyer Schools*, 56 YALE L. J. 1303, 1303 (1947).

80. *Id.* at 1304.

81. *Id.* at 1304; *see also* Jerome Frank, *Clinical Law School*, 81 U. PA. L. REV. 907 (1932–33); Jerome Frank, *Both Ends Against the Middle*, 100 U. PA. L. REV. 20 (1951) (hereinafter *Both Ends*).

82. Jerome Frank, *Are Judges Human?* 80 U. PA. L. REV. 17, 30 n.31 (1931).

83. Frank, *supra* note 79, at 1303; *see also* Douglas D. McFarland, *Self-Images of Law Professors: Rethinking the Schism in Legal Education*, 35 J. LEGAL EDUC. 232, 233 n.4 (1985).

84. Costonis, *supra* note 61, at 164.

and in the further fact that the businesses named in the ordinance were the 'businesses of a public laundry or washhouse where articles are washed and cleansed for hire'—businesses at that time almost completely usurped by Chinese. Racial prejudice was the true basis of the decision. According to the historians, had the court accurately reported the reasons for the decision, the opinion would have read: 'Chinese are obnoxious yellow aliens who should stay where they belong and not come into 'white' neighborhoods.' But the conventions proscribed such faithful reporting of the reasons for decisions. Instead, the opinion states, in due form, rules which are syllogistically linked to facts so as to seemingly compel the decision.[85]

Rejecting Langdell's visions of law as a pristine science of rules embodied in judicial decisions, Frank also rejected Langdell's approach to legal education as an academic discipline to be studied in the law library. In its place, Frank proposed a clinical lawyer-school which he described in this way:

> Each law school would build its teaching around a legal clinic. The clinic would be in charge of full-time professors who had varied experience in practicing law…. The students, as apprentices, would engage in every kind of legal service rendered by law offices…. Theory and practice would constantly intertwine.[86]

In Frank's view, substantive courses should be sharply reduced because they only serve to teach the case method which he thought could be achieved with intensive training in just one or two subjects.[87] (Frank suggested contracts and torts.) The other substantive courses could be better learned through reading texts on many legal topics.[88] Frank's opponents argued that this approach limited the time available for studying legal doctrine through case analysis. Frank responded that the "relatively simple technique" of analyzing appellate cases could be learned "in about six months."[89] In his view, the three years of law school "is squandered by bored students, in applying that technique over and over again—and never with reference to a live client or a real lawsuit—to a variety of matters."[90]

---

85. Frank, *supra* note 82, at 37 (footnotes omitted).

86. *Both Ends*, *supra* note 81, at 29–30, *construed in* Costonis, *supra* note 61, at 164.

87. *See* Costonis, *supra* note 61, at 165.

88. *Both Ends*, *supra* note 81, at 31, *construed in* Costonis, *supra* note 61, at 165.

89. JEROME FRANK, COURTS ON TRIAL 225,*quoted in* Steven H. Leleiko, *Legal Education—Some Crucial Frontiers*, 23 J. LEGAL EDUC. 502, 509–10 (1971).

90. *Id.*

Thus, as we trace the academic and apprenticeship approaches historically, we see how they shape the content and structure of legal education today. In the Langdell tradition, large classes of students study appellate cases as a scholarly body of knowledge. Law schools today also recognize the value of interdisciplinary study as advocated by Reed. And, as Frank urged, students learn practical skills and apply them in the context of actual practice in law school clinics. And the ABA and the AALS have somewhat paradoxically supported all three approaches. As we have seen, these organizations were founded to improve the professionalism of the bar and vigorously supported Langdell's model of heightened academic standards for admission to practice. But now, the ABA and the AALS are vocal advocates of the view that law schools should also prepare students for the actual practice of law through interdisciplinary studies as well as clinical and skills training.[91]

1.2.3 Late Twentieth-Century Developments

The late twentieth century brought two new fields into the mainstream of legal education: (1) professional ethics and responsibility; and (2) transnational legal perspectives. This section will outline these developments.

First, following the Watergate scandal of the 1970s, the public demanded that law schools provide formal instruction in legal ethics, and the ABA ultimately adopted an accreditation standard to achieve that goal.[92] The ABA standard requires that every student "receive substantial instruction in ... the history, goals, structure, values, rules and responsibilities of the legal profession and its members."[93] In addition, in 1996, the ABA adopted an additional standard calling on law schools to "offer substantial opportunities for ... student participation in pro bono activities."[94] We'll briefly consider both these standards.

---

91. *MacCrate Report, supra* note 1, at 138–40.

92. N. William Hines, *Ten Major Changes in Legal Education Over the Past Twenty-Five Years,* AALS News, Aug. 2005, at 4–5.

93. ABA Standards and Rules of Procedure for Approval to Law Schools, Standard 302(a)(5), http://www.americanbar.org/content/dam/aba/publications/misc/legal_education/Standards/2012_standards_chapter_3.authcheckdam.pdf (last visited Apr. 5, 2012).

94. ABA Standards and Rules of Procedure for Approval to Law Schools, Standard 302(b)(2), http://www.americanbar.org/content/dam/aba/publications/misc/legal_education/Standards/2012_standards_chapter_3.authcheckdam.pdf (last visited Apr. 5, 2012).

Under Standard 302(a), law schools offer a professional responsibility course addressing the formal regulation of lawyers, including requirements for bar admission and mechanisms for discipline. The course examines the ABA Model Rules of Professional Conduct and other professional responsibility codes. It helps students understand the special—and sometimes conflicting—responsibilities a lawyer bears as both a zealous advocate and an officer of the court. In addition to covering the formal regulation of lawyers, the course attempts to sensitize students to the hidden pitfalls of practice that can trip up even the most well-intentioned lawyer. This formal course is supplemented—albeit somewhat sporadically—by teachers who integrate ethical issues into other law school courses so that professional responsibility issues are pervasive in the curriculum.

The standard encouraging students to participate in pro bono activities is designed to make the exhortation to devote time to pro bono service more than an empty platitude. As Mark Twain recognized, "To do right is noble. To advise others to do right is also noble and much less trouble to yourself."[95] Pro bono opportunities in law school serve several goals including educating students about their professional responsibility to provide pro bono representation, delivering legal services to underrepresented groups, providing students with practical experience, and exposing students to the shortcomings of our legal system.[96]

Simply put, our legal system fails to provide equal justice. Studies find that four-fifths of the civil legal needs of the poor are unmet and that a huge number of indigent criminal defendants receive inadequate representation.[97] Underrepresented groups include victims of domestic violence, criminal defendants, juveniles facing delinquency charges, immigrants seeking asylum, children needing special education, elders baffled by social services and health care bureaucracies, communities threatened by environmental hazards, and poor people with healthcare and housing needs.[98] Proponents of pro bono opportunities in law school believe that students who participate in pro bono service will better understand their ethical obligation to provide legal services to the indigent and generate "long term commitments that will 'trickle up' to the profession generally."[99]

---

95. Deborah L. Rhode, *Professionalism in Professional Schools,* 27 Fla. St. U. L. Rev. 193, 193 (1999).

96. *Id.* at 200–01.

97. Deborah L. Rhode, *Pro Bono in Principle and in Practice,* 53 J. Legal Educ. 413, 431 (2003).

98. Report, AALS Equal Justice Project 1 (2002).

99. Rhode, *supra* note 95, at 200–01.

The second development, the incorporation of transnational perspectives, recognizes that today we live in a global legal environment. One legal education scholar placed "Globalization of Law and Legal Practice" at the top of his list of ten major changes in legal education over the past twenty-five years.[100] International law is no longer an exotic field for a few specialized practitioners. Commercial transactions, intellectual property rights, pandemic medical responses, security from terrorism, and environmental regulation are just a few obvious areas needing transnational legal approaches. United States lawyers play important roles in both public and private international law. To be effective practitioners, increasingly United States lawyers must understand international law and must be sensitive to transnational perspectives. As Professor Sexton observed:

> [W]e can be certain that over the next century the world will become smaller and increasingly interdependent; and we can be sure that law will provide the basis of economic interdependence and the foundation of human rights. The rule of law will permeate an emerging global village, touching societies it never has touched. And, importantly, the success of this new community will depend in large part upon the integration and accommodation of disparate traditions through law.[101]

Lawyers in the global legal community are committed to promoting human rights, stable justice systems, and economic growth through the rule of law.[102] The ABA, for example, has established a Center for Rule of Law Initiatives and is expanding programs in Africa, Asia, Central Europe, Eurasia, and Latin America.[103] These programs strive to promote judicial reform, develop independent legal systems, improve legal education, combat corruption and human trafficking, and promote gender equality.[104] Through these programs, ABA members have contributed more than $150 million in pro bono assistance in the past fifteen years.[105] The recent ABA International Law Symposium convened over 400 judges, lawyers, and leaders from more than forty countries on five continents to consider "how the rule of law can help solve

---

100. N. William Hines, *Ten Major Changes in Legal Education Over the Past 25 Years,* AALS News, Nov. 2005, at 4–5.

101. John A. Sexton, *'Out of the Box': Thinking About the Training of Lawyers in the Next Millennium,* 43 S. Tex. L. Rev. 623, 626 (2002).

102. Michael S. Greco, *Advancing the Rule of Law,* A.B.A. J., Jan. 2006, at 6.

103. *Id.*

104. *Id.* You may wish to check out the symposium website at www.rolsymposium.org.

105. *Id.*

our pressing global problems, from terrorism and corruption to disease and poverty."[106]

The AALS has recognized the need to adopt a global legal perspective, and at its 2005 annual meeting it offered two related programs: "Educating Lawyers for Transnational Challenges," and "Transnational Law: What is it? How Does it Differ from International Law and Comparative Law."[107] At the conclusion, the AALS unanimously adopted a resolution approving the formation of the International Association of Law Schools (IALS).[108] Since 2005, the IALS has provided a forum for its members to meet regularly to discuss the importance of legal education in an increasingly globalized world. Its Mission Statement lists its goals as:

(a) To foster mutual understanding of and respect for the world's varied and changing legal systems and cultures as a contribution to justice and a peaceful world;

(b) To enhance and strengthen the role of law in the development of societies through legal education;

(c) To serve as an open and independent forum for discussion of diverse ideas about legal education;

(d) To contribute to the development and improvement of law schools and conditions of legal education throughout the world;

(e) To contribute to the better preparation of lawyers as they increasingly engage in transnational or global legal practice, and when they pursue careers other than private practice, including governmental, non-governmental, academic, and corporate careers;

(f) To share experience and practices regarding legal education.[109]

Legal education has responded to this challenge in a number of ways. First, many schools have increased their offerings in international and comparative law.[110] Second, others have adopted a pervasive approach, integrating inter-

---

106. *Id.*

107. Louis Del Duca, *Introduction to Educating Lawyers for Transnational Challenges,* 23 Penn St. Int'l L. Rev. 741 (2005).

108. Carl Monk, *What Kind of Machinery Can Be Set in Place on an International Basis so that the Process Can Continue in a Constructive Manner in the Years Ahead?* 23 Penn St. Int'l L. Rev. 749, 750 (2005).

109. International Association of Law Schools, http://www.ialsnet.org/ (last visited April 5, 2012).

110. Claudio Grossman, *Techniques Available to Incorporate Transnational Components Into Traditional Law School Courses: Integrated Sections; Experiential Learning; Dual J.D.s; Semester Abroad Programs; and Other Cooperative Agreements,* 23 Penn St. Int'l L. Rev. 743, 745 (2005).

national perspectives throughout the curriculum.[111] Third, many schools have initiated international programs which follow a number of different models. Some attract students, lawyers, and graduates from around the world to study in either the basic three-year program or in advanced degree or summer programs. Others have education-abroad or student-exchange programs, either for a semester, an academic year, or for the summer.[112] Some schools are using their network of faculty and alumni contacts to encourage scholarly exchange programs and international conferences.[113] Fourth, students from around the world participate in international moot court competitions.[114] And finally, some law schools have helped establish clinical programs to serve emerging democracies and developing countries or to litigate international human rights cases.[115] New ideas and innovations in legal education are emerging to tackle the need for transnational understanding, discourse, and cooperation.[116]

1.3 Legal Education Today

Legal education today draws from and builds on Langdell's Harvard tradition, Reed's interdisciplinary approach, and Frank's clinical model. The historical tension between the academic and the practical aspects of legal education survives, but with a growing recognition that both are appropriate and necessary components of a professional education. In addition, law schools today instruct their students in professional ethics and responsibilities so that they can navigate their way through the ethical challenges they will inevitably face. And, finally, legal education today seeks to incorporate transnational legal perspectives so that law graduates will be able to practice effectively in a global legal environment.

---

111. Stephen H. Legomsky, *Globalization and the Legal Educator: Building a Curriculum for a Brave New World,* 43 S. Tex. L. Rev. 479, 487–89 (2002).

112. Grossman, *supra* note 111, at 745.

113. Dean John B. Attanasio, *Partnerships, Joint Ventures and Other Forms for Building Global Law Schools,* 18 Dick. J. Int'l L. 483, 486–87 (2000).

114. Grossman, *supra* note 111, at 745.

115. *See, e.g.,* Lawrence M. Grosberg, *Clinical Legal Education in Russia: "Da and Nyet,"* 7 Clinical L. Rev. 469 (2001); Haider Ala Hamoudi, *Toward a Rule of Law Society in Iraq: Introducing Clinical Legal Education into Iraqi Law Schools,* 23 Berkeley J. Int'l L. 112 (2005); Grossman, *supra* note 111, at 745–46.

116. Louis F. Del Duca, *Symposium on Developing Mechanisms to Enhance Internationalization of Legal Education,* 22 Penn St. Int'l L. Rev. 393 (2004); see also *Globalizing Legal Education—Symposium,* 23 Penn St. Int'l L. Rev. 741–807 (2005).

1.3.1 The Academic Context of Legal Education

In the Langdell tradition, many law schools are university-based. Like Langdell's Harvard, they generally require an undergraduate degree, require attendance for three years, divide the curriculum into substantive legal topics, have large class sizes, and assign grades based on final examinations. Although contemporary scholars reject Langdell's view that law is a science, many courses continue to be taught using cases as the raw material for examining legal doctrines. Moreover, law schools today have expanded the scope of doctrinal instruction to new fields including environmental law, intellectual property, and international law. Reflecting the growing inclusion of women and minorities in law school communities, feminist jurisprudence and critical race theory have emerged to challenge fundamental assumptions about law and the legal system. In this way, Langdell's academic tradition has evolved to encompass developing areas of the law and legal analysis.

This expansion of the academic side of legal education has led to wide-ranging interdisciplinary inquiries which Alfred Zantzinger Reed would have applauded. Recent decades have seen in the expansion of a host of "Law and ..." courses, including Law and Psychology, Law and Medicine, Law and Economics, Law and Literature, and Law and Technology. Indeed, in 2004, more than 800 full-time law faculty members in law schools around the nation held PhDs along with their law degrees.[117] This interdisciplinary approach reflects our growing recognition of the interrelationship between law and other fields. It also serves as a bridge between Langdell's view of law as a self-contained science discernible from legal materials alone and Reed's view that legal education should be interdisciplinary and policy oriented.

On the other hand, in the Frank tradition and in response to pressure from the practicing bar, law schools have developed extensive skills and clinical instruction to better prepare their students for the actual practice of law. Indeed, skills instruction is considered by some to be "the most significant development in legal education in the post-World War II era."[118] Courses in pretrial skills, client counseling, negotiations, trial practice, and alternative dispute resolution (ADR) have become an established part of the curriculum. In addition to classroom instruction in lawyering skills, simulated exercises and live-client clinics are widespread as are externship opportunities with judges,

---

117. N. William Hines, *Ten Major Changes in Legal Education Over the Past 25 Years*, AALS News, Nov. 2005, at 1.

118. *MacCrate Report, supra* note 1, at 6.

criminal defense attorneys and prosecutors, government agencies, public interest firms, and other practitioners.

The importance of skills instruction in legal education was underscored by the ABA's Task Force on Law Schools and the Profession: Narrowing the Gap, which was formed to study and improve the ways new members of the profession are prepared for practice. In 1992, the Task Force issued its report entitled *Legal Education and Professional Development—An Educational Continuum* which is generally referred to as the MacCrate Report after its editor Robert MacCrate. The report describes the legal profession and considers the fundamental skills and values of a competent and responsible lawyer.

The MacCrate Report encourages law schools to provide instruction to help students develop ten fundamental lawyering skills:

1. Problem solving;
2. Legal analysis and reasoning;
3. Legal research;
4. Factual investigation;
5. Communication;
6. Counseling;
7. Negotiation;
8. Litigation and alternative dispute resolution procedures;
9. Organization and management of legal work; and
10. Recognizing and resolving ethical dilemmas.[119]

In addition to identifying and describing these skills, the MacCrate Report is designed to serve as a prospectus for law students entering law school and to increase their appreciation of the need to acquire professional skills.

In the decade after the MacCrate Report was issued, law schools responded. While law faculties initially resisted its recommendations, studies show that law school curricula have changed significantly in response to the report. For example, a recent ABA report on curricular changes from 1992 to 2002 concluded:

> [O]ne pronounced trend has been the growth in opportunities for students to gain practical experiences in representing clients within supervised clinical settings and the proliferation of courses emphasizing discrete professional skills, such as factual investigation, interviewing, counseling, negotiation, mediation, and litigation—the core agenda of the MacCrate Report.[120]

---

119. *Id.* at 138–40.
120. Hines, *supra* note 118, at 2.

As skills instruction in law schools developed to train students to be both legal scholars and also legal professionals, law schools have faced the vexing question of their mission. If we are preparing students to practice law, what should we be teaching them beyond the substantive law? The academic dimension trains students to understand and analyze the law and legal problems. The skills curriculum teaches students to apply that knowledge to solving a client's problem. This combination of academic and skills instruction reflects one conception of a successful legal education:

> Legal education, when it is done successfully and well, will produce graduates who will be good lawyers, technically proficient in, at, and with the law—persons who understand how to engage in legal analysis and the construction and assessment of legal argument, who understand and can employ adeptly and imaginatively legal doctrines and concepts, and who can and will bring skills and knowledge of this sort regularly and fully to bear upon any matter of concern to any client willing and able to employ them in order to further the client's interest, provided only that they, as lawyers do not do what the law prohibits lawyers from doing for clients.[121]

1.3.2 Law School Values and Ethics

But many condemn a model of professional education which ignores or marginalizes professional responsibilities and values, especially in light of the legal profession's privilege and power. Since lawyers have a monopoly on access to our legal system, we are responsible for the rule of law and the quality of justice in our country. As explained above, the ABA has adopted standards requiring the formal teaching of professional standards, ethics, and values.[122]

In your view, is this instruction in ethics, responsibilities, and values appropriate in law school? Is it possible? If so, what values should we teach? How? What about the values that brought you to law school? Why are you here? What do you expect of your legal education? What do you expect from

---

121. Richard Wasserstrom, *Legal Education and the Good Lawyer*, 34 J. Legal Educ. 155, 156 (1984).

122. ABA Standards, Interpretations, and Rules of Procedure of the Section of legal Education and Admission to the Bar, Standard 302(a)(5), http://www.aba net.org/legaled/standards (last visited Jan. 2, 2006).

a legal career? As you begin your professional education, reflect on your personal goals and values. What do you expect law school to contribute to fulfilling your goals and informing your values?

Historically, students enter law school for a number of reasons listed here in descending order: (1) to continue intellectual growth; (2) to increase earning power; (3) to enter a profession with high prestige; (4) to better serve humanity; (5) to satisfy employment requirements; (6) to improve one's ability to change society; (7) to engage in political activities; (8) to study law for its intrinsic interest; (9) to see whether one likes it; (10) to prepare for an academic career; (11) to find oneself.[123]

Another survey reflects alternative goals for you to consider.[124] Of the 300 students who participated, 41% said that being admired for their honesty and integrity was their main professional goal.[125] Twenty-six percent hoped to contribute to important legal decisions.[126] Sixteen percent wanted to be recognized for their professional accomplishments.[127] Eight percent aspired to attain high-level management positions.[128] And only 5% said their main goal was to become wealthy.[129] As you think about your education, consider these reasons and any others that brought you to law school and how they reflect your personal values.

In reflecting on your personal values, consider the values stressed by legal education today, which include rationality, accountability, and process.[130] As Professor Auerbach explains, most law teachers would agree that rationality is a basic value because "[a] body of law is more rational and civilized when every rule it contains is referred articulately and definitely to an end which it subserves, and when the grounds for desiring that end are stated or are ready to be stated in words."[131] This is not to say that moral sensitivity, personal values, and social awareness are excluded from the analysis. Rather, rationality requires that they be explicitly exposed and evaluated. For example, one could

---

123. Carl Auerbach, *Legal Education and Some of Its Discontents*, 34 J. LEGAL EDUC. 43, 52 (1984).

124. Jennifer L. Reichert, *Law Students Are Altruists at Heart*, TRIAL, Jan. 1999, at 100 (reporting on the Key Education Resources survey of 300 law students).

125. *Id.*

126. *Id.*

127. *Id.*

128. *Id.*

129. *Id.*

130. Auerbach, *supra* note 124, at 58–65.

131. *Id.* at 58 (quoting Oliver W. Holmes, *Path of the Law, in* COLLECTED LEGAL PAPERS 186 (1920)).

argue in support of anti-discrimination laws on the grounds that bigotry is morally wrong and that elimination of bias will create a more just society. This argument is based on morality, personal values, and social awareness; it is also completely rational.

Official accountability is the second value Professor Auerbach identifies in legal education.[132] The legal order in a democratic society demands accountability. In law schools across the country, virtually every significant exercise of public power is subjected to constant analysis and debate. While they frequently disagree on specific issues, law professors would uniformly support the value of this academic scrutiny of our governmental institutions. Some call on law schools to serve as the conscience of the legal system and its administration.[133]

A third value identified by Professor Auerbach is process.[134] Law school studies conflicts—between individuals, between citizens and their government, and between the branches of government. Because the conflicts reflect fundamental differences in our views of ourselves and our institutions, for our system to enjoy the confidence and respect of society, we must believe that the mechanisms for resolving these conflicts are fair. As a democratic society, we agree to abide by decisions with which we disagree because we accept the process and hope that through this process we will ultimately prevail through peaceful change, not revolution. For this reason, in legal education, process is highly valued and rigorously examined.

While rationality, accountability, and process are hallmarks of legal education, they do not address the values necessary to practice law responsibly. The MacCrate Report undertook the task of identifying and examining the fundamental values of the profession. It identified four fundamental values:

1. As members of a profession dedicated to serving clients, lawyers should be committed to attaining and maintaining a level of competence in their field of practice and representing clients competently.[135]
2. As members of a profession bearing a special responsibility for the quality of justice, lawyers should promote justice, fairness and morality in their daily practice, contribute to fulfilling the profession's responsibility to ensure that legal services are available to those who cannot afford to pay for them, and contribute to fulfilling the profession's

---

132. *Id.*
133. Wasserstrom, *supra* note 122, at 160–61.
134. Auerbach, *supra* note 124, at 65.
135. *MacCrate Report, supra* note 1, at 207–12.

responsibility to enhance the capacity of the law and legal institutions to do justice.[136]

3. As members of a self-governing profession, lawyers should participate in activities designed to improve the profession, assist in the training of new lawyers, and strive to rid the profession of bias based on race, religion, ethnic origin, gender, sexual orientation, or disability.[137]

4. As members of a learned profession, lawyers should seek out opportunities to increase knowledge and improve skills while selecting employment that will allow professional development and the pursuit of personal goals.[138]

Do these values reflect your understanding of a lawyer's responsibilities? In particular, what do you think of the view that lawyers should promote justice, fairness, and morality in their daily practice? Should law school concern itself with your moral education?

In 2003, the steering committee of the Best Practices project of the Clinical Legal Education Association added a provision articulating the goal for law schools to strive to develop the characteristics of good lawyers.[139] If the goal of legal education is to train good lawyers, then we need to understand what a good lawyer is.[140] In Professor Wasserstrom's view, the concept of a good lawyer would include "care always to assure just and decent treatment of clients and all other persons affected by the client, concern always manifested about the justness and goodness of the choices made concerning the claims vindicated and defended, and interest and concern for the justness and goodness of the existing system of law."[141] To Professor Wasserstrom, a responsible person does not assist another in achieving some objective without considering the moral worth of the goal. The morality question does not vanish simply because one is charging a fee for the assistance; indeed, this exacerbates the problem. Moreover, a responsible person considers the morality not just of the end but also of the means. And a responsible person develops and nurtures character traits of cooperativeness, compassion, and honesty. Thus, a responsible lawyer must consider the moral worth of every professional undertaking and strive to serve goodness and justice. This view would require

---

136. *Id.* at 213–15.

137. *Id.* at 216–17.

138. *Id.* at 218–21.

139. MacCrate, *supra* note 25, at 823–24.

140. Wasserstrom, *supra* note 122, at 155.

141. *Id.*

legal education to undertake a normative assessment of legal doctrine and its application in order to promote justice and goodness. The moral context is central; for as Justice Holmes observed, the law "is the witness and external deposit of our moral life."[142]

Professor Wasserstrom's concept of the good lawyer tackles directly the notion of a lawyer as an amoral hired gun. How does the good lawyer practice in our adversary system which assumes that the truth emerges from the clash of spirited advocacy and that the lawyer must subordinate personal values in deference to client autonomy? This question has no simple nor single answer. For some, the solution is to limit their practice to causes which are consistent with their conceptions of the public interest.[143] Others are willing to serve clients with whose goals they disagree so long as they refuse to take any action on behalf of a client that the lawyer would not take on his or her own behalf with a clear conscience.[144] And still others will serve any client's interests so long as the representation does not violate the law or the rules of professional conduct. Are they all good lawyers?

While lawyers disagree on what is required to be a good lawyer, we all share the special responsibility for performing pro bono service. A few years ago, the AALS appointed a commission to examine how law schools should achieve the goal of ensuring that their students understand the obligation to perform pro bono legal services.[145] The AALS Commission on Pro Bono and Public Service Opportunities concluded:

> Our central recommendation is that law schools make available to all law students at least once during their law school careers a well-supervised law-related pro bono opportunity and either require the students' participation or find ways to attract the great majority of students to volunteer.[146]

This Commission's conclusion is supported by a survey revealing that 95% of the deans of American law schools shared the belief that "it is an important goal of law schools to instill in students a sense of obligation to perform pro

---

142. Auerbach, *supra* note 124, at 62 (quoting Oliver W. Holmes, *Path of the Law, in* COLLECTED LEGAL PAPERS 186 (1920)).

143. *Id.* at 60 (explaining Joseph L. Rauh, Jr.'s personal ethical standard).

144. *Id.* at 61.

145. "Learning to Serve," The Findings and Proposals of the AALS Commission on Pro Bono and Public Service Opportunities (AALS October 1999) (copy on file with author).

146. *Id.* at 4.

bono work during their later careers."[147] Unfortunately, a 2005 survey of 3,000 law graduates by Professor Deborah L. Rhode suggests that law schools are falling short of this goal.[148] It found that only 1% of the sample reported that pro bono issues were addressed in orientation programs or professional responsibility courses.[149] Moreover, only 3% of the graduates felt that their faculty supported pro bono service or that their school provided adequate opportunities for public interest work.[150] As Professor Rhode concluded, "Equal justice under law is an ideal exalted in law schools' commencement rhetoric and marginalized in their curricula."[151]

But some positive developments may help law schools better fulfill this goal. Specifically, the AALS Equal Justice Project convened nineteen colloquia across the nation.[152] The colloquia explored ways that law schools can more effectively address the equal justice issues which plague our country.[153] The Project's report catalogues the many equal justice activities undertaken in American law schools today, highlights the best programs, and could stimulate a new commitment to equal justice work in law schools. It proposes the "creation of a permanent network of law schools and faculty dedicated to the promotion of equal justice work."[154]

While the debate continues to be refined,[155] law schools have reached a fair degree of consensus as to their mission. First, we must provide instruction in law and legal institutions, skills, and legal doctrine. Second, we must provide students with an understanding of their professional responsibilities. And third, we must ensure that students understand their special responsibility to provide access to justice for the poor and underrepresented. In fact, most of us agree with Professor Merryman that teaching students the existing law is only the starting point for legal education. More importantly, our goal is to develop our students' abilities to discharge their ethical and professional responsibilities, to perform legal analysis, to distinguish the relevant from the irrelevant, to deal with a mass of facts in an authori-

---

147. *Id.* at 2.

148. Deborah L. Rhode, *Survey Indicates Little Emphasis on Public Service,* NAT'L L. J., Sept. 12, 2005, at 18.

149. *Id.*

150. *Id.*

151. *Id.*

152. Report, AALS Equal Justice Project, *supra* note 146, at 1.

153. *Id.*

154. *Id.*

155. *The Professional Responsibilities of Professional Schools,* 49 J. LEGAL. EDUC. 23, 23–95 (1999).

tative way, to put together careful and persuasive arguments on any side of a legal question, and to think constructively about social problems and their solution.[156]

Indeed, the dialogue exploring conflicting values and social morality is essential to solving legal problems in a healthy democracy. And the peaceful resolution of these conflicts under the rule of law is the goal of our legal institutions. As Justice Anthony Kennedy explained: "Law cannot live in the consciousness of a people without an abiding belief in the principles of individual responsibility, rationality, and civility. No group is more eager or more receptive to a recommitment and a rededication to the rule of law and to these principles than the present generation of law students and those who have just graduated."[157]

Today, our responsibilities extend beyond our own legal institutions. United States lawyers play an increasingly important role internationally, and legal education is responding to enable lawyers to practice effectively in a global environment. Terrorism, torture, and human rights abuses respect no boundaries and require international solutions. Global warming, protection of endangered species, and air and water pollution are just a few of the many international environmental problems. In the internet age, international crimes—including financial con games and the transmission of child pornography—are easy to commit and hard to stop. The global tragedy of AIDS and the potential threat of a flu pandemic require international responses to protect human life without sacrificing human freedom. And in the commercial context, United States lawyers negotiate contracts and litigate commercial disputes around the world. Free trade agreements and the global agenda of the World Trade Organization promise to increase the internationalization of all commercial activity. As these examples illustrate, we live in an age of interaction and interconnection which the world has never known. Addressing global problems and conflicts will require respect for and understanding of transnational perspectives to achieve cooperative and collaborative legal solutions.

1.3.3 Tuition Costs and Law School Rankings

A clear understanding of your reasons for attending law school is perhaps more important today than ever before. Law school tuition rates have been

---

156. John H. Merryman, *Legal Education There and Here: A Comparison*, 27 Stan. L. Rev. 859, 871 (1975); *see also* Costonis, *supra* note 61, at 169; Auerbach, *supra* note 124, at 43.

157. Justice Anthony M. Kennedy, *Law and Belief*, Trial, July 1998, at 26.

rising dramatically in recent years. Between 1987 and 2005, the average cost of tuition at public law schools increased by 448%.[158] In 1986, tuition and fees at public law schools averaged $2,063 (roughly $4,000 when adjusted for inflation).[159] By 2008 this cost had risen to $16,836.[160] Rapidly rising tuition rates have led many students to borrow extremely large sums of money in order to finance their education. According to the Office of Management and Budget, the total balance of unpaid student loans in the United States was $730 billion dollars in 2010.[161] These massive levels of debt are of particular concern to many recent law school graduates who have struggled to find work in the wake of the most recent economic recession.

In 2000, more than 90% of graduates from ABA-accredited law schools were employed.[162] Most of these graduates worked in private practice at firms that offered progressively increasing salaries.[163] However, the percentage of employed law school graduates has steadily declined each year since 2007, and fell more than 4% from 2009 to 2011.[164] In fact, a recent report by the Bureau of Labor Statistics predicted that the legal services sector will most likely add the fewest number of new jobs among all the professional occupations over the next ten years.[165]

In spite of these alarming employment trends, law school applications continue to rise. In 2009, for example, 86,600 aspiring lawyers submitted applications to law schools, a 4% increase from the previous year.[166] Of these, 58,400 candidates were admitted to at least one law school, and 48,900 matriculated—a 5% increase from the previous admission cycle.[167] Moreover, the ABA accredited three new law schools in 2008, increasing the number of future law school graduates by over 400.[168] And as of 2011, five new law schools are in the process of awaiting ABA approval.[169]

---

158. William S. Howard, *The Student Loan Crisis and the Race to Princeton Law School*, 7 J.L. Econ. & Pol'y 485, 486–87 (2011).

159. *Id.*

160. *Id.*

161. *Id.*

162. Daniel S. Harawa, *A Numbers Game: The Ethicality of Law School Reporting Practices*, Geo. J. Legal Ethics 607, 609 (2011).

163. *Id.*

164. *Id.* at 610.

165. *Id.* at 611.

166. *Id.*

167. *Id.*

168. *Id.*

169. *Id.*

These figures raise an interesting question: with competition for admission so high and post-graduation employment prospects so low, why are students applying to law schools in greater numbers than ever before? A 2011 article in the Journal of Law, Economics and Policy examined this question and concluded:

> "Factors such as social misperceptions of the legal profession, a feeling of imperviousness to the legal recession, and lack of available jobs post college graduation all probably contributed to the increase in law school applications, despite frightening employment prospects. What also has likely contributed is a lack of holistic knowledge on the part of the prospective students ... many students financed expensive educations under the assumption that the post-graduation jobs and average salaries advertised by schools and school ranking magazines would be available to them."[170]

In recent years, the reporting practices used by law schools to provide information to encourage students to attend law school have come under attack. According to Standard 509 of the ABA Standard for Approval of Law Schools, all ABA-approved law schools are required to "publish basic consumer information [that] shall be published in a fair and accurate manner reflective of actual practice."[171] This information, which is published on school websites and in brochures for prospective students, includes admission data, bar passage rates for the school, the percentage of students employed upon graduation, and other salary information. In theory, any school that fails to report accurate information is in danger of losing its accreditation status.[172] However, in real life there is an enforcement gap and most schools are not held accountable for their reporting methodologies.[173]

For example, even though a reported 87.6% of the class of 2010 were employed at nine months after graduation, a closer examination by NALP revealed that 29% of those were neither full-time nor permanent jobs, and only 68.4% of those jobs required bar passage.[174] Furthermore, roughly 2.7% of

---

170. *Id.* at 612.

171. Standard 509 of ABA Standard for Approval of Law Schools, available at: http://www.lawschooltransparency.com/documents/ABA_Standards/2011-2012/2011-2012_Chapter5.pdf.

172. Daniel S. Harawa, *A Numbers Game*, at 608.

173. *Id.*

174. Debra Cassens Weiss, *A Record Low for 2010 law Grads: Only 68% Have Jobs Requiring Bar Passage*, ABA JOURNAL (June 1, 2011, 7:57 AM), http://www.abajournal.com/news/article/a_record_low_for_2010_law_grads_only_68_have_jobs_requiring_bar_passage.

these jobs were created by law schools themselves in order to raise employment numbers, meaning the real employment rate for the class of 2010 would have otherwise been closer to 85%.[175] Unfortunately, many law schools are not making these important distinctions when reporting and publicizing employment data.[176] As one recent article explained, "a number of schools hire recent graduates temporarily to coincide with reporting deadlines. Graduates that are waiting tables, performing temp work reviewing documents, and volunteering are all considered employed for reporting purposes."[177]

Perhaps a degree of distortion can be expected, and might even be tolerated were it not occasionally accompanied by even greater misrepresentations. Unfortunately, it has now been revealed that some schools are going beyond simply relying on questionable reporting practices and have actually been reporting false and misleading information. For example, in 2011, Villanova Law School admitted it had been "knowingly" reporting false information to the ABA for "years".[178] Despite this open admission, the ABA has failed to discipline Villanova Law School and is allowing the school to retain its accreditation status notwithstanding the school's clear violation of the ABA Standards of Accreditation.[179]

Unquestionably, there are strong incentives for schools to publish favorable statistics regardless of their accuracy. As one law school dean recently explained, "[t]here are millions of dollars riding on students' decisions about where to go to law school, and that creates real institutional pressure."[180] Furthermore, the information reported to the ABA under Standard 509 is the same information the schools must use when reporting to the U.S. News and World Report for their rankings.[181]

Each year, the U.S. News & World Report uses the information reported to the ABA to compile the rankings of American law schools, and a recent survey of law students revealed that the single most important factor in their decision to select a law school was the school's ranking.[182]

---

175. Id.

176. Daniel S. Harawa, A Numbers Game, at 610.

177. Id.

178. Id. at 612.

179. Id.

180. Id.

181. Id. at 615.

182. Shocked About Kaplan's Survey Results? New Information Comes to Light, Law School Transparency (Dec 3, 2010, 12:04 PM), http://www.lawschooltransparency.com/2010/12/shocked-about-kaplans-survey-results-new-information-comes-to-light.

As one article aptly summarized:

> "The legal education system is caught in a vicious cycle that favors (if not encourages) the gaming of statistics. The best students want to go to the highest ranked schools, so that they in turn will get the most prestigious and highest paying jobs, and therefore as alumni will have more money to donate back to the school. For law schools, therefore, the higher they are in the rankings, the better situated they are as profit-making enterprises ... This then creates a continually perpetuated cycle because the only enforcement mechanism in place is the practically non-existent risk of a law school losing accreditation."[183]

Recently, the *US News & World Report's* director of data research, Robert Morse, publicly recognized the need to portray a more accurate picture of legal employment in its next annual rankings.[184] However, unless the ABA takes a firmer stance on regulating self-reporting practices by law schools, a commitment by *U.S. News* may not do very much to solve the problem.[185]

1.4 Discussion Questions

1. For many years, you have served as legal counsel to the members of a family in a variety of matters. When the parents died, their son Samuel and daughter Dena each inherited about $750,000. Samuel is unmarried but has an 11-year-old child, Clara, who lives in his home under his care. You now represent Samuel in business, investment, and estate planning matters. From things Samuel has told you in confidence and from things you have observed about him, you have concluded that he has developed a serious drug addiction that makes him unfit to take care of himself, his estate, and Clara. Now Dena has come to you and asked you to do something about the situation.[186]

You research the California law of conservators and discover that a relative such as Dena is allowed to petition the court for appointment of a conservator for a person in Samuel's position; the conservator is authorized to run the

---

183. Daniel S. Harawa, *A Numbers Game*, at 612–13.

184. *Id.* at 615.

185. *Id.*

186. Reprinted from M.D. Schwartz, R.C. Wydick, R.R. Perschbacher & D.L. Bassett, Problems in Legal Ethics (9th ed. 2010) and R.C. Wydick, R.R. Perschbacher & D.L. Bassett, California Legal Ethics (7th ed. 2010) with permission of the West Group.

person's affairs until the court orders otherwise.[187] If Samuel does not want a conservator, he can oppose the petition and turn the matter into an adversary proceeding. You know from your prior dealings with Samuel that he will adamantly oppose the petition.

In talking with Dena, you are concerned about a possible conflict of interest and fear that any proceedings may involve information you obtained from Samuel in confidence. After talking with Dena, you research the applicable rules of professional responsibility. Under the ABA Model Rules:

> When the lawyer reasonably believes that the client has diminished capacity, is at risk of substantial physical, financial or other harm unless action is taken and cannot adequately act in the client's own interest, the lawyer may take reasonably necessary protective action, including consulting with individuals or entities that have the ability to take action to protect the client and, in appropriate cases, seeking the appointment of a guardian ad litem, conservator or guardian.[188]

On the other hand, three California ethics committees have concluded that the lawyer must *not* petition the court to have a guardian appointed. These opinions reason that petitioning for a guardian would involve the misuse of client information and create a conflict of interest since the lawyer would be bringing an action against a present client. Further, the lawyer must not permit the interest of others (like Dena and Clara) to undermine loyalty to the client.

   a. What should you do? Is the problem solved by simply following the California ethics opinions?

   b. Does your answer depend on whether you are acting as a lawyer for Samuel or whether you are a close friend and influential advisor?

   c. If you believe the answer is different depending on your role as a lawyer or a friend, how can that be?

   d. Should law school teach you to answer these questions? If law school should teach you to answer these questions, how should it do that?

2. You are a probate lawyer who has written a will for an elderly client, Ellen, who has several grown children. Her health is quite fragile and failing. Her will provides that her estate shall be divided equally among her children. One day Ellen phones to ask you to change the will because the youngest child, Daniel, has just taken part in a public celebration of same-sex partnerships

---

187. CAL. PROB. CODE §§ 1800–1835 (West 1991).
188. MODEL RULES OF PROFESSIONAL CONDUCT RULE 1.14(b) (2002).

which received widespread media attention, including photographs and news footage of Daniel and his partner. Ellen wants to disinherit Daniel. You know from your past consultations with Ellen that she has always dearly loved Daniel and that she tends to react impulsively to events and then to regret decisions made in anger. You understand that Ellen is upset about Daniel's participation in the ceremony and the resulting publicity. But you believe that in time she will change her mind about disinheriting Daniel and would deeply regret the hurt it would cause him. You fear that if you change the will, Ellen might die or become incapacitated while the will excluding Daniel is operative. In your view, this will would not reflect Ellen's true long-term wishes and would be extremely emotionally painful to Daniel. What should you do?

a. Should you follow your client's instructions and rewrite the will since the underlying mother/child relationship is really not your concern and beyond your professional expertise?

b. Should you raise these issues and discuss them with your client? ABA Model Rule 2.1 provides that as an advisor "a lawyer shall exercise independent judgment and render candid advice. In rendering advice, a lawyer may refer not only to law but to other considerations such as moral, economic, social and political factors, that may be relevant to the client's situation." What does this rule require you to do in Ellen's case?

c. Should you delay rewriting the will, giving Ellen an excuse about the time it will take to accomplish the job in order to give her a cooling off period?

d. Should your own personal views on same-sex partnerships influence your handling of the matter? If not, how can you prevent your views from influencing—perhaps very subtly—your view of the matter and your relationship with your client?

e. Should law school teach you to answer these questions? If law school should teach you to answer these questions, how should it do that?

CHAPTER 2

INTRODUCTION TO THE UNITED STATES LEGAL PROFESSION

In this chapter we will provide an overview of the legal profession by outlining a number of its most significant features including: (1) the regulation of lawyers; (2) the number of lawyers in the United States; (3) the gender and racial diversity of the bar; and (4) the settings in which lawyers practice.

2.1 The Regulation of Lawyers

In the United States, lawyers are regulated by the individual states in which they practice. Thus, to be licensed to practice in New York, lawyers are required to meet New York admission requirements and pass the New York bar examination. There is no official American or national bar association. The "American bar" refers to all the lawyers in the United States, each licensed by state law. And the American Bar Association (ABA), as we learned in the last chapter, is a voluntary professional organization devoted to the improvement of the profession and the administration of justice.

Since each state determines the requirements for admission to practice, there is some variation nationally. The requirements are usually established by the state supreme court or the state legislature or both. As you know, most states require graduation from an accredited law school, but others accept other qualifications. In addition to the educational requirements, applicants must take a state bar examination which generally lasts two or three days. Finally, applicants must satisfy the state's moral character standards which are designed to screen out potentially unscrupulous practitioners. Once they are admitted to practice, lawyers are generally governed by the state's official bar association to which all the state's lawyers belong. These associations are usually authorized by the state legislature or supreme court to handle bar admissions and discipline. In many states, the legislature has given the state supreme court jurisdiction over these matters which it delegates to the state bar, subject to supreme court review.

Unlike England where lawyers are licensed as barristers or solicitors, in the United States lawyers are authorized to engage in any type of law practice without meeting specialization requirements. Today, however, specialization is increasing to keep pace with the increasing complexity of the law. Reflecting this trend, many states have developed programs to recognize specialists. For example, in California all lawyers may appear in state appellate courts. But lawyers who satisfy additional training and experience requirements may qualify as "certified specialists" in appellate practice. Now that lawyer advertising is permitted, this certified specialty may become a valuable marketing tool.

What if a lawyer admitted in one state has a client who is sued in another state? Can the lawyer represent the client in that dispute? Generally, the lawyer cannot appear without being admitted in the sister state. Occasionally, a court may admit a lawyer to appear in a particular case (*pro hac vice*) if there is a special need. But in most cases, states have historically limited the practice of law to members of their own state bar. Apart from appearing in court, can lawyers who are not licensed in a state give legal advice to clients in that state? The historical answer is that advising a client in a state where one is not licensed would constitute the unauthorized practice of law. A few states recognize other states' lawyers under reciprocity agreements, but most do not.

Recently, these restrictions have come under attack. Critics argue that they are economically inefficient,[1] and are "largely motivated by parochial attempts to protect lawyers from outside competition."[2] Today, in recognition of the practical realities of interstate and international practice, a number of states are relaxing the historical restrictions.[3] In 2002, after two years of effort,[4] the ABA adopted a model rule for multijurisdictional practice (MJP) in specified situations.[5] Since Model Rule 5.5 was promulgated, fourteen states have adopted the rule more or less verbatim, and twenty-nine have adopted some version

---

1. Michael J. Thomas, *The American Lawyer's Next Hurdle: The State-Based Bar Examination System*, 24 J. Legal Prof. 235, 236 (2000).

2. Arthur F. Greenbaum, *Multijurisdictional Practice and the Influence of Model Rule of Professional Conduct 5.5—an Interim Assessment*, 43 Akron L. Rev. 729, 768 (2010).

3. Mark Hansen, *MJP Picks up Steam*, A.B.A. J. (Jan. 1, 2004 2:19AM), http://www.abajournal.com/magazine/article/mjp_picks_up_steam.

4. *Id.*

5. Model Rules of Professional Conduct Rule 5.5.

of it.[6] Even some additional states that have not yet officially adopted this rule have elected to follow it in certain cases.[7]

However, state variations in MJP regulation have created some confusion and conflicts.[8] For example, under the California rule, MJP is limited to lawyers who work as in-house counsel for businesses and public interest lawyers.[9] Separate provisions allow attorneys admitted in other states to practice in California temporarily.[10] But other jurisdictions remain opposed to relaxing the traditional restrictions. Montana, one of the most restrictive states, has not only rejected proposed MJP rules, but also instituted a lifetime limit of two *pro hac vice* admissions.[11] As one scholar noted, "You can drive through Montana, but that's all."[12] The disparity in *pro hac vice* limitations among jurisdictions (Florida: three per year; Rhode Island: three in five years; Virginia: twelve in a twelve-month period; and in forty-one other states: zero numerical limits)[13], illustrates the discrepancy that results from leaving MJP regulation to individual states.

Things are about to become even more complicated. The United States and nearly 150 other countries entered into the General Agreement on Trade in Services (GATS) which took effect in 2005.[14] Under GATS, member countries must publish rules regulating practice within their borders by foreign lawyers. This presents terrific opportunities for United States firms which opened at least thirty new foreign offices in 2002, reflecting the fact that "[l]egal services is one of the areas where the United States has a huge surplus in its trade with other countries."[15] As Justice Brennan once observed, rock-and-roll, blue jeans, and law are our three biggest international exports.[16] But since lawyers in the

---

6. Greenbaum, *supra* note 2, at 735.

7. See, e.g. Colmar, Ltd. v. Fremantlemedia N. Am., Inc., 344 Ill. App. 3d 977, 988, 801 N.E.2d 1017, 1026 (Ill. App. Ct. 2003).

8. *Lawyers Engaging in Cross-Border Practice Must Take Care to Know other States' Rules,* U.S. L. Week, June 21, 2005, at 2764–65.

9. California Rules of Professional Conduct Rule 964.

10. California Rules of Professional Conduct Rule 966–967.

11. Greenbaum, *supra* note 2, at 768.

12. *Lawyers Engaging in Cross-Border Practice Must Take Care to Know other States' Rules,* U.S. L. Week, June 21, 2005, at 2765.

13. Greenbaum, *supra* note 2, at 768.

14. Hansen, *supra* note 2, at 46.

15. Martha Neil, *Over There,* A.B.A. J., Apr. 2003, at 56.

16. United States v. Verdugo-Urquidez, 494 U.S. 259, 281 (Brennan, J., dissenting) (quoting Grundman, *The New Imperialism: The Extraterritorial Application of United States Law,* 14 Int'l Law. 257, 257 (1980).

United States are regulated by the individual states, our compliance with GATS will require a delicate accommodation of state regulations and international obligations. The ABA has previously adopted a Model Rule for Licensing Legal Consultants and a Model Rule for Temporary Practice by Foreign Lawyers.[17] States are developing rules to address this issue. For example, a proposed rule in Florida sets out conditions under which lawyers who are not licensed in the United States may provide temporary services in Florida.[18] An ABA task force is studying issues raised by the GATS agreement.[19]

While many see state restrictions as archaic and anti-competitive, state regulators clearly need the power to discipline lawyers for misconduct. States have traditionally been responsible for ensuring that only competent lawyers are admitted to practice and for disciplining lawyers who fall below acceptable standards. Moreover, the independence of the bar is one of its strongest traditions which requires that lawyers be free from external control except by the courts. Lawyers can only be disciplined or disbarred by their state bar or their highest state court. Some critics have argued against this tradition of independence on the grounds that nonlawyers should play a role policing the bar which might otherwise simply act as a self-protecting guild. But to many, this tradition of independence is considered essential to safeguard zealous advocacy and individual liberties and to ensure that lawyers are free to represent unpopular causes. How will this work when out-of-state and foreign lawyers are permitted to practice at least temporarily in a state without passing the state bar examination, meeting other admission standards, or joining the state bar association? What regulatory scheme can accommodate the emerging trend toward multinational practice, while ensuring professional accountability and independence? Clearly, these developments present both opportunities and challenges for the United States legal profession. One scholar notes "the United States, the leader in pushing for open legal services markets, has one of the most complicated and difficult systems for foreign lawyers. While the United States seeks to establish international standards applicable to the practice of law, internally it has fifty-four jurisdictions with fifty-four sets of requirements to practice law."[20]

---

17. *ABA Delegates Approve Proposals to Allow Some Multijurisdictional Practice by Lawyers,* U.S. L. Week, Aug. 20, 2002, at 2107.

18. *Proposed Florida Rule Would Permit Temporary Multinational Practice,* U.S. L. Week, Jan. 20, 2004, at 2411.

19. *Id.*

20. Stewart M. Young, *Whistleblowing in a Foreign Key: The Consistency of Ethics Regulation Under Sarbanes-Oxley with the WTO GATS Provisions,* 32 Denv. J. Int'l L. & Pol'y 55, 66 (2003).

In short, lawyers in the United States are admitted to practice and regulated on a state-by-state basis. Generally, lawyers are entitled to practice in any area they select, although increased specialization is altering that tradition. To ensure the independence of the profession and yet protect clients from unscrupulous practitioners, most states have adopted disciplinary systems overseen by their state supreme courts. Finally, although multijurisdictional practice is a relatively new and as yet unresolved area for regulation, it is clearly the emerging reality in today's global legal environment.

2.2 The Number of Lawyers

Many criticize the growth of the bar and condemn it as an anchor slowing progress. Indeed, some years ago a California state senator urged that the University of California law schools should all be shut down as waste of taxpayers' money. As he explained, "There is no reason the people of California should continue to pay millions of dollars a year to produce more lawyers [because] more lawyers seldom produce anything but more delay in the ongoing process of government, law, and business."[21]

In some ways, the senator was correct, for the number of lawyers has exploded since World War II. Specifically, according to the MacCrate Report, in 1947–48, there were 169,489 lawyers in the United States, a ratio of one lawyer for every 790 people.[22] This ratio was roughly the same as it had been since 1880.[23] By 1995, there were 857,931 lawyers in the United States, a ratio of one lawyer for every 303 people.[24] According to the American Bar Foundation, in 2000 there were 1,066,328 lawyers in the United States, a ratio of one lawyer for every 264 people.[25] Stated differently, since the American Bar Foundation began statistical reporting in 1949, the lawyer population has quadrupled while the general population has not even doubled.[26]

---

21. Carl Auerbach, *Legal Education and Some of Its Discontents*, 34 J. LEGAL EDUC. 43 (1984).

22. MacCrate et al., *Legal Education and Professional Development—An Educational Continuum*, 1992 ABA SEC. LEGAL EDUC. & ADMISSION TO THE B. 15 (hereinafter *MacCrate Report*).

23. *Id.* at 14–15.

24. CLARA N. CARSON, THE LAWYER STATISTICAL REPORT; THE U.S. LEGAL PROFESSION IN 1995 1(1999).

25. Barbara A. Curran & Clara N. Carson, *Growth and Gender Diversity—A Statistical Profile of the Legal Profession in 2000,* 16 RESEARCHING L. 1 (2005).

26. CARSON, *supra* note 20, at v.

As might be expected, these lawyers are not dispersed evenly throughout the country. For example, according to the 2005 ABA compilation of active, resident lawyer populations by state, Alaska had 2,309 lawyers, California had 139,371 lawyers, New York had 142,538 lawyers, and North Dakota had 1,302 lawyers.[27] Moreover, the ratio of population to lawyer varies from state to state. In 2005, for example, California had 147,100 lawyers or one practicing lawyer for every 243 people, ninth in the country.[28] This ratio may be contrasted to that of the District of Columbia which has the highest ratio of one lawyer for every ten people[29] and in last place South Carolina with one lawyer for every 463 people.[30]

Happily for all these lawyers, the growth in their ranks has been matched by the growing demand for their services. According to one survey, the growing demand for legal services has occurred in expanding or entirely new fields of practice including new business formation, mergers and acquisitions, international trade and finance, malpractice, consumer protection, environmental law, tax reform, and litigation.[31] But here again there is some truth to the senator's observations because many of these new and expanding areas of law have been designed by lawyers and reflect increased regulation of business and the economy. This increased regulation is most evident when there is competition for scarce resources (e.g., the fishing and oil industries) or conflict over social policy (e.g., toxic waste and zoning).[32] But despite the drag increased regulation arguably places on business development, since World War II "economic activity vastly expanded, new business enterprises multiplied and the number of transactions in every segment of the economy proliferated."[33] Indeed, the legal profession itself is an example of this remarkable growth climbing from a $4.2 billion-a-year service activity in 1965 to an estimated $91 billion-a-year industry in 1990.[34] And while the profession ebbs and flows with economic currents, the overall trend is for the profession to grow along with the national and international economies.

---

27. American Bar Association: Lawyer Count by State, http://www.americanbar.org/content/dam/aba/migrated/marketresearch/PublicDocuments/lawyer_count_by_state_20012011_1.authcheckdam.pdf (last visited Apr. 8, 2012).

28. Clara N. Carson, The Lawyer Statistical Report; The U.S. Legal Profession in 2005 34 (2005).

29. *Id.* at 271.

30. *Id.* at 214.

31. T. C. Fischer, Legal Education, Law Practice and the Economy: A New England Study 77 (1990) quoted in *MacCrate Report, supra* note 18, at 17 n.12.

32. *Id.*

33. *MacCrate Report, supra* note 18, at 17.

34. *Id.* at 18.

Despite this boom in the legal profession, we are failing to serve significant and unmet legal needs. The raw number of lawyers obscures the unavailability of legal services for many. Studies suggest that 90% of poor people cannot obtain legal help for their serious legal problems.[35] Today, nationally there is one legal aid attorney for 6,861 poor people.[36] In some areas the unmet need is even greater. For example, in Los Angeles, there are one million poor people eligible for legal aid, but only forty legal aid lawyers.[37] As one observer remarked, "No matter how you cut it, forty lawyers cannot meet the needs of a million people."[38] And the soaring cost of legal services makes lawyers out of reach for middle-class people and small businesses as well. A critical challenge to our profession is developing programs to meet these needs.

2.3 The Gender and Racial Diversity of the Bar

In 1970s and 1980s, law schools began to enroll significant numbers of women along with racial and ethnic minorities. Their presence has changed legal education, the law, and the legal profession in both subtle and striking ways. In this section, we will briefly review this historic development and sketch out some of the challenges still impeding the profession's goals of eliminating gender and racial bias and fully serving our diverse country.

2.3.1 Gender Diversity

The entry of women into law schools and the legal profession has been dramatic and accelerating. In each year before 1971, less than 3% of lawyers were women.[39] By 1980 women amounted to only 8% of the bar (44,185 women lawyers). By 2000 they comprised 27% of the bar (288,060 women lawyers),[40]

---

35. Scott L. Cummings, *Access to Justice in the New Millennium—Achieving the Promise of Pro Bono*, Hum. Rts., Summer 2005, at 8.

36. Anat Rubin, *Study: Legal Aid Cannot Meet Needs of Most Poor People*, Daily Recorder, Oct. 10, 2005, at 2.

37. *Id.*

38. *Id.*

39. Barbara A. Curran & Clara N. Carson, *Growth and Gender Diversity—A Statistical Profile of the Legal Profession in 2000*, 16 Researching L. 1, 7 (2005).

40. *Id.*

and in 2010, 31% of bar members were women.[41] The number of women enrolling in law school continues to climb. In 1965, 4.2% of J.D. candidates were women (2,374 women law students);[42] in 1980, 33% of J.D. candidates were women (40,834 women law students);[43] and in 2010, 44% of J.D. candidates were women (68,502 women law students).[44] Given their late entry into the bar, it is not surprising that the median age for women lawyers is younger than for men lawyers. Specifically, in 2000 the median age of men lawyers was forty-eight years and the single largest group was fifty-two years old.[45] In contrast, in 2000 the median age of women lawyers was forty years and the single largest group was thirty-nine years old.[46]

As they began to enter the profession, women followed different career paths than men. A smaller percentage entered private practice while a larger percentage of women went into government, private associations, legal aid, and public defender offices.[47] While employment patterns are tending to converge in recent years, women lawyers remain overrepresented in government, legal aid, public defender programs, judicial support staff, and among law firm associates.[48] They remain underrepresented as judges and law firm partners.[49] Today women attorneys comprise only 16% of corporate general counsel at Fortune 500 companies.[50]

Today in the judiciary, women comprise just 26% of all federal and state-level judgeships (or 5,015 seats), while men occupy 74% of all seats (14,335).[51] In some jurisdictions, the numbers are even more disproportionate. For example, in the U.S. Northern District of New York (a region with 26 counties), there are no women judges despite a pool of 359 female candidates serving as judges on New York State benches.[52]

---

41. The A.B.A. Commission on Women in the Profession—A Current Glance at Women in the Law 2011, http://www.americanbar.org/content/dam/aba/uncategorized/2011/cwp_current_glance_statistics_2011.authcheckdam.pdf (last visited Apr. 8, 2012).
42. *MacCrate Report, supra* note 18, at 18.
43. *Id.*
44. A Current Glance at Women in the Law, *supra* note 42.
45. Curran & Carson, *supra* note 35, at 8.
46. *Id.*
47. *MacCrate Report, supra* note 18, at 20.
48. Curran & Carson, *supra* note 35, at 9.
49. *Id.*
50. The White House Project—By the Numbers, http://benchmarks.thewhitehouseproject.org/page/by-the-numbers (last visited Apr. 8, 2012).
51. A Report of the Center for Women in Government & Civil Society—Women in Federal and State Level Judgeships Spring 2010, http://www.albany.edu/womeningov/judgeships_report_final_web.pdf.
52. *Id.*

Despite remarkable progress over the past two decades, women continue to struggle to overcome bias and to break through the glass ceiling which impedes their progress to the higher echelons in private practice. Each year, The National Association of Women Lawyers (NAWL) conducts a national study that tracks the professional progress of women in the nation's 200 largest law firms.[53] According to NAWL:

> Women play a surprisingly small role in the highest levels of law firm leadership ... The average firm's highest governing committee counts women as only 15% of its members—and about 14% of the nation's largest firms have no women at all on their governing committees ... The advancement of women lawyers into the role of managing partner is even more disproportionate. In 2006, only 5% of managing partners in the largest firms in the country were women. Three years later, in 2009, only 6% of women occupy this role.[54]

Moreover, given the same qualifications, men are still twice as likely to be offered a partnership in law firms,[55] and women attorneys that do advance to the highest levels of partnership still find that they earn less, on average, than their male counterparts. In 2009, the median compensation for male equity attorneys was $565,200 and the median compensation for female equity attorneys was $499,350[56]—meaning that, on average, female equity partners earn only 88% of ($65,859 less than) their median male counterparts.[57] According to NAWL, "The highest compensated lawyer in the nation's largest firms continues to be male, 99% of the time. Clearly women lawyers are virtually nonexistent among the elite group of those who are compensated the most by their firms." These figures raise concerns that the average law firm in America today has not yet adopted effective strategies or practices to narrow the gap in gender inequality.[58]

As they entered the profession, women have changed the law, the practice of law, and the study of law. For example, women lawyers and scholars have

---

53. *Report of the Fourth Annual National Survey on Retention and Promotion of Women in Law Firms.* National Association of Women Lawyers and The NAWL Foundation, http://nawl.timberlakepublishing.com/files/2009%20Survey%20Report%20FINAL.pdf (last visited Apr. 8, 2012).

54. *Id.*

55. *Id.*

56. NAWL Foundation Report, *supra* note 53.

57. *Id.*

58. *Id.*

challenged previous legal standards relating to pregnancy, rape, domestic violence, and sexual harassment.[59] Women in practice have challenged the traditional structure which creates conflicts between work and family; women have sought to modify the structure to accommodate pregnancy leaves and parenting responsibilities by instituting more flexible schedules and alternative career tracks.[60] Women in academia have challenged conventional jurisprudence with feminist jurisprudence which examines legal doctrine through the lens of women's life experience.[61]

2.3.2 Racial Diversity

As law schools and the legal profession began extending opportunities to women, they also gradually began to open their doors to racial and ethnic minorities. Legal education and the legal profession were historically exclusionary. Until segregation was prohibited and civil rights legislation was passed, African Americans had few opportunities to study law. Indeed, as late as 1983, four predominately black law schools had trained the majority of the country's African-American lawyers.[62] But between 1971–72 and 1991–92, minority enrollment increased from 5,568 to 19,410.[63] In 2009, minority enrollment reached 32,505 or 22.4% of J.D. candidates.[64] Mirroring this progress, the number of African-American lawyers and judges climbed between 1980 and 1990 from 14,839 to 25,704.[65] And the percentage of all minorities in the profession has nearly doubled from about 5% in 1980 to 9.7% in 2000.[66]

While this progress has been real, minorities remain drastically underrepresented in the legal profession. Specifically, in 1970, African-American lawyers were only 1% of the total number of lawyers; by 1990 this number

---

59. *Id.* at 22.
60. *Id.*
61. *Id.*
62. *Id.* at 23.
63. *Id.* at 24.
64. ABA Statistics—First Year J.D. and Total J.D. Minority Enrollment, http://www.americanbar.org/content/dam/aba/migrated/legaled/statistics/charts/stats_8.authcheckdam.pdf (last visited Apr. 8, 2012).
65. *MacCrate Report, supra* note 18, at 25.
66. Geoffrey A. Campbell, *Slow Progress for Minorities in Law*, A.B.A. J., Sept. 1998, at 82; Miles to Go, Progress of Minorities in the Legal Profession—http://www.law.harvard.edu/programs/plp/pdf/Projects_MilesToGo.pdf.

had only risen to 3.3% of the total.[67] By 2008, the figure had risen only slightly to 4.6%.[68] The 2005 report of the ABA Commission of Racial and Ethnic Diversity in the Profession, entitled *Miles to Go: Progress of Minorities in the Legal Profession,* found that the legal profession lagged behind other key professions in terms of diversity. Specifically, less that 9.7% of lawyers in the United States are minorities, while they make up 20.8% of accountants and auditors, 24.6% of physicians and surgeons, and 18.2% of college and university professors.[69] As the ABA study concluded, although more minority students are attending law school, they continue to enter private practice at lower rates than whites, to enter fewer judicial clerkships, and to be "grossly underrepresented in top level jobs, such as law partner and corporate general counsel."[70]

Minority students remain underrepresented in law schools as well. In 2009, there were only 10,173 African Americans enrolled in J.D. programs (comprising just 7% of total enrollments),[71] and only 7.2% of law school staff and faculty members (1,635 out of 22,844 total) were African American.[72] Latinas and Latinos are also underrepresented. Specifically, in 2009 only 2,592 Mexican Americans were enrolled in J.D. programs.[73] American Indian and Alaska Native enrollment was only 1,273 in 2009.[74] On the other hand, Asian and Pa-

---

67. *MacCrate Report, supra* note 18, at 25.

68. ABA Statistics, Household Date Annual Averages, http://www.americanbar.org/content/dam/aba/migrated/marketresearch/PublicDocuments/cpsaat11.authcheckdam.pdf (last visited Apr. 8, 2012).

69. Molly McDonough, *A Long March—Report Says the Legal Profession's Efforts to Achieve Diversity Still Are at a Crawl,* A.B.A. J., Feb. 2005, at 59.

70. Theresa Osterman Stevenson, *Progress for Minority Lawyers Lacking,* Litig. News, July 2005, at 1 (quoting *Miles to Go: Progress of Minorities in the Legal Profession* by the ABA Commission on Racial and Ethnic Diversity in the Legal Profession).

71. ABA Statistics, African-American J.D. Enrollment, http://www.americanbar.org/content/dam/aba/migrated/legaled/statistics/charts/stats_13.authcheckdam.pdf (last visited Apr. 8, 2012).

72. ABA Statistics, Total Male and Female Staff & Faculty Members, http://www.americanbar.org/content/dam/aba/migrated/legaled/statistics/charts/facultyinformationbygender.authcheckdam.pdf (last visited Apr. 8, 2012).

73. ABA Statistics, Mexican American J.D. Enrollment, http://www.americanbar.org/content/dam/aba/migrated/legaled/statistics/charts/stats_14.authcheckdam.pdf (last visited Apr. 8, 2012).

74. ABA Statistics, Native American or Alaska Native J.D. Enrollment, http://www.americanbar.org/content/dam/aba/migrated/legaled/statistics/charts/stats_11.authcheckdam.pdf (last visited Apr. 8, 2012).

cific Islander enrollment was 11,327.[75] To put these numbers in perspective, it's helpful to compare them to the general population:

Table 2.1 Minorities and Women in the California Legal Profession[76]

	% of California Population	% of California Lawyers	% at UC Law Schools
Caucasian	46.7	83.0	46.1
Asian	10.9	6.0	20.3
Latino	32.4	3.7	7.7
African-American	6.7	2.4	3.3
Women	50.2	32.0	55.6

Unfortunately, the lack of racial and ethnic diversity in the profession is stark. Most recently, in 2010, a NALP data analysis of roughly 129,000 lawyers at more than 785 U.S. law firms found a slight decrease in the percentage of minority attorneys for the first time since data began being collected in the 1990s.[77] According to NALP Executive Director James Leipold,

> While the actual drop in the representation of women and minorities is quite small, the significance of the drop is of enormous importance because it represents the reversal of what had been, up until now, a constant upward trend. Prior to the recession law firms had struggled to recruit and retain a diverse workforce of attorneys, but there were small gains year after year which, over time, had begun to make a significant change in law firm workplaces. The reversal of that trend underscores how important it is for law firms to redouble their diversity efforts at this time.[78]

What explains the slow progress in achieving diversity? In the past, the ABA has cited restrictions on affirmative action and the resulting cuts in minority admissions to law schools, along with the soaring costs of higher education as primary factors.[79] Today, however, law firms primarily point to the current slump in economic conditions.[80]

---

75. ABA Statistics, Asian or Pacific Islander J.D. Enrollment, http://www.americanbar.org/content/dam/aba/migrated/legaled/statistics/charts/stats_12.authcheckdam.pdf (last visited Apr. 8, 2012).

76. *Diverse Is Yet to Come*, CAL. LAW., Nov. 2002, at 13.

77. http://www.callawyer.com/story.cfm?eid=913836&evid=1.

78. Law Firm Diversity Among Associates Erodes in 2010—http://www.examiner.com/law-schools-in-los-angeles/law-firm-diversity-among-associates-erodes-2010#ixzz1RX8eYCy9.

79. Campbell, *supra* note 66.

80. Minority Law Journal, *Diversity Scorecard 2009*, http://www.law.com/jsp/mlj/PubArticleMLJ.jsp?id=1202430425120&hubtype=Spotlight&slreturn=1&hbxlogin=1 (last visited Apr. 8, 2012).

In an effort to encourage diversity in US law firms, the Minority Law Journal has released diversity rankings for the nation's 250 largest and highest-grossing law firms.[81] The Journal's latest survey methodology reflects not only the percentage of minority attorneys at a firm, but also the percentage of minority attorneys in partnership positions.[82] The survey suggests that the current financial crisis has hindered diversity efforts. "The biggest challenge to building diversity in the past year was the economic downturn," answered O'Melveny & Myers (ranked among the top 20 firms for diversity). "The state of the economy has made us ever more mindful of the need to control expenses and ensure that the internal programs we develop and facilitate, as well as the external programs we sponsor, are the best use of our resources."[83] As the pressure for billable hours increases, mentoring and recruiting efforts tend to decrease, leading to further impediments in the push for diversity.[84] These factors, combined with the reality of a lower number of minority candidates to begin with, all contribute to the slowed growth in minority representation in the legal profession.

Despite the slow progress, there are some reasons for cautious optimism that the picture will improve. In a recent landmark decision, the United States Supreme Court upheld a law school admissions policy designed to increase minority enrollment and found that diversity in legal education was a compelling state interest.[85] As Justice O'Connor explained, diversity breaks down racial stereotypes, enlivens class discussion, and promotes cross-racial understanding for students of all races. In reaching this conclusion, the Court relied on numerous studies showing that student body diversity promotes learning outcomes, and "better prepares students for an increasingly diverse workforce and society, and better prepares them as professionals." This view was supported by major American businesses which filed a friend-of-the-court brief arguing that in today's increasingly global marketplace, necessary skills can only be developed through exposure to widely diverse people, cultures, ideas, and viewpoints. The Court emphasized the importance of education in preparing students for work and citizenship, sustaining our political and cultural her-

---

81. Minority Law Journal, *Defining Diversity: Methodology*, http://www.law.com/jsp/mlj/PubArticleMLJ.jsp?id=1202430426360.

82. *Id.*

83. Diversity Scorecard, *supra* note 80.

84. *Id.*

85. Grutter v. Bollinger, 539 U.S. 306 (2003). In 2012 the United States Supreme Court granted certiorari in Fisher v. University of Texas (docket #11-345) which means next year the Supreme Court will reconsider the use of affirmative action in university admissions.

itage, and maintaining the fabric of society. Justice O'Connor explained that law schools in particular are the training ground for our country's leaders and that all members of our heterogeneous society must believe in the openness and integrity of these institutions and have access to this gateway to leadership.

In recognition of the importance of improving diversity in the profession, the organized bar, law firms, law schools, and the business community are developing and implementing programs to address the slow progress. For example, the ABA Council on Racial and Ethnic Justice has adopted multiple strategies to further its mission.[86] It uses national news events like the law school affirmative action case to spotlight the need for equal access to justice and diversity in the profession.[87] It works with other ABA entities, state, local and ethnic bar associations, public officials, and community groups to reach young people and motivate minority students to become lawyers.[88] It held a successful conference, Diversity in the Legal Profession: Opening the Pipeline, to identify and develop strategies for increasing diversity in the profession.[89] The new ABA Diversity Center coordinates all ABA diversity initiatives and manages the Legal Opportunity Scholarship Fund.[90] Another recent conference, co-sponsored by the ABA and the Law School Admission Council, called Embracing the Opportunities for Increasing Diversity Into the Legal Profession: Collaborating to Expand the Pipeline is the beginning of a broad, new initiative among lawyers, corporate counsel, judges, law schools, and others seeking to advance diversity in the profession.[91]

Law firms, while still lacking in diversity, now understand that "diversity is key for talent, business and quality of life reasons."[92] Many firms are working with law schools to increase placement of diverse law students in summer associate programs.[93] They are also sponsoring programs for diverse law student associations, coaching moot court competitions, mentoring students, providing interviewers for mock interview programs, running job fairs, and hosting networking events.[94] Some firms have minority fellowship programs and offer part-time clerkships during the school year to help ease financial bur-

---

86. Robert A. Stein, *Working to Wipe Out Bias*, A.B.A. J., Jan. 2004, at 63.

87. *Id.*

88. *Id.*

89. *Id.*

90. Michael S. Greco, *Profession's True Colors*, A.B.A. J., Feb. 2006, at 6.

91. *Id.*

92. Patrick Lynch and Elaine Arabatzis, *Recruiting Diverse Attorneys*, NAT'L L. J. , Apr. 18, 2005, at R1.

93. *Id.* at R22.

94. *Id.*

dens. The D.C. Road Show is a program founded by African-American attorneys which presents panels around the country about private practice, interviewing techniques, and networking opportunities.[95] The group hosts a reception each summer for African-American summer associates in the Washington area.[96] These initiatives hold real promise for increasing diversity in the profession.[97]

Law schools, in addition to adopting affirmative action programs when possible, have undertaken a number of initiatives to improve diversity. Many have developed outreach programs to encourage undergraduates to consider law school and to provide them with educational support to improve their prospects for law school admission. "Street Law" classes are offered to spark high-school students' interest in legal careers. Law schools are working with law firms, minority bar associations, and individual alumni to provide networking and mentoring programs. To help financially disadvantaged students, law schools provide financial support, scholarships, and loan repayment assistance programs.

Finally, the business community recognizes that the United States population will become "majority minority."[98] In response, corporate clients are increasingly demanding that their law firms more closely reflect the diversity of their customers and clients. For example, Sara Lee Corp.'s general counsel has circulated a letter to his fellow general counsel asking them to pledge to reward law firms with good diversity records and to fire those that lack diversity.[99] This follows the 1999 letter by Charles Morgan, then general counsel of BellSouth Corp., signed by more than 500 general counsel, urging law firms to hire more women and minorities.[100] As Morgan explained, "I want diversity to look like a 707 on law firms' [radar], as opposed to a Piper Cub."[101] The general counsel for Shell Oil Company took the pledge a step further by issuing diversity report cards and then dropping hundreds of firms with failing grades.[102]

---

95. *Id.*

96. *Id.*

97. In 2010 NALP produced a detailed report of law firm diversity by major urban areas in the United States, available at: http://www.nalp.org/uploads/PressReleases/10NALP-WomenMinoritiesPressRel.pdf.

98. Stevenson, *supra* note 73, at 1.

99. Lisa Lerer, *Sara Lee GC Seeks to Turn Up Heat on Diversity*, Nat'l L. J., Aug. 30, 2004, at 10.

100. *Id.*

101. *Id.*

102. Terry Carter, *Coming Out of Her Shell — This Oil Company's General Counsel Spoke Out and Became a Champion of Diversity*, A.B.A. J., Dec. 2004, at 31.

While their numbers remain relatively small, minority lawyers have made substantial contributions to legal scholarship. Just as the prism of gender has focused legal scholarship on previously ignored areas of the law, the prism of race and ethnicity has invigorated debate over issues of concern to minority communities. As we will see in later chapters, minority scholars are taking a fresh look at established legal doctrine and challenge the conventional underpinnings of the legal system by exploring the ways in which race, ethnicity, and class influence the law.

2.4 The Settings in Which Lawyers Practice

The MacCrate Report canvassed the settings in which lawyers practice and the American Bar Foundation regularly publishes a statistical report on the legal profession. In this section we shall present a summary of this information. As you read it, consider the practice settings that are the most attractive to you in terms of your personal values and professional goals.

2.4.1 Historical Overview

Historically, American lawyers were independent sole practitioners providing general legal services according to their private clients' needs. Many only practiced law part-time and also engaged in other activities such as real estate, banking, or politics. While some lawyers shared office space or formed loose partnerships, law firms were unusual. Indeed, as late as 1872, a study reported that only fourteen law firms in the entire country had even four lawyers, three had five lawyers, and one had six.[103]

The twentieth century dramatically altered the structure of practice. In the early years of the century, businesses hired increasing numbers of lawyers to serve as in-house counsel. The progressive era focused public attention on law and social issues which led a growing number into government service. The depression era and New Deal continued this trend. By the end of World War II, three-quarters of the lawyers were in private practice.[104] Three-quarters of these practitioners were in solo practice and more that 98% of them were in solo practice or firms of fewer than nine lawyers.[105] The remaining one-quarter of the bar was in government service or employed as in-house counsel.[106]

---

103. *MacCrate Report, supra* note 18, at 30.
104. *Id.*
105. *Id.*
106. *Id.*

The second half of the century saw a steady movement from solo practice and smaller firms into larger units.[107] In the past decade, that trend has reversed. In 1995, for the first time since 1960, the proportion of private practitioners who practiced solo grew while that of practitioners in law firms dropped.[108] Moreover, between 1990 and 2000, the growth rate for both solo and firm lawyers slowed, but more so for firms than for solos.[109] Firm size and practice settings are directly related to the clients served, the type of law practiced, and the financial compensation received. Generally, solo and small firm practitioners serve predominately individual clients; larger firms in urban settings work predominately for business clients.[110]

As growing firms focused increasingly on business clients, new organizations have been developing to provide legal services to individuals of modest means and new ways to finance such services. Increasing numbers of sole and small-firm practitioners are participating in these new programs which the MacCrate Report found provided potential access to legal services for more than 70 million middle-income Americans.[111] Moreover, new organizations have expanded legal services to the poor, including publicly funded legal service programs, public defender offices, pro bono panels, public interest firms, and law school clinics.[112]

The following sections will provide an overview of these diverse practice settings. As the MacCrate Report explained, this information can be useful to you in planning your legal education and your future career. It should help you design your course of study to find employment that fits your interests and talents. Moreover, as one study concluded, "the nature of the first law job generally determines the field of substantive law in which a lawyer will specialize."[113] For this reason, to map out a well-informed and satisfying professional career, you need information about the opportunities available to you. For a quick overview of the employment prospects in the various practice settings, consider Table 2.2.[114]

---

107. *Id.* at 31; In the Spotlight, *supra* note 47, at 2.

108. *Id.*

109. Curran & Carson, *supra* note 21, at 8.

110. *MacCrate Report, supra* note 18, at 31.

111. *Id.* at 68.

112. *Id.* at 50–57.

113. *Id.* at 35 (citing F. Zemans and V. Rosenblum, The Making of a Public Profession 79 (1981)).

114. Carson, *supra* note 24, at 7.

Table 2.2 Employment Prospects[115]

% of lawyers in ...	1980	1991	2000	2005
Private Practice	68%	73%	74%	75%
Government	10%	9%	7%	8%
Private Industry	10%	9%	8%	8%
Retired/Inactive	5%	5%	5%	4%
Judiciary	4%	3%	3%	3%
Education	1%	1%	1%	1%
Legal Aid/Public Defender	2%	1%	1%	1%
Private Association	1%	1%	1%	1%

We'll now turn to a summary of these practice settings.

2.4.2 Sole Practitioners and Small Firms

As the preceding overview and table show, private practice continues to be the most numerous segment of the legal profession. According to the American Bar Foundation, as of 2005, 75% of lawyers nationwide are in private practice.[116] Of those, roughly 332,500 are solo practitioners, and 93,600 are small firm lawyers (2–5 lawyers). According to NALP, the number of recent law school graduates entering the work force as solo practitioners increased from 3.5% in 2008 to 5.5% in 2009.[117] This was the biggest one-year jump since 1982.[118] Most recently, for the class of 2010, this percentage increased to 5.7%, the highest it has been in 13 years.[119] These numbers are not surprising, given the job market faced by recent law school graduates. The recent recession has been called the worst economic stagnation since the great depression of the 1930s.[120] According to the Bureau of Labor Statistics, jobs in the legal services sector have declined by over 54,000 since May 2008.[121] Despite the decline, the employment opportunities in firm practice and solo practice have remained very stable.

---

115. Compiled by the ABA Market Research Department from *The Lawyer Statistical Report, American Bar Foundation*, 1985, 1994, and 2005 editions.

116. Carson, *supra* note 28, at 5.

117. Anika Anand, *Law Grads Going Solo and Loving It*, MSNBC (June 20, 2011 12:22 PM), http://www.msnbc.msn.com/id/43442917.

118. *Id.*

119. *Id.*

120. Cynthia Baker & Robert Lancaster, *Under Pressure: Rethinking Externships in A Bleak Economy*, 17 Clinical L. Rev. 71, 74 (2010).

121. Anand, *supra* note 117.

Table 2.3 Private Practitioners[122]

% of private practitioners ...	1980	1991	2000	2005
Solo	49%	45%	48%	48%
2–5 lawyers	22%	15%	15%	14%
6–10 lawyers	9%	7%	7%	6%
11–20 lawyers	7%	7%	6%	6%
21–50 lawyers	7%	5%	4%	6%
51–100 lawyers	7%	5%	4%	4%
101+ lawyers	*	13%	14%	16%

Solo practice, like small firm practice, primarily involves resolving disputes for individuals and small businesses in a variety of legal areas. According one study, individual disputes involved in order of frequency: post-divorce; tort (personal injury, wrongful death, etc.); property; government; debt; landlord-tenant; discrimination; and consumer complaints.[123]

Solo and small firm practice is diverse, and work setting varies with the landscape in which the firm or practice is located. Some of these lawyers work in rural communities while others are in major cities; some work in their home offices while others work in high-rise office towers; some specialize in one area of practice while others are generalists.

In recent years, the increasing complexity of the law has led to specialization among solo practitioners and small firm attorneys. As a survey by the ABA Young Lawyers Division concluded, 55% of the sole practitioners responding to the survey reported that they spent 50% or more of their time in one substantive area.[124] For those who spent three-fourths of their time in one field, the most common specialties were real estate, probate and trust, family law, torts and insurance, intellectual property, criminal law, and taxation.[125]

Often these solo practitioners and small firms market their services to middle-income clients needing relatively routine types of legal services.[126] Since the United States Supreme Court struck down bans on lawyer advertising, enterprising lawyers began setting up legal clinics to represent individuals for fixed-fees using standardized procedures which reduced costs.[127] This standardization is especially effective in highly specialized offices such

---

122. *MacCrate Report*, supra note 18; AND—2005 lawyer statistical report
123. *Id.* at 39–40.
124. *Id.* at 41.
125. *Id.*
126. *Id.* at 59.
127. *Id.*

as those handling conveyancing, personal bankruptcies, and worker's compensation, where paralegals under the lawyer's direction can handle the word-processing and form-completion chores at fees lower than a traditional law firm would charge.[128]

Criminal defense practice deserves a special comment. Today, full-time public prosecutors initiate all proceedings, and most private defense lawyers are sole and small-firm practitioners. Typically, these private defense lawyers gained experience in a prosecutors' or public defenders' office before hanging out a shingle or joining a small firm. This pattern has developed because of the difficulty of competently entering practice without substantial post-law-school training and supervision.

In fields other than criminal law, recent graduates have difficulty obtaining this professional training. As the ABA Task Force on Solo and Small Firm Practitioners cautioned, "The biggest problem that solos and smalls have is isolation."[129] Understandably, recent graduates without a mentor rely heavily on their legal education. Yet, law schools are frequently criticized for focusing on students who will join larger firms where supervision will be provided while failing to adequately prepare the students who will be practicing solo or in small firms. As the MacCrate Report concluded, "The transition from law school into individual practice or relatively unsupervised positions in small offices ... presents special problems which the law schools and the organized bar must address."[130] In response to this challenge, the ABA recently hosted the first Leadership Coalition for Solo and Small Firm Lawyers at the 2010 ABA Midyear meeting.[131] The goal of the Coalition was to discuss ways to develop policies and programs within the ABA that would promote solo and small firm lawyer success and participation in the ABA.[132] The Coalition is committed to assisting attorneys by coordinating with state and local bars, as well as by making sure that solo and small firm issues are considered at all levels of the ABA decision-making process.[133] Fortunately, the Internet is becoming a valuable resource for solo practitioners and small firms, providing networking, educational, and mentoring programs. Solo practitioners, in particular, are increasingly relying on social networking sites such as Twitter,

---

128. *Id.*

129. *Id.* at 47.

130. *Id.*

131. American Bar Association Publications: GP Solo Magazine Jan/Feb 2011, http://www.americanbar.org/publications/gp_solo/2011/january_february/division_news.html.

132. *Id.*

133. *Id.*

LinkedIn, and Facebook to generate business.[134] Online schools such as Solo Practice University[135] provide services such as website design and maintenance support, connecting recent law grads with faculty mentors, and offering hands-on courses designed to fill in the practical gaps in legal education. For an idea of the resources to solo practitioners available online, you may wish to visit the website of the ABA General Practice, Solo & Small Firm Division which includes a law student section.[136]

Finally, while small firm practice may involve litigation, television and the movies have given the public a mistaken impression of the number of lawyers actively appearing in court. Actually, in all practice settings the number of lawyers actually engaging in litigation is relatively small, and most rarely appear in courtrooms.[137] In civil litigation, much of the lawyer's time is spent in pretrial practice including interviewing and counseling clients, drafting pleadings and motions, taking depositions of witnesses, propounding and responding to interrogatories (written questions about the case), and negotiating settlements. Similarly, in criminal cases most of the lawyer's time is spent investigating the facts, negotiating the charges and plea, and working out a sentencing plan. Thus, although a precise estimate is impossible, only a fraction of the practicing bar of American lawyers regularly conducts trials or presents appellate arguments.[138]

2.4.3 Middle-Sized and Large Firms

Table 2.3 above displays the number of firms and the number of lawyers in small, middle-sized and large firms reported in American Bar Foundation surveys.[139] As you can see, less than one-third of private practitioners are in middle-sized or large law firms. We'll turn now to a discussion of these larger practice settings.

2.4.3(a) Middle-Sized Firms

According to the ABA's most recent edition of The Lawyer Statistical Report, which contains data for the year 2000, middle-sized firms of eleven to

---

134. Aviva Cuyler, *Generate Business with Twitter, LinkedIn, and Facebook*, GP Solo Magazine June 2011, http://www.americanbar.org/publications/gp_solo/2011/june/social_networkingleveragingtwitterlinkedinandfacebook.html.

135. You may wish to visit http://solopracticeuniversity.com.

136. *See* http://www.americanbar.org/groups/gpsolo.html.

137. Daniel J. Meador, American Courts 69 (2d ed. 2000).

138. *Id.*

139. Compiled by the ABA Market Research Department from *The Lawyer Statistical Report, American Bar Foundation*, 1985, 1995, and 2005 editions.

100 lawyers employed about 16% of the nation's private practitioners.[140] These firms provide a wide array of services to a diverse client base, representing both individuals and businesses. Some specialize in specific substantive areas while others offer a full line of services. They are a cross-section of private practice.[141]

Middle-sized firms can choose between competing with larger firms in providing a wide range of services to primarily business clients, or they can limit their practice by focusing on limited clients and substantive areas. Those that elect to specialize often focus on one industry such as entertainment, health, sports, publishing, or intellectual property. Others specialize in a specific area of litigation such as aviation accidents or product liability.

Middle-sized firms face different opportunities and challenges than larger firms. They generally have lower overhead costs than large firms, allowing them to charge clients lower rates than large firms.[142] Attorneys at middle-sized firms may feel closer and more connected with one another than lawyers in a huge firm.[143] Middle-sized firms may also be more flexible and better able to adapt to the specific needs of clients than large, rigid law firms.[144] On the other hand, middle-sized firms often lack the resources to handle extremely large cases spanning multiple or international jurisdictions, meaning that large firms often end up taking many of the most complex and expensive cases.[145]

While these firms recognize the necessity of adopting effective law office management to remain competitive with large firms, they have continued to view law first as a profession and second as a business, resisting the institutionalization of practice in a rigid bureaucratic model.[146] Thus, lawyers from middle-sized firms are frequently involved in bar activities to enhance the professionalism of practice and provide leadership for bar associations.[147] Because large firms have thrived since the 1960s, some experts predicted that they would overshadow and eventually replace middle-sized firms all together.[148] However, many middle-sized firms grew in size and continued to

---

140. *Id.*

141. *MacCrate Report, supra* note 18, at 73.

142. Carol M. Sanchez and Patrick E. Mears, *How the Mid-sized Survive: Survey Shows a Smaller Path for Smaller Law Firms amid The Giants*, Business Law Today, Vol. 11, Sept/Oct 2001, available at: http://apps.americanbar.org/buslaw/blt/bltsept01_sanchezmears.html.

143. *Id.*

144. *Id.*

145. *Id.*

146. *Id.* at 74.

147. *Id.*

148. Sanchez, *supra* note 142.

yield healthy profits during times when larger firms struggled to sustain profitability.[149]

2.4.3(b) Large Firms

The large firms of more than 100 lawyers have been called the "critical catalysts" of recent change in the profession.[150] The leading architect of the large firm was Paul D. Cravath who founded a New York City firm early in this century. Under his system, the firm hired top graduates right out of law school who began as associates and later were expected to become partners in the firm. They were provided a salary and training, but were let go if they failed to be promoted to partner. In this system, clients retained the firm, not the individual lawyers within the firm.[151]

Cravath's system grew and spread from New York to Chicago and Washington D.C. In part in response to the heightening of regulatory activity during the 1930s, these corporate law firms were in heavy demand. The prosperous years of the post-war period brought increased economic activity that further fueled the growth of corporate firms. By the 1950s these firms were well established, and in the 1960s they entered their "Golden Age."[152]

The 1970s and 1980s saw a transformation of the large law firm. Both the number of large firms and their size grew dramatically: the number of firms with more than 100 lawyers grew from forty-five in 1975 to 247 in 1987, and the average size of the twenty largest firms grew more than fourfold from 1968 (128 lawyers) to 1987 (527 lawyers).[153] This exponential growth reflected the system which promoted an increasing number of associates to partners and required replacing those new partners with still more associates.[154] Sustaining this growth required attracting new business. As a result, large firms became more competitive and profit-oriented.[155] They opened branch offices, marketed their services, and instituted business-like management policies.[156] The competition extended both to attracting clients and also to attracting top law school graduates through summer associate programs and generous compen-

---

149. *Id.*

150. *Id.* at 75, quoting R. H. Sander & E. D. Williams, *Why Are There So Many Lawyers? Perspectives on a Turbulent Market,* 14 LAW & SOC. INQUIRY 478 (1989).

151. *MacCrate Report, supra* note 18, at 76.

152. *Id.*

153. *Id.* at 78.

154. *Id.*

155. *Id.* at 78–79.

156. *Id.* at 79–81.

sation packages.[157] The economic consequences of the emergence of these huge firms have been extensively studied. Between 1972 and 1987, the average receipts of the twenty largest firms grew from $14.7 million to $158 million.[158] According to analysts, even adjusting for inflation, this is a fourfold increase in revenues in just fourteen years.[159] This economic growth was mirrored in the rapid increase in lawyer income in the large firms.

Because these firms depend heavily on business clients, the 1990–1992 economic downturn caused a corresponding decline in the demand for large-firm services.[160] Following the example of their corporate clients, many large firms were forced to downsize both through reducing the hiring of new lawyers and also terminating associates and even partners.[161] This downsizing created a pool of experienced lawyers with first-rate academic credentials competing for jobs with recent graduates, creating a temporary glut.[162] The downsizing of the early 1990s was at least partially offset as large firms enlarged their markets by opening branch offices in both the United States and abroad.[163] Indeed, the globalization of law practice, as discussed in Chapter 1, is one of the most striking recent developments in the profession.

The close of the 1990s saw the return of boom times. According to one survey, the growth rate for U.S. law firms for 1998–1999 doubled over the preceding year.[164] The stampede was on to hire new associates to keep up with the demand. For example, in 1999, California's largest firm, Wilson Sonsini Goodrich & Rosati (500-lawyers plus), hired fifty-five rookies.[165] Because of the high demand for associates in the late 1990s, compensation packages skyrocketed. In 1998, the average staring salary for first-year associates was $55,000, up 10% from the year before.[166] Beginning in 2000, several major firms began paying first-year associates between $100,000 to $155,000.[167] As one Silicon Valley firm explained, because it was competing with its clients

---

157. *Id.* at 79.

158. *Id.* at 81.

159. *Id.*

160. *Id.* at 83.

161. *Id.* at 84.

162. *Id.*

163. *Id.* at 85.

164. Amar Bhatia, *Did You Know?*, FED. LAW., Sept. 1998, at 15 (citing Aspen Law & Business Of Counsel 700 survey).

165. *Id.*

166. Mark Hansen, *Starting Out in Style*, A.B.A. J., Sept. 1999, at 24.

167. Leslie A. Gordon, *Brobeck Boosts Starting Pay to Potential $155K*, DAILY RECORDER, Jan. 25, 2000, at 5.

for top legal talent, it decided "to benchmark the firm to the new dot-com economy" as opposed to other law firms.[168] Other competitive firms quickly followed suit.[169] Competition for talented lawyers grew so fierce that one Silicon Valley firm added a provision to its fee agreement charging clients a fee for luring away lawyers.[170] In the end, in 2000, first-year associates at one of these high-flying Silicon Valley firms earned more than the Chief Justice of the California Supreme Court.[171]

But the dot-com bust led to waves of lawyer layoffs. Fenwick & West — which had hired twenty-seven new associates in 1999[172] — laid off thirty-two associates in 2001.[173] In 2002, Gray Cary laid off forty-five associates.[174] And, as you surely suspected, with the economic downturn, salaries dipped. In 2002, both Gray Cary and Pillsbury Winthrop cut first-year associates salaries by $10,000.[175] In 2003, salaries remained flat.[176] But given the reality of hundreds of lay offs, most associates were relieved to keep their jobs even though salaries remained flat for three years.[177] For a while things looked as if they would improve; toward the end of 2005, two large firms announced for the first time in years that they were raising first-year associate salaries by $5000.[178] And in January, 2006, Gibson Dunn & Crutcher was reported to be raising first-year salaries to $135,000, a $10,000 boost.[179] At the time, experts expected that these increases would force other large firms to raise salaries.[180] However, this trend was short lived, and the year 2008 marked the beginning of what became the greatest economic recession since the great depression of the 1930s.[181]

---

168. Steph Paynes, *The Gold*, CAL. LAW., July 2000, at 41.

169. *Id.*

170. Jill Schachner Chanen, *Pay to Hire Away*, A.B.A. J., Aug. 2000, at 20.

171. *See* Paynes, *supra* note 142, at 41–42.

172. Leslie A. Gordon, *To Be Young and Rich*, CAL. LAW., Mar. 1999, at 20.

173. Erik Cummins, *Dot-Com Crashes Motivates Fenwick to Announce Layoffs*, DAILY RECORDER, Sept. 11, 2001, at 1, 7.

174. Donna Huffaker, *Gray Cary Employees Shocked by Historic Layoffs*, DAILY RECORDER, Jan. 7, 2002, at 1.

175. *Law Firms Cutting First-Year Salaries*, S.F. CHRON., Mar. 17, 2002, at J5.

176. Martha Neil, *What Goes Up ... Starting Associate Salaries Are Flat for Now, and the Future Is Uncertain*, A.B.A. J., Feb. 2003, at 24.

177. Renee Deger, *Diminished Expectations*, DAILY RECORDER, Sept. 8, 2003, at 1.

178. Marie-Anne Hogarth, *Stagnant Firm Salaries May Be Moving Up in California*, NAT'L L. J., Oct. 10, 2005, at 10.

179. Kellie Schmitt, *Gibson Dunn Applies Pressure by Hiking First-Year Pay*, NAT'L L. J., Jan. 9, 2006, at 12.

180. *Id.*

181. Neil J. Dilloff, *The Changing Cultures and Economics of Large law Firm Practice and Their Impact on Legal Education*, 70 MD. L. REV. 341, 342 (2011).

The financial meltdown resulted in thousands of lost jobs in the legal services sector. The slowed economy forced many large firms to lay off vast numbers of lawyers, paralegals and other staff for the first time in many years.[182] In fact, a survey published by the National Association of Women Lawyers revealed that between February 2008 and June 2009, 95% of large firms engaged in involuntary terminations.[183] At large firms alone, an estimated 12,100 employees were laid off in 2009.[184] The Wall Street Journal even called the 2009 job market "one of the worst ... in decades."[185] Large law firms also suffered financially, as dismal new economic realities made it increasingly difficult to sustain profitability. As a result, revenue-per-lawyer—which is generally considered to be the most reliable indicator of a firms overall financial health— stagnated or declined for the majority of the Am Law 100[186] between 2007 and 2009.[187] Partner profits at major firms also declined. Even DLA Piper—ranked as the largest firm in the world by numbers—experienced an 11.5% drop in partner profits for 2009,[188] and many other firms have experienced similar losses.

What does this mean for aspiring law students hoping to work in a large firm setting after graduation? To say the least, landing a prestigious salaried job at a large corporate law firm is certainly more difficult today than it has been in the past. The National Association for Law Placement (NALP) reported that the median number of job offers to recent law school graduates at large firms of more than 700 lawyers has dropped from 30 to 18.5.[189]

As one scholar described in a recent article:

> The U.S. legal profession no longer has a shortage of sophisticated business lawyers ... and many large corporate clients no longer want to pay the billing rates of junior associates who are learning on the

---

182. NAWL Foundation Report, *supra* note 53.

183. *Id.*

184. Lawshucks, *Life in and after Big Law* (Jan 3, 2010), http://lawshucks.com/2010/01/the-year-in-law-firm-layoffs-2009.

185. Nathan Koppel, *Bar Raised for Law-Grad Jobs*, Wall St. J., May 5, 2010, at A3.

186. The Am Law 100 is a list of the world's largest law firms by revenue, and is published each year by The American Lawyer magazine.

187. William D. Henderson & Rachel M. Zahorsky, *Law Job Stagnation May Have Started Before the Recession—And It May Be a Sign of Lasting Change*, ABA J. (July 1, 2011 4:40 AM), http://www.abajournal.com/magazine/article/paradigm_shift.

188. Cynthia Baker & Robert Lancaster, *Under Pressure: Rethinking Externships in A Bleak Economy*, 17 Clinical L. Rev. 71, 72 (2010).

189. *Id.*

job, excluding first- and second-year associates from working on their matters. In response, law firms have reduced the number of entry-level lawyers, turning the traditional pyramid structure into a diamond with many senior associates and nonequity partners composing the broad middle.[190]

In spite of the competitive conditions at large firms, the opportunity to work in other legal services areas and in diverse practice settings is greater today than ever before.[191] Although jobs at large firms generally pay more than jobs at smaller firms, the expectations placed upon associates at large firms can be stressful and intense. The high salaries in private practice are supported by high hourly rates for services. One survey revealed that most law firm partners bill at $300 per hour or more.[192] And the high salaries require increased billable hours. Billable hour requirements can reach well over 2000 hours per year, which requires the lawyer to work between 60 and 80 hours per week.[193] In short, to earn the enormous salaries, lawyers must often sacrifice their personal lives by coming in early, skipping lunch, staying late, and working weekends.[194]

As a result of these demanding working conditions, many new associates leave their large firm jobs within a short period of time. In fact, the most recent NALP study on attrition revealed that over half of associates at firms with more than 500 attorneys leave within three years,[195] and over 80 percent leave within five years.[196] At top New York firms, the average attrition rate for first-year associates is 25%. The reason is simple: the high salaries lead to increased demands for billable hours. That means that associates are working longer hours, and partners have little time to spend training them. As reported in the ABA Journal, new associates are leaving because of "grueling schedules combined with lack of training and mentoring."[197] An ABA Survey found that quality of life issues were crucial in the associate's decision to leave.

---

190. Henderson *supra* note 188, at 44.

191. *Id.* at 40.

192. *Survey Reveals Law Firm Billing Practices*, 69 U.S.L.W. 2261 (Nov. 7, 2000).

193. Choo, *supra* note 53, at 60.

194. Patrick Mahoney, *The Pyramid*, Cal. Law., July 2000, at 47, 49.

195. Becky Beaupre Gillespie & Hollee Schwartz Temple, *Hunting Happy in Grim Times, A Search for Joy in Law Practice Gains Ground*, ABA J. (February 1, 2011 5:39 AM), http://www.abajournal.com/magazine/article/hunting_happy_in_grim_times_a_search_for_joy_in_law_practice_gains_ground.

196. Luis J. Diaz, Patrick C. Dunican Jr., *Ending the Revolving Door Syndrome in Law*, 41 Seton Hall L. Rev. 947, 968 (2011).

197. *Id.*

According to the ABA's Commission on Billable Hours, work expectations rose from 1,100 hours annually in 1950 to an average of 1,900 in 2000, with many large firms expecting 2,500 hours or even more.[198] United States Supreme Court Justice Breyer described this workload as "a pace which … is like drinking from a fire hose."[199] These high hourly expectations rob attorneys of time for their families and pro bono activities.

An empirical study of the correlation between income and job satisfaction in the legal profession quantifies the problem.[200] According to the data collected from University of Michigan alumni, "Attorneys in large private practices report the highest annual income…. At least when examined according to type of practice, job satisfaction seems to have roughly the negative relationship with annual income predicted by the simple economic model: the high-earning practitioners in large private practices report the lowest job satisfaction…."[201] According to Douglas O. Linder, author of *The Happy Lawyer,* over two-thirds (68%) of lawyers who work in the public service sector are satisfied with their career and work-life balance, while only 44% of corporate lawyers report the same.[202] Not surprisingly, in a 2009 ABA Survey with over 2,300 respondents, 84% reported that they would be willing to receive less income in exchange for a lower billable hours requirement.[203]

Clearly, some changes are necessary and firms are devising strategies to address the problem. According to a former Harvard Business School professor, law firms need to modernize their management polices. Some firms are heeding this advice and retaining management experts to help them improve in many areas. For example, some firms have employed teams of nonlawyer business professionals to streamline operations, plan for the future, and free up the lawyers' time to serve clients rather than managing the practice.[204] According to the managing partner of a 330-lawyer firm, "It may be feasible for lawyers without real formal business training to run small law firms, but as

---

198. *Id.*

199. *Id.*

200. Kenneth G. Dau-Schmidt & Kaushik Mukhopadhaya, *The Fruits of Our Labors: An Empirical Study of the Distribution of Income and Job Satisfaction Across the Legal Profession,* 49 J. LEGAL EDUC. 342, 343 (1999).

201. *Id.* at 346.

202. NANCY LEVIT & DOUGLAS O. LINDER, THE HAPPY LAWYER: MAKING A GOOD LIFE IN THE LAW 9 (2010).

203. Levit *supra* note 202 at 173; ABA 2009 National Lawyer Population Survey, available at: http://www.abanet.org/marketresearch/2009_NATL_LAWYER_by_state.pdf.

204. Ingrid Becker, *Going Corporate,* CAL. LAW., Mar. 1999, at 23.

enterprises increase in size the management of those firms is a business problem as much as a legal problem."[205] Some firms have retained ombudspersons to provide confidential help to associates.[206] They have initiated evaluation systems to enable associates to snitch on oppressive partners who are then given counseling to help them become better managers.[207] Some require all partners to have management training.[208] Other firms are improving their continuing legal education and mentoring programs.[209] And still others are developing alternative career tracks.[210]

Some feared that another consequence of the high salaries would be a decreased commitment to pro bono service because as lawyers were required to bill more hours, they would have less time for pro bono work.[211] This appeared to be the case at the height of the big firm boom in 2000, when only eighteen of 100 firms surveyed had met the ABA guideline of fifty hours of pro bono service per lawyer per year.[212]

But recently firms have shown a renewed commitment to pro bono service. A 2005 ABA study found that two-thirds of lawyers give nearly a full work week of free legal services per year and that 46% met the ABA's goal of fifty hours per year.[213] Of those performing pro bono work, 46% gave 150 hours of time, three times the ABA goal.[214] And some of the largest law firms are leaders in pro bono service. Many have institutionalized their pro bono programs and some have dedicated attorneys to full-time pro bono practice.[215] According to one survey, in 2004, New York City's top firms provided over 650,000 hours of pro bono service.[216]

There are several explanations for the pro bono trend. Apart from the professional responsibility to provide pro bono service, "pro bono work has be-

---

205. *Id.* at 24.

206. Terry Carter, *A New Breed*, A.B.A. J., Mar. 2001, at 37, 39.

207. *Id.*

208. *Id.*

209. Jill Schachner Chanen, *You Rang, Sir?*, A.B.A. J., Oct. 2000, at 82.

210. Terry Carter, *Your Time or Your Money*, A.B.A. J., Feb. 2001, at 26.

211. Mark Hansen, *Trickle-Away Economics*, 86 A.B.A. J., July 2000, at 20.

212. Scott L. Cummings, *Access to Justice in the New Millennium*, Hum. Rts., Summer 2005, at 6.

213. Kenneth Davis, *ABA Releases First Survey on Pro Bono Work*, Daily Recorder, Aug. 3, 2005, at 1.

214. Dee McAree, *ABA Study: Two-Thirds Give Free Public Service*, Nat'l L. J., Aug. 15, 2005, at 6.

215. Terry Carter, *Building a Pro Bono Base*, A.B.A. J., June 2003, at 30.

216. Cummings, *supra* note 176, at 6.

come an essential component of an attractive career program for today's top law school graduates. Indeed, it has become a recruiting, training and retention imperative."[217] It is also a good marketing tool since the *American Lawyer* magazine uses a firm's pro bono rating to account for one third of its overall ranking in the "A-List" of the country's top twenty law firms.[218] In part, however, this increased devotion to pro bono service reflects the decrease in paid work due to the economic downturn,[219] and one can only hope that when economic prosperity returns, the firms will maintain their commitment to pro bono service.

2.4.4 In-House Counsel

Corporations are artificial persons under the law which exist independently of their owners and which have independent powers and liabilities. Lawyers not only created corporations—they also serve corporations by working as full-time legal advisors, known as in-house counsel. Beginning in the late 19th century, as the need for corporate legal services grew, a few large corporations began hiring their own full-time lawyers to work within the corporation as salaried employees.[220] In time these corporate lawyers were replaced with full-scale legal departments, and today, private corporations employ approximately 8% of the legal profession.[221] The chief lawyer of an in-house legal department is usually referred to as a "general counsel."

In the early years of this century, lawyers were hired to cope with the increased pervasiveness of government regulations.[222] As the New Deal era spawned increasingly complex regulatory controls, the need for legal advice in virtually every industry became clear.[223] These specialists would keep up with regulatory controls and keep their clients out of trouble. Other in-house legal departments in railroad and insurance companies were hired to handle the large volume of routine matters including leases and damage claims.[224] The expansion

---

217. Ivan Dominguez, *Pro Bono As Recruiting Imperative for Firms*, NAT'L L. J., Apr. 18, 2005, at R2.

218. Deborah L. Rhode, *Rethinking the Public in Lawyers' Public Service: Pro Bono, Strategic Philanthropy, and the Bottom Line*, FORDHAM L. REV. 1435, 1441 (2009).

219. Renee Deger, *Pro Bono Bonanza*, DAILY RECORDER, Aug. 2002, at 1.

220. *MacCrate Report*, *supra* note 18, at 88.

221. ABA Miscellaneous Statistics, *supra* note 39.

222. *MacCrate Report*, *supra* note 18, at 89.

223. *Id.*

224. *Id.*

of in-house employment continued through about 1970 and has remained roughly constant since that time, comprising 8–11% of legal employment.[225]

Although lawyers often start their careers at traditional law firms, many are attracted to corporate legal departments because they are seen as less hierarchical and competitive than large law firms.[226] These departments often stress contributions to the company over individual advancement.[227] Some corporate departments assert that corporate law departments cost half as much per hour as outside counsel.[228] These lawyers have no incentive to run the meter on their clients, have special expertise in their industry, and are comfortable with their corporate culture. An increasingly important responsibility of in-house counsel, especially in the wake of the recent economic recession, is to assure that their companies receive cost-effective legal services. As one recent article described, "In the corporate realm, general counsel are increasingly expected to achieve what other departments and businesses do—get better results at lower costs. No longer viewed as purveyors of the law, in-house lawyers are problem solvers and key business strategists."[229] Indeed, the salaries of many general counsels are directly linked to their ability to control legal costs.[230] Increasingly, in large corporations, in-house lawyers account for their time by charging it to internal clients.[231] Corporate legal departments are also seen as more willing to hire minority and women lawyers and to be more flexible with regard to part-time work, family leave, and other personnel policies.[232]

The size of these corporate legal departments ranges from one to nearly 500 lawyers.[233] According to the MacCrate Report, roughly one-third of in-house lawyers work for companies with one to three lawyers; another third works for companies with four to fifty lawyers; and the final third works for companies with over fifty lawyers. Most of these lawyers work for Fortune 500 industrial companies or in one of the Fortune 50 largest companies in selected industries.[234]

The late 1990s saw an increase in the use of in-house counsel. For example, Maxicare Health Plans, a Los Angeles based company, slashed its number of

---

225. ABA Miscellaneous Statistics, abanet.org/legaled/statistics (last visited Jan. 2, 2006).
226. *MacCrate Report, supra* note 18, at 92.
227. *Id.*
228. *Id.* at 94.
229. Henderson *supra* note 188, at 45.
230. *MacCrate Report,* supra note 18 at 94.
231. *Id.* at 93.
232. *Id.* at 92.
233. *Id.* at 93.
234. *Id.* at 92–93.

outside firms from eight to two and enjoyed a cost savings of more than half a million dollars a year.[235] Reflecting the value of this use of in-house counsel, Maxicare's in-house lawyers have seen their salaries double since the 1980s.[236] According to one survey, this reflects a national trend of companies to use more in-house lawyers and to increase their compensation in order to compete with outside firms for top law school graduates.[237]

Lawyers within these companies may face a special set of ethical problems and challenges to their independence. This issue has been raised in a number of recent lawsuits challenging the trend of insurance companies to use in-house counsel to represent policyholders.[238] The problem, according to critics, is that the lawyers who should be loyal to their clients, the policyholders, are, in fact, loyal to their employers, the insurance companies. While this potential conflict arises in every insurer-policyholder claim, it is increased where the lawyer is totally dependent on the insurer. As one plaintiff explained:

> Inherently there is a conflict. Staff counsel and insurance companies are one and the same.... When you sign up for a policy of insurance they are supposed to give you someone [as a lawyer] who is independent and will represent you. They would like you to believe that the lawyer's loyalty is to the client. But when [staff lawyers] get a paycheck solely form one source, I can't imagine that would not adversely affect you.[239]

While the creation of a corporate legal department provides obvious advantages to industry and may create a positive working environment, this employment creates a tension between the lawyer's role as a corporate officer and as a responsible professional.[240] After all, the lawyer is bound by ethical constraints and obligations which are not imposed on the corporation itself. In-house counsel face some unique ethical issues. As one commentator wrote:

> In-house lawyers face unique ethical issues in labor and employment law matters. In-house lawyers are also full-time employees of the corporation and thus are likely to encounter difficult questions of professional independence not faced by outside counsel. Additionally,

---

235. Vivien Lou Chen, *Outside in the Cold*, DAILY RECORDER, April 7, 1999, at 1.
236. *Id.*
237. *Id.*
238. Deborah Baker, *A Grab for the Ball*, A.B.A. J., Apr. 1999, at 42.
239. *Id.* at 44–451.
240. *MacCrate Report, supra* note 18, at 95.

corporate counsel often confront challenging issues regarding identi-fying the "client" among the various managers, employees and other constituencies within the corporation. And unlike outside lawyers, in-house lawyers are more likely to assume multiple roles as business adviser and legal adviser, or both. The blending of managerial and legal duties makes issues of confidentiality more difficult as a practi-cal matter.[241]

2.4.5 Lawyers for the Government

At least 89,476 different governments operate in the United States, in-cluding federal and state governments along with counties, municipalities, townships, school districts and special taxing districts.[242] While all of these units require legal services, most hire private attorneys as needed. But just as large corporations have found it cost-effective to create in-house legal de-partments, larger government entities have also established legal departments staffed by full-time salaried employees. In addition to following the general rules of professional conduct, these lawyers often have special responsibili-ties including duties of public trust, as when the prosecutor exercises pros-ecutorial discretion. To prepare students to assume these public roles, law schools need to provide special instruction in these public obligations.[243] We'll now briefly examine the employment of lawyers by government, be-ginning with the judicial branches and then turning to lawyers for local, state, and federal governments. We'll close this section with a discussion of the fi-nancial squeeze created by low government salaries and high law school debt and an overview of some programs designed to enable lawyers to pursue pub-lic service careers.

2.4.5(a) Lawyers in the Judiciary

While judges are the most important lawyers in the judiciary, their work is supported by the efforts of numerous other lawyers and assistants includ-ing law clerks and staff attorneys. This section will briefly describe these judges and lawyers who serve the judicial system. We will return to consider some ad-

---

241. Dennis P. Duffy, *Ethical Problems in Employment Litigation* (Nov 7, 2010) available at: http://apps.americanbar.org/labor/annualconference/2007/materials/data/papers/v1/017.pdf.
242. U.S. Census Bureau 2007: Local Governments and Public School Systems by Type and State, http://www.census.gov/govs/cog/GovOrgTab03ss.html.
243. *Id.* at 101–102.

ditional aspects of the state and federal judiciary in the next chapter of these materials.

In the United States, unlike many other countries, judges generally are appointed or elected to the bench after extensive experience in legal practice. Their backgrounds and areas of practice vary; many were prosecutors or government lawyers, some were civil litigators, and some were even academics. And, unlike many other countries, these judges may enter the judiciary at any level, even the highest level. In this sense, there is no required ladder in the judiciary from trial court judge to appellate court judge to Supreme Court judge. While some follow that path, the majority spends their judicial career on the same benches where they began.

In other countries, the tradition is different. For example, in England, judges are experienced barristers who enter the judiciary at the lowest level and then are customarily promoted to the next level if successful in the appointment.[244] In this way they can expect to move up through the court system. By contrast, in the civil law systems of Western Europe, judges begin their professional careers as judges after completing their university studies and a short period of training.[245]

Compared to these other systems, in the United States the methods for judicial appointment are varied.[246] Specifically, four methods are used: (1) judges are nominated by the chief executive and confirmed by a legislative body; (2) judges are appointed by the chief executive from a short list certified by an independent commission; (3) judges gain office in popular elections; and (4) judges are elected by the legislature.[247] Many critics have argued that the political nature of the process fails to insure that the judges will be persons of great integrity and competence. Rather, they may simply be large campaign contributors. For this reason, in recent years there has been a persistent agitation for merit selection plans.[248]

In addition to the variation in the method of selection, the terms of office vary considerably from terms as short as four years to life tenure.[249] Historical notions of judicial independence support the adoption of life tenure or at least lengthy terms with difficult removal procedures. Generally, we want our courts to be free from active control by political forces, even the popular will of the

---

244. MEADOR, *supra* note 117, at 55.
245. *Id.*
246. *Id.*
247. *Id.* at 57.
248. *Id.* at 58–59.
249. *Id.*

moment. After all, we don't want timid judges taking public opinion polls before ruling on legal questions so that they can be sure to retain their seats in the next election. We want strong people of integrity and principle acting objectively and fairly without regard to political whims. To assure this independence, federal judges enjoy life tenure. On the other hand, in a democracy the people are sovereign and judges—like all public officials—must be accountable to the people.[250] To ensure accountability, many states have adopted provisions for frequent judicial elections. Since these two competing values— independence and accountability—cannot be completely reconciled, different systems have struck the compromise in different ways.

The goal of safeguarding judicial independence is also evidenced by long-standing customs relating to the judge's relationship to parties and politicians. Specifically, it is well understood that no one should communicate with a judge about a pending case, other than the litigants and their attorneys acting through established procedures.[251] It would similarly be highly improper for a governor or legislator to attempt to influence a court in any way.[252]

Today, because of the burden of growing dockets, law clerks and staff attorneys assist judges in the decision-making process. Law clerks are usually recent law school graduates with strong academic records. They typically serve only a year or two before moving on. These clerks work closely with their judge in chambers researching the law, writing memoranda, and sometimes drafting opinions. For this reason, they are often referred to as the judge's "elbow clerks." A clerkship provides a new graduate with a unique opportunity to see behind the bench and to hone analytic and writing skills. Clerkships also maximize future career opportunities. Let us put in a plug right now: aim for a clerkship when you graduate from law school.

Beginning in the 1960s, judges needed even more help to manage their caseloads.[253] To fill this need, courts began hiring permanent central staffs of attorneys. Unlike elbow clerks who usually serve one particular judge for a year or two, staff attorneys often serve the entire court and may spend their entire career in that capacity.[254] These attorneys often write memoranda, draft proposed dispositions in routine cases, and screen the docket for cases which can be readily resolved.[255] While most admit that delegation of some of the judi-

---

250. *Id.* at 60.
251. *Id.* at 61.
252. *Id.* at 62.
253. *Id.* at 63.
254. *Id.* at 64.
255. *Id.*

cial process to staff attorneys is an unavoidable reality in response to burgeoning caseloads, critics worry that excessive delegation could impair the quality of the judicial process. This concern is yet another reason that we need to ensure that the judges appointed to the bench are people of high integrity and conscientious dedication.[256]

2.4.5(b) Lawyers for Local Governments

Lawyers employed by local governments serve many legal needs and handle a broad range of legal matters.[257] Law enforcement and criminal justice are paramount. According to the National District Attorneys Association, in 1991 there were between 20,000 and 22,000 district attorneys and assistant district attorneys in the United States.[258] Other salaried attorneys employed by local governments in the criminal justice system serve in probation, parole, and public defenders' offices. On the civil side, one reasonable estimate is that local governments employ at least 50,000 attorneys.[259] These lawyers serve departments of education, school boards, hospital districts, transportation agencies, revenue services, water boards, and a host of other local entities. They advise local governments and often litigate disputes on their behalf.

2.4.5(c) Lawyers for State Governments

At the state level, the primary legal office is that of the Attorney General. According to a 1991 survey, these offices employed 8,278 full-time and 236 part-time attorneys.[260] The attorney general is usually the chief law enforcement officer for the state. In addition to criminal matters, in many states the attorney general's office is involved in consumer protection and civil rights enforcement.[261] While it varies from state to state, the attorney general's office may also provide legal services to a number of other state agencies including those responsible for child welfare, civil rights, corrections, occupational licensing, liquor control, health, highway and occupational safety, parole, taxation and workers compensation.[262] Where the attorney general's office does

---

256. *Id.* at 65.
257. *MacCrate Report, supra* note 18, at 96.
258. *Id.* at 97.
259. *Id.*
260. *Id.* at 97–98.
261. *Id.* at 98.
262. *Id.*

not provide these services, the outside agencies frequently employ their own full- or part-time lawyers.

The legislative branch also employs a staff of attorneys to draft and review legislation, to review administrative regulations, to serve legislative committees, and to assist with constituent services.[263] With the advent of term-limits and the resulting turnover in representatives, these attorneys with their expertise and institutional memory play an increasingly vital role in the legislative process.

2.4.5(d) Lawyers for the Federal Government

Beginning with the Founding Fathers, lawyers have played a prominent role in the federal government. Indeed, a majority of the delegates to the Constitutional Convention were trained in the law.[264] With the growth of the federal government, especially after the New Deal and World War II, the number of lawyers in federal service increased. By 1980, the federal government employed more than 20,000 lawyers.[265] By 1990, by some reasonable estimates, the number of lawyers in federal service had climbed to over 40,000.[266] While nearly 20% of these lawyers are probably employed by the Department of Justice, others are found in the Internal Revenue Service, the Department of Defense and Armed Services, the Department of Health and Human Services, the National Labor Relations Board, Congress, the Veterans' Administration, the various other cabinet departments, and a host of other departments and agencies.

2.4.5(e) Making Ends Meet in Public Service

Many law students and lawyers are attracted to public service. A survey found that lawyers enter public service careers for several reasons including the opportunity to contribute to society, helping people directly, the nature of the work, and the quality of life.[267] But relatively low government salaries make this choice a financial sacrifice and high law school debt may make it an impossibility.[268]

---

263. *Id.*

264. *Id.* at 99.

265. *Id.*

266. *Id.* at 101.

267. Karla Smith, *The Public Interest Versus the Private Sector: The Debt Factor*, FED. LAW., Mar./Apr. 2005, at 46.

268. Robert E. Hirshon, *Graduating Under Pressure*, A.B.A. J., Nov. 2001, at 6; Smith, *supra* note 233, at 46.

The National Association for Law Placement conducted two studies spotlighting the salary gap between public service and private practice:

Table 2.4 Median Salaries for Attorneys[269]

Years of Experience	Public Defender	Prosecuting Attorney	Private Practice
Entry Level	$39,000	$40,574	$95,000
5 years	$50,000	$47,700	$115,250
8 years	*	*	$135,000
11–15 years	$65,000	$68,139	*

Given the salary disparity, it is not surprising that 66% of students responding to a survey said law school debt was a deterrent when considering a government job or that 68% of government employers had difficulty recruiting new attorneys.[270] Students in 2009 graduated with an average education debt of $68,827 at public schools and $106,249 at private schools.[271] More than 20% owe more than $100,000 at graduation,[272] and most graduates pay an average monthly loan payment of $1,100.[273] This means that the average student can expect to pay over $13,000 annually in student loans—a significant percentage of the 2008 median starting salary of $40,000 for public service jobs.[274]

Three proposals are gaining support to address this problem: (1) the adoption of loan repayment assistance programs (LRAPs); (2) the creation of percentage-based student loan programs; and (3) proposed legislation providing for government assistance for public servants to pay law school debt. First, LRAPs are increasingly being adopted across the country. In 2006, about 100 of the approximately 190 American law schools had LRAP, compared to only forty-seven in 2000.[275] These programs pay part or all of the debt for students who enter public interest or public service careers with low salaries. Unfortunately, only half of the ABA accredited law schools have LRAPs and many

---

269. *Id.*

270. Hirshon, *supra* note 269.

271. ABA Report: Average Amount Borrowed for Law School, http://www.american-bar.org/content/dam/aba/administrative/legal_education_and_admissions_to_the_bar/council_reports_and_resolutions/2001_2010_avg_amt_borrowed.authcheckdam.pdf (last visited Apr. 8, 2012).

272. Rhonda McMillion, *A Lighter Load*, A.B.A. J., Aug. 2005, at 64.

273. Smith, *supra* note 233, at 46.

274. 2008 NALP Press Release: "New Report on Salaries for Public Sector and Public Interest Attorneys", http://www.abajournal.com/files/NALP_Press_Release.pdf (last visited Apr. 8, 2012).

275. Philip G. Schrag, *Federal Student Loan Repayment Assistance for Public Interest Lawyers and Other Employees of Governments and Nonprofit Organizations*, 36 Hofstra L. Rev. 27, 61 (2007).

of them are underfunded.[276] But at least twenty more schools are developing LRAPs,[277] and many are working very well.[278]

Second, Professor Robert B. Reich of Brandeis University and former Secretary of Labor has proposed percentage-based student loan programs to enable graduates to choose public service careers. In such a program, loan payments would be based on income and all students would pay the same percentage. In other words, a new prosecuting attorney would pay the same percentage as the new law firm associate, but the amount would be substantially lower. Under Professor Reich's proposal, private lenders would provide the loans which would be guaranteed by the federal government.

Finally, in 2003 the ABA reported that a two-year study by the ABA Commission on Loan Repayment and Forgiveness found that loan debt was a road block for law graduates who would otherwise go into public service.[279] In 2005, based on the study, the ABA submitted two recommendations to Congress. First, it recommended improvements to an existing repayment program that is percentage-based along the lines suggested by Professor Reich.[280] Second, it recommended increasing the amounts students may borrow under another program which offers special terms and highly competitive interest rates.[281] In 2007, Congress passed the College Cost Reduction and Access Act (CCRAA). The act did two things—first, it adopted an "income-based repayment" plan, similar to the program endorsed by Professor Reich. Second, the act entitled students committed to public service jobs to have a significant portion of their student debt forgiven after making light payments during a ten-year period of full-time employment. Additionally, some states and public service employers, including several federal agencies, have instituted their own LRAPs to assist specific types of lawyers.[282]

2.4.6 Public Interest Lawyers

According to the MacCrate Report, over the past thirty years new organizations have developed to supplement the provision of legal services to the poor and to persons of modest means. These organizations include legal serv-

---

276. *Id.*
277. Tresa Baldas, *Paying the Way,* Nat'l L. J., July 5, 2004, at 1.
278. *Id.*
279. McMillion, *A Lighter Load, supra* note 237, at 64.
280. *Id.*
281. *Id.*
282. Schrag, *supra* note 276.

ices agencies, public defender offices, law school clinics, pro bono programs, and group legal services. In this section we will trace the historical roots of these service providers and briefly summarize the characteristics of these practice settings.

2.4.6(a) The Historical Antecedents

For more than 100 years, lawyers have wrestled with the problem of providing legal services to the poor and have generally failed to make adequate access available. In 1876, German-American immigrants founded the earliest organization in New York City.[283] By 1900, six cities had legal aid societies formed by bar associations and civic groups, and by 1917 forty-one legal aid organizations were operating.[284] But while these organizations handled 117,201 cases in 1916, this effort fell far short of fulfilling the need.[285] Moreover, these organizations refused criminal cases which left indigent criminal defendants without representation.[286]

In 1893, Clara Shortridge Foltz, the first woman admitted to practice in California, launched the public defender movement to require the government to provide counsel for indigent criminal defendants.[287] Despite her efforts, few offices were established. By 1917 there were five public defender offices, and by 1949 there were only twenty-eight.[288] Real change only came after the Supreme Court recognized the right to counsel in federal court in 1938, which was extended to felony cases in state court in 1963, and to cases supporting a prison sentence in 1972.[289]

With respect to civil matters, entire communities have historically been denied access to justice in our system. From the early 20th century, organizations formed by lawyers and political activists have attempted to address these group needs, including the American Civil Liberties Union and the NAACP Legal Defense and Education Fund.[290] But the development of a segment of the bar devoted to what is now called "public interest law" did not emerge until the activist decade of the 1960s.

In the following sections, we will trace the progress of programs to provide lawyers for the poor and the emergence of public interest law practice.

---

283. *MacCrate Report, supra* note 18, at 48.
284. *Id.*
285. *Id.*
286. *Id.*
287. *Id.* at 49.
288. *Id.*
289. *Id.*
290. *Id.* at 50.

2.4.6(b) Lawyers for the Poor

The history of the provision of legal services to the poor can only be understood with reference to the constitutional requirement of legal representation for indigent criminal defendants. Since the Supreme Court has held that the states and federal government are constitutionally required to provide legal counsel, counsel is provided at the taxpayers' expense.[291] However, since there is no constitutional requirement of counsel in civil cases, these services are generally not provided to any significant extent by public entities. This section will first discuss the provision of legal assistance in criminal cases and then turn to the provision of civil legal assistance to the poor.

In a series of cases beginning in 1932, the United States Supreme Court announced that the constitutional requirement of due process of law required that indigent criminal defendants be provided legal counsel in serious cases. The Court's landmark *Gideon* decision in 1963, coupled with the passage of the Criminal Justice Act of 1964, finally recognized that publicly funded compensation of these defense services was required.[292] Thereafter, public defender programs grew dramatically. In 1967, the state and federal governments spent a total of $20 million to represent defendants charged with felonies; by 1988 the expenditures reached $1.4 billion.[293] According to one directory, in 1991–1992 there were 1,529 main and branch offices providing representation to indigent defendants.[294] These services are supplemented by a significant number of private practitioners working on a retainer, as well as on a publicly subsidized or pro bono basis.[295]

While the availability of representation has improved since the days when Clara Shortridge Foltz began her campaign, the problem of providing adequate representation has not been solved. Both the federal and state governments have crushing caseloads of drug and drug-related offenses with a gross disparity between resources available for prosecution compared to those available for defense.[296] As the MacCrate Report concludes, "Many public defender offices are today overburdened and underpaid, with high turnover, and unprepared to handle their massive caseloads."[297] As a result, innocent people get convicted of crimes they did not commit. Since 1992, the Innocence Project

---

291. *Id.* at 55.
292. *Id.*
293. *Id.*
294. *Id.*
295. *Id.* at 56.
296. *Id.*
297. *Id.* at 56–57.

founded by Barry Scheck and Peter Neufeld at Cardozo Law School has exonerated 172 inmates through DNA evidence.[298]

The need for competent representation is especially critical in death penalty cases. Recent reports documenting the poor quality of representation in a number of these cases are alarming. According to one report, serious reversible errors occurred in 68% of the capital punishment cases reviewed.[299] Moreover, the study found 87 inmates who had been released from death row as factually or legally innocent.[300] One of the most common errors was found to be "egregiously incompetent defense lawyering."[301]

Turning to civil cases, the lack of adequate legal representation for poor people is perhaps even more acute than in the criminal arena. In the 1960s, the "War on Poverty" included a commitment to fund legal services for the poor.[302] Thus, in 1965, the Office of Legal Services was founded within the Office of Economic Opportunity. From 1965 to 1973, the federal Legal Services Program, with the enthusiastic support of the bar, brought lawyers into poor neighborhoods. By 1973, the Program included 250 community-based agencies staffed by more than 2,600 full-time lawyers who had served over five million clients and argued a hundred appeals in the United States Supreme Court.[303] During this period and until 1981, the Program extended services to farm workers, Native Americans, the elderly, and the disabled.[304] Through these programs, a distinct body of poverty law was created.[305]

The 1980s brought a sharp reversal in federal support. Beginning in 1981, many of the federal programs were redesigned to transfer operations and control to state governments.[306] And in 1982, the budget was cut by 25%.[307] For the rest of the decade, the challenge for proponents of legal services, including the American Bar Association was to maintain funding at the 1982 level.[308] By 1996, federal funding for the Legal Services Corporation had been cut in 50%

---

298. The Innocence Project, http://www.innocenceproject.org (last visited Apr. 8, 2012).

299. *Error Rate in Capital Punishment System is at "Epidemic Proportions," Study Charges,* 68 U.S.L.W. 2762 (June 20, 2000) (reporting on study conducted by Professor James S. Liebman of Columbia University School of Law).

300. *Id.*

301. *Id.*

302. *MacCrate Report, supra* note 18, at 51.

303. *Id.*

304. *Id.* at 51–52.

305. *Id.* at 52.

306. *Id.* at 52–53.

307. *Id.* at 52.

308. *Id.* at 52.

from its highest level in 1980.[309] Most recently, in 2011, the Legal Services Corporation budget faced a $104 million cut in fiscal year 2012.[310] The proposed cut reduced financial support by 26%, bringing back Legal Services Corporation funding to a level not seen since 1999.[311] Unfortunately, Legal Services Corporation—still the nation's largest source of funding for civil legal aid to the poor—faces these drastic cuts at a time when the demand for legal aid to the poor is higher than ever. LSC's initial estimates reveal that roughly 235,000 low-income Americans eligible for legal aid at LSC-funded programs would be denied if the proposed cuts are enacted.[312]

The lack of funding makes it difficult for law school graduates to pursue poverty law careers for two reasons. First, jobs are scarce, and, second, they don't pay well. In fact, poverty and public interest lawyers make even less than government lawyers:

Table 2.5

Years of Experience	Legal Services	Public Interest Firm	Prosecuting Attorney	Private Practice
Entry Level	$34,000	$36,656	$40,574	$95,000
5 years	$40,000	$46,313	$47,700	$115,250
8 years	*	*	*	$135,000
11–15 years	$51,927	$64,000	$68,139	*

As discussed above, a number of initiatives are under way to provide relief from heavy debt burdens so that law graduates can pursue public interest careers.

In addition to the legislative initiatives, private philanthropy offers another alternative. The Bill and Melinda Gates Foundation recently gave $33 million to the University of Washington School of Law to support aspiring public interest lawyers.[313] The gift is designed both to cover expenses for the legal education of 400 students over 80 years, and also to raise awareness for the need for public interest lawyers.[314] According to David Sten, chief executive of Equal

---

309. Cummings, *supra* note 176, at 6.

310. Debra Cassens Weiss, *Legal Services Corp Faces Potential 26% Budget Cut; ABA President Voices Concern*, ABA JOURNAL (July 19, 2011, 9:50 AM), http://www.abajournal.com/news/article/legal_services_corp._faces_potential_26_budget_cut_aba_president_voices_con.

311. *Id.*

312. Arkansas Legal Services Partnership, *Proposal Would Cut Legal Aid by $104 Million*, http://www.arlegalservices.org/node/705 (last visited Apr. 8, 2012).

313. Leigh Jones, *A $33M Investment in Public Interest Lawyers*, NAT'L L. J., Jan 9, 2006, at 6.

314. *Id.*

Justice Works, a nonprofit group that promotes public interest law, the Gates Foundation gift should "inspire other donors to realize the debt obstacle and similarly inspire them to give grants."[315]

To fill the gap left by the pared down Legal Services Corporation, over 1,000 institutionalized pro bono programs have been created.[316] The ABA exercised strong leadership in this effort by adopting the 1993 revision to the Model Rules which provides that every lawyer "should aspire to render at least (50) hours of pro bono publico legal services per year" of which the "substantial majority should be in serving people of limited means or organizations that advocate on their behalf."[317] The ABA's Commission on the Evaluation of the Rules of Professional Conduct (Ethics 2000) later amended Model Rule 6.1 to provide that "[e]very lawyer has a professional responsibility to provide legal services to those unable to pay."[318] As discussed above, many of the most elite firms have institutionalized pro bono programs and provide substantial pro bono services.[319] These efforts are complemented by a trend for government agencies to adopt policies to encourage and facilitate the provision of pro bono services by their lawyers.[320] In addition to these volunteer lawyers, law schools make a significant contribution to the provision of civil legal services through live-client clinics.

But publicly funded services, even supplemented by volunteer efforts, have not kept up with the need. In 2005, Legal Services Corporation released a report finding that nationally 80% of the civil legal needs of the poor are unmet.[321] According to the State Bar of California's report, *The Path to Justice,* "only 28% of California's poor have access to justice" while "a million and a half poor families ... do not have access to justice when their rights to employment, housing, health care, transportation or other basic human needs are denied."[322] It also found that only one lawyer is available for every 10,000 poor Californians.[323] Clearly, we need to do better.

---

315. *Id.*

316. Cummings, *supra* note 176, at 6.

317. Model Rules of Professional Conduct Rule 6.1.

318. *Id.*; Cummings, *supra* note 176, at 6.

319. *Id.*

320. David Jackson Devries, *Public Sector Obstacles Are Vanishing,* A.B.A. J., Dec. 2000, at 66.

321. Anat Rubin, *supra* note 32; Rhonda McMillion, *It's That Time Again,* A.B.A. J., Mar. 2006, at 61.

322. *The Path to Justice: A Five-Year State Report on Access to Justice,* Press Release, Nov. 20, 2002, http://www.calbar.ca.gov/LinkClick.aspx?fileticket=QhMjgCPh4gg%3D&tabid=216 (last visited Apr. 8, 2012).

323. *Id.*

2.4.6(c) Advocates for Group Legal Rights

Since a landmark United States Supreme Court decision in 1963, public interest advocates have used litigation to vindicate group legal rights.[324] As Justice Brennan explained in recognizing the significance of this development, "[L]itigation may well be the sole practicable avenue open for a minority to petition for redress of grievances."[325] The advocates for group legal rights practice in three interrelated settings: public interest law firms; cooperating private attorneys and firms; and government agencies.

Public interest law firms, funded by individuals and foundations, represent clients and causes. Some focus on a particular client group including children, the disabled, women, the elderly, gays and lesbians, minorities, farmworkers, and poor people.[326] Others focus on causes including the environment, civil liberties, human rights, consumer protection, and government reform.[327] These firms run the political and ideological gamut. Compliance with IRS regulations affords them tax-exempt status.[328]

The work of these public interest firms is supplemented by the volunteer efforts of private practitioners. Under the sponsorship of the National Legal Aid and Defender Association and the ABA Litigation Section, with funding from the Ford Foundation, the Litigation Assistance Partnership Project facilitates this cooperation.[329] These partnerships have tackled complex poverty litigation and other litigation for the benefit of the poor.

Finally, government agencies provide representation to disadvantaged groups. For example, the New Jersey Department of the Public Advocate operates as a "combination public defender, ombudsman and trouble-shooter—a triple threat champion for citizens beset by arrogant bureaucratic and self-aggrandizing private interests."[330]

Law schools have a special obligation to instill in their students the responsibility for improving and extending our legal system to serve all of soci-

---

324. *MacCrate Report, supra* note 18, at 70.

325. *Id.* (quoting NAACP Legal Defense Fund, Inc. v. Button, 371 U.S. 415, 430 (1963)).

326. *MacCrate Report, supra* note 18, at 70–71.

327. *Id.* at 71.

328. *Id.*

329. *Id.; see also* David B. Barber, *Pro Bono Project Provides Opportunities for Lawyers,* Litig. News, Jan. 2006, at 7. You may wish to visit the Project's website at http://www.abanet.org/litigation/lapp.

330. *MacCrate Report, supra* note 18, at 72 (quoting Bierbaum, *On the Frontiers of Public Interest Law: The New Jersey State Department of the Public Advocate—The Public Advocacy Division,* 13 Seton Hall. L. Rev. 475, 481 (1983)).

ety and to provide equal justice under law. Since we are providing our students with the privilege of a monopoly on access to our legal system, we must teach our students of their special responsibility for the quality and availability of justice in our country.[331] One way to achieve this goal is to educate our students about legal programs for the poor and public interest law. As Justice Thurgood Marshall explained:

> Public interest law seeks to fill some of the gaps in our legal system. Today's public interest lawyers have built upon the earlier successes of civil rights, civil liberties, and legal aid lawyers, but have moved into new areas....
> They also represent neglected interests that are widely shared by most of us as consumers, as workers, and as individuals in need of privacy and a healthy environment.... More fundamentally, perhaps, they have made our legal process work better. They have broadened the flow of information to decision makers.... And, by helping open doors to our legal system, they have moved us a little closer to the ideal of equal justice for all.[332]

---

331. *MacCrate Report, supra* note 18, at 140.

332. *Id.* at 72 (quoting Justice Thurgood Marshall, *Financing Public Interest: Law: The Role of the Organized Bar,* Address to the Award of Merit Luncheon of the Bar Activities Section of the American Bar Association (August 10, 1975)).

CHAPTER 3

INTRODUCTION TO THE
UNITED STATES LEGAL SYSTEM

Much of the special challenge involved in mastering the law of the United States is understanding the unique structure of the United States government. As you know, the United States is a republic of fifty states. Each state has a complete government consisting of three branches—the legislative, the executive, and the judicial. In addition to these state governments, the federal government has its own three branches. How do these state and federal systems fit together? How does one determine whether the federal government or a state government controls a legal area? What if two governments both adopt laws pertaining to a single issue? For example, Congress passed the Brady Bill to regulate the sale of handguns, but California also has gun control laws. Similarly, while the federal government prohibits the possession of marijuana, California allows the possession of marijuana for medical purposes. The proper relationship between the state and federal governments underlies our concept of "federalism."

After determining which government has authority to act, how does one determine which branch should act? For example, the Food and Drug Administration—an agency of the executive branch—attempted to regulate the sale of tobacco as a drug. But in 2000 the United States Supreme Court concluded that this exceeded the FDA's jurisdiction because Congress did not intend to give the agency this authority.* This is an example of how the Supreme Court reviews actions of the legislative and executive branches to determine whether they exceeded their authority. It also illustrates the interplay between the three branches of government. The basic yet difficult question of the interrelationship of the three branches of a government is addressed under the doctrine of "separation of powers."

---

* FDA v. Brown & Williamson Tobacco Corp., 529 U.S. 120 (2000). In July 2009 Congress passed the "Family Smoking Prevention and Tobacco Control Act" to explicitly authorize the FDA to regulate the sale of tobacco as a drug.

In this chapter, we will introduce basic notions of federalism and separation of powers. We will begin by considering the multiple sovereignties that make up our legal system and their relationship to each other. We will then turn to a description of the federal and state systems with a special emphasis on the courts and the judicial process. Finally, we will outline some of the complications and resulting accommodations that arise in our complex system of multiple sovereignties.

3.1 Multiple Sovereignties

To understand the United States legal system, one must first understand the fundamental elements of the government. Strictly speaking, there is no single United States government; there are two levels of government—federal (or national) and state—that coexist and operate simultaneously at most points within the United States. In addition to the fifty state governments, analogous governments exist for the District of Columbia, the Commonwealth of Puerto Rico, and the territories of the Virgin Islands, Guam, American Samoa, and the Northern Mariana Islands. Thus, the "government of the United States" is really one federal government and the more than fifty state and territorial governments, each of which has its own set of laws and its own court system. In addition to these fifty plus governments, there are innumerable local governments—cities, counties, regional boards, etc. To resolve a legal problem, a lawyer may have to consult local codes and ordinances, one or more state's law, federal law, and, increasingly, the laws of foreign countries. In fact, this system of multiple governments gives the United States legal system much of its richness, diversity, complexity, and conceptual challenge.

3.1.1 Federalism

The major governmental and legal division in the United States is the federal-state division of authority. We have a federal system of government, that is, governmental responsibility is divided between one national government and a coexisting set of state governments. "Federalism" refers to the relationship, often one of dynamic tension, between the federal and state governments which share governmental functions in the United States.

Our fidelity to federalism is not simply a matter of historical accident. As Justice Black explained, federalism entails:

(a) a proper respect for state functions;

(b) a recognition that the country is made up of a union of separate state governments; and

(c) a continuation of the belief that the National government will fare best if the states are left free to perform their separate functions in their separate ways.[1]

The principal source of this division of power between the federal and state governments is the United States Constitution. The Founding Fathers feared the accumulation of centralized power—after all, they had just fought the Revolutionary War against King George III. Representatives of the original thirteen sovereign states created a limited federal government by adopting the Constitution. In other words, the Constitution did not create the states; the states created the Constitution. Since the states preceded the federal United States government, they retain that first-in-time character. They are the repositories of residual governmental power in our federal scheme. The primordial and residual state power means that, unless limited by the United States Constitution, the states have all the governmental powers to which any sovereign is entitled. The Constitution limits the powers of the federal government vis-à-vis the states, primarily through the enumeration of specified federal powers, leaving those powers not granted to the federal government to the states. The Tenth Amendment to the Constitution specifically addresses the federal-state relationship, expressly stating what is implicit in the structure of the Constitution itself, "The powers not delegated to the United States by the Constitution, nor prohibited by it to the States, are reserved to the States respectively, or to the people."

Yet, while the Constitution carefully preserves the primacy of the states and created a limited federal government, it also limits the powers of the states. The Supremacy Clause provides that the United States Constitution and federal laws are the supreme law of the land. For this reason, when the state and federal laws conflict, federal law prevails. For example, the United States Supreme Court struck down a Massachusetts law barring state agencies from buying goods from Burma.[2] The Court held that in foreign affairs state law is preempted by the federal government and application of the state prohibition would therefore violate the Supremacy Clause. And when the Constitution protects individual liberties, the states must afford at least as much protection as the Constitution requires. The states are free to provide greater protection, but not less.

---

1. Younger v. Harris, 401 U.S. 37, 44 (1971).
2. Crosby v. National Foreign Trade Council, 530 U.S. 363, 366 (2000).

Despite the Founding Fathers' care in creating a limited federal government, the federal-state relationship has been a dynamic one, and historically the trend has been one of increasing federal power at the expense of the states. Most importantly, the Civil War and its aftermath dramatically realigned the balance of power between the federal and state governments. The post-Civil War Amendments to the Constitution—the Thirteenth, Fourteenth, and Fifteenth Amendments—revised both the relationship of the federal government to the state governments, and also the relationship between the states and their citizens.

Specifically, the Fourteenth Amendment includes the Due Process Clause and the Equal Protection Clause which extended the protections of the Bill of Rights to the states. Originally, the Bill of Rights only restricted the power of the federal government, not the states. Thus, the Fourteenth Amendment had the effect of imposing fundamental restrictions on state power in order to protect individual constitutional rights. These amendments and the vigorous exercise of federal leadership during the New Deal era of President Franklin Roosevelt created the powerful federal government we have today.

The prior existence of state government affects the relationship between federal and state courts as well. State courts are referred to as courts of "general jurisdiction." This means that presumably they can hear any case brought before them unless it can be shown that the case belongs to the relatively small category of cases of exclusive federal jurisdiction. In contrast, federal courts always require a showing that they possess judicial power to hear a particular matter because it comes within their limited subject matter jurisdiction. Generally, this means that the party wishing to litigate a case in federal court must show that it involves either (1) a federal right or (2) an interstate or international dispute. Moreover, the federal courts have adopted self-imposed restrictions on their jurisdiction in deference to federalism principles.

The abstention doctrines provide an excellent example of the federal courts' reluctance to overstep their limited role, especially when intruding on the states' power is not absolutely necessary. For example, numerous adult entertainment establishments have challenged state criminal prosecutions under obscenity laws as interfering with their rights under the First Amendment which guarantees freedom of expression. Generally, the federal courts will abstain from interfering with the state prosecution, even if they believe that the defendant's claim might be valid. Out of respect for the state court, the federal court will abstain in the belief that the state court is every bit as competent and zealous in protecting constitutional rights as the federal court would be. Thus, the state court will be given the first opportunity to adjudicate the case, and the federal courts will only intervene if the defendant can demonstrate bad faith in the state prosecution.

Of course, federal deference to state courts might on occasion be misplaced where the state court is reluctant to declare that a popular state law is unconstitutional (like an obscenity law) in order to protect an unpopular cause (like the First Amendment Rights of topless bars). Does abstention mean that the defendant's constitutional rights are left without federal protection? No, because if the defendant is convicted under an unconstitutional state statute, the conviction can then be challenged by a petition for *certiorari* to the United States Supreme Court or a federal action in a district court for a writ of habeas corpus (an order from the federal court to release the prisoner). Thus, the federal courts will abstain from interfering in an on-going state prosecution, but they have the power to later provide relief in the event the state court allows an unconstitutional conviction. This example illustrates the intersection of two traditional federal court concerns—limited federal jurisdiction and respect for state governments. It also shows the federal courts' effort to balance their obligation to vigorously enforce federal constitutional protections against the countervailing policies of federalism and respect for state governments. You will study these abstention principles in depth in your courses in Constitutional Law, Civil Rights, and Federal Jurisdiction.

3.1.2 Substantive Law Areas of the Multiple Sovereigns

While the laws of the multiple sovereigns complement, overlap, and sometimes outright conflict with each other, we'll introduce federalism with a simplified historical overview. It is much tidier than reality, but it should help you understand the main outlines of federal versus state authority. We will return to add some details to this sketch in later sections of this chapter.

As a starting point, much of the business of the federal government reflects those areas of law assigned to it by the Constitution. Most of the federal legislative authority derives from the enumerated powers found in Article I, section 8 of the Constitution which include the powers to impose taxes, regulate commerce, control immigration, punish counterfeiting, protect intellectual property, and establish an army and navy. In contrast to these limited areas carved out for federal control, originally the Constitution left everything else for the states to control. Specifically, criminal law—murder, rape, robbery, arson, etc.—was exclusively a matter of state law. Similarly, state law governed business transactions including contracts, partnerships, and corporations. State law determined both real and personal property rights including land use, real property conveyancing, landlord-tenant relations, and the purchase and sale of goods. And state law governed tort law (liability for misconduct causing injury) which included assault, battery, false imprisonment, trespass, malpractice, negligence, libel, and slander. State law also controlled all matters relating to family law and estates including marriage, divorce, custody, wills, trusts, and probate.

In the 20th century, Congress enacted major statutory schemes that extended the reach of federal law. Federal statutes now regulate labor relations, business (including antitrust protections and securities transactions), transportation, banking, broadcasting, telecommunications, and the Internet. In other areas, federal statutes today provide for civil rights in employment, housing, and public accommodations, protect the environment, regulate public health and safety, including drug safety, and fund major public works including federal buildings, dams, bridges, and interstate highways. Finally, Congress has increasingly adopted criminal statutes that overlap with state criminal laws in areas such as bank robbery, kidnapping, securities transactions, and drug trafficking.

As a result of this trend, federal law has an increasing presence in areas traditionally left to the states. The number of federal crimes has expanded well beyond the handful that existed in the first fifty years of the federal government. And, with extensive federalization of crime, federal criminal law has become almost coextensive with state criminal law outside of traditional, usually violent felonies (murder, rape, robbery, assault, larceny and burglary). Many regulatory offenses are also federal crimes in the business, securities, banking, and environmental areas. With mixed success, federal law now also reaches into education at all levels, driven by federal funding programs. Congress has attempted to make domestic violence a federal offense and is attempting to regulate tort law, traditionally a state concern, by limiting damages and setting liability rules for products manufacturers, gun dealers, and health care professionals. Overall, today there is almost as much overlapping authority across federal and state bounds, as there is exclusively federal or exclusively state authority.

With all the overlapping laws, conflicts inevitably arise. For example, California voters passed a proposition banning the use of certain traps to capture or kill wildlife. But federal agencies under the authority of the Endangered Species Act sometimes permitted the use of these traps where necessary to protect endangered species. Could California prevent federal agencies from using the traps? The answer is no. Under the Supremacy Clause of the United States Constitution, Congress may preempt states from adopting laws that conflict with federal laws so long as the federal law is within Congress' constitutional

---

3. National Audubon Society v. Davis, 144 F. Supp.2d 1160, 1181 (N.D. Cal. 2000).

authority.[3] Moreover, so long as the federal law is within congressional authority, states cannot adopt laws infringing on federal foreign affairs powers. For example, Massachusetts passed a law barring state agencies from buying goods from Burma (Myanmar) because of human rights abuses. Three months later, the federal government passed a statute imposing certain sanctions on Burma. The United States Supreme Court held that the state law was preempted by the federal law under the Foreign Commerce Clause of the United States Constitution.[4] Similarly, a federal court struck down a California statute providing compensation to victims of slave labor regimes imposed during World War II on the grounds that it infringed on the federal government's exclusive power over foreign affairs.[5]

Just as the Court sometimes concludes that a state has overstepped its authority by intruding into areas reserved to the federal government, at other times the Court finds that the federal government has improperly intruded into areas reserved to the states. For example, the Court has concluded that Congress exceeded its authority in adopting the Gun-Free School Zones Act which made it a crime to have a gun within 1,000 feet of a school.[6] In the Court's view, the law improperly extended federal authority to a general police power which is reserved to the states. And following the same reasoning, the Court struck down the Violence Against Women Act.[7] That law, the Court found, improperly extended federal authority to issues of local crime which are reserved to the states' police power under the Constitution.

In short, while the historical dividing lines between areas of federal law and areas of state law were fairly crisp, today the two systems overlap, intersect, and, occasionally conflict. Despite the large and, until recently, growing presence of the federal or national government in our lives, much of United States government remains state government. In these next sections, we look in more detail first at the federal government and then state governments.

3.2 The Federal Government

Although created by representatives of the states, today we think of the federal government as "the government of the United States." As our high

---

4. Crosby v. National Foreign Trade Council, 530 U.S. 363 (2000).

5. *In re* World War II Era Japanese Forced Labor Litigation, 164 F. Supp. 2d 1160 (N.D. Cal. 2001).

6. United States v. Lopez, 514 U.S. 549 (1995).

7. United States v. Morrison, 529 U.S. 598 (2000).

school civics texts taught us, the federal government is created by and, to a considerable extent, regulated by the United States Constitution. It consists of three separate but interrelated branches: the legislative, the executive, and the judicial.

3.2.1 United States Constitution

The Constitution, formally adopted in 1789, but amended in important respects since, established the federal government, including in Article I the Congress with its Senate and House of Representatives, in Article II the Presidency, and in Article III the United States Supreme Court. Article VI of the Constitution contains the Supremacy Clause which declares that "[t]his Constitution, and the Laws of the United States which shall be made in Pursuance thereof, and all Treaties made, or which shall be made under the Authority of the United States, shall be the supreme Law of the Land, and the Judges in every State shall be bound thereby, any Thing in the Constitution or Laws of any State to the Contrary notwithstanding." In other words, where the Constitution speaks to an issue, it is the primary law of the United States, and overrides all contrary state laws. The Constitution also defines the outer limits of the powers of the federal government and each of its three branches.

Other parts of the Constitution declare certain areas off limits. For example, Article I, section 9 declares, "No Bill of Attainder or ex post facto Law shall be passed." And amendments to the Constitution impose even more important limitations on federal authority. The first ten amendments, which you know as the Bill of Rights, prohibit Congress from interfering with protected rights. Specifically, under the First Amendment, Congress is prohibited from making laws establishing a religion or prohibiting the free exercise of a religion or abridging freedom of speech or of the press. The Fourth Amendment protects the right of the people to be secure in their persons, houses, papers, and effects, against unreasonable searches and seizure. The Sixth Amendment provides criminal defendants the right to a speedy and public trial and the right to assistance of counsel. And the Eighth Amendment prohibits excessive bail, excessive fines, and cruel and unusual punishment.

In short, the Constitution creates the three branches of federal government, specifies the duties and powers each branch possesses, outlines the relationship between the federal government and the states, and limits the powers of both the federal and state governments. We'll now take a closer look at each of the three branches of the federal government.

3.2.2 The Three Branches of Government

Under the United States Constitution, federal (national) powers are distributed among the legislative, executive, and judicial branches of government. These three branches are the subjects of the first three articles of the Constitution. Each branch has specific powers assigned to it by the Constitution, and each branch has means available to check the powers of the other branches.

Specifically, Article I creates the national legislature, the Congress, consisting of the House of Representatives and the Senate. The legislature alone has the ability to pass legislation (statutory laws) for the United States. Article II establishes that the President is the chief executive and commander in chief of the armed forces of the United States. While Congress alone can pass legislation, the President can veto legislation passed by Congress and thereby prevent it from becoming law. Congress, in turn, upon a two-thirds vote of the House and the Senate, can override the President's veto. Under Article III, the federal courts exercise the judicial power of the United States. As determined by the United States Supreme Court in an early decision, *Marbury v. Madison,* this power includes the power to declare unconstitutional (contrary to the United States Constitution), and thus unenforceable, acts of the Congress and the President. But, to check the power of the judicial branch, Congress has the authority to create and fund the courts and, for the most part, to regulate federal court jurisdiction.

Thus, under the Constitution, each branch has its own specified area of authority and also its own responsibility for checking the exercise of authority by the other branches. As we will see, this division of power into three branches reflects the Founding Fathers' distrust of concentrated federal power and gives rise to the separation-of-powers principles applied by the courts to restrain the legislative and executive branches from overstepping their proper authority.

3.2.2(a) The Legislative Branch

Under Article I, section 1 of the United States Constitution, "[a]ll legislative Powers herein granted shall be vested in a Congress of the United States, which shall consist of a Senate and House of Representatives." Section 8 of Article I lists the "enumerated powers" of the legislature. These include the power to tax, to regulate interstate commerce, to declare war, to control immigration, to protect intellectual property, and to establish federal courts in addition to the Supreme Court.

A longstanding debate concerns the scope of Congress' power, "[t]o make all Laws which shall be *necessary and proper* for carrying into Execution the foregoing Powers...." In the landmark decision *McCulloch v. Maryland,* the Court was asked to determine whether the Necessary and Proper Clause included the power to establish a federal bank which would facilitate the exercise of the taxing and spending powers.[8] Alexander Hamilton believed that "necessary and proper" meant convenient and useful; Thomas Jefferson believed that it meant required or essential. Chief Justice John Marshall accepted Hamilton's expansive interpretation, thereby granting Congress great latitude to legislate within its enumerated powers.

While all its powers are important, two enumerated powers dominate the legislative agenda: (1) the power to regulate interstate commerce; and (2) the power to tax and fund (or decline to fund) government programs, including programs and operations of the executive and judicial branches. First, the power to regulate interstate commerce gives Congress the authority to reach all commercial transactions in the United States, from the smallest mom-and-pop shop to the largest multinational conglomerate. In addition, Congress's Commerce Clause power limits the states' ability to regulate commerce within their borders. So, for example, when New York adopted provisions restricting the direct sale of wine to New Yorkers by out-of-state wineries, the Court struck the statute down for improperly exercising state control over interstate commerce, which only Congress can do.[9] Second, the power to tax and spend gives Congress the power of the purse over every federal dollar spent for the military, interstate highways, airports, national parks, judicial salaries and courthouses, health and welfare programs, education, immigration and naturalization, national security, the arts, the space program, and scientific and medical research. Through the vigorous exercise of these powers in the 20th century, the federal government and its relationship to the states and its citizens have been transformed.

3.2.2(b) *The Executive Branch*

Under Article II, section 1 of the Constitution, "[t]he executive Power shall be vested in a President of the United States of America." Section 2 of Article II declares the President "Commander in Chief of the Army and Navy of the United States," and gives the President power "by and with the Advice and Consent of the Senate, to make Treaties" and to nominate ambassadors, "Judges of the Supreme Court, and all other Officers of the United States, whose Appointments are not herein otherwise provided for, and which shall be established by Law...."

---

8. McCulloch v. Maryland, 17 U.S. (4 Wheat.) 316 (1819).
9. Granholm v. Heald, 544 U.S. 460 (2005).

In fact, today the President's executive branch has greatly expanded powers from the earliest days of the federal government. Much of this expansion has been accomplished by the creation of executive departments, including the presidential cabinet (not mentioned in the Constitution) consisting of the departments of Agriculture, Commerce, Education, Energy, Housing and Urban Development, Interior, Labor, State, Defense, Transportation, Treasury, Justice, Veterans, and Health and Human Services. Moreover, presidential advisors head numerous organizations including the National Security Advisor, Council of Economic Advisors, and Office of Management and Budget. And finally, Congress has created numerous administrative agencies, which are part of the executive branch. Currently, administrative agencies, such as the Food and Drug Administration, Environmental Protection Agency, and Securities and Exchange Commission, possess enormous rule-making (legislative-like) and adjudicative (judicial-like) powers. They may even be considered a separate branch of the federal government because they act like legislatures, executives, and the judiciary in their many roles in government.

3.2.2(c) The Judicial Branch

Under Article III, section 1 of the Constitution, "[t]he judicial Power of the United States, shall be vested in one supreme Court, and in such inferior Courts as the Congress may from time to time ordain and establish." In other words, the Constitution does not establish any federal courts except the Supreme Court. And it does not specify a structure for the Supreme Court; for example, it does not prescribe a certain number of Justices. But the very first Congress created lower federal courts, and we have had them ever since. Another part of Article III, section 1 declares that United States federal judges "shall hold their Offices during good Behavior." Thus federal judges are appointed by the President, with confirmation by the Senate, for life and can be removed only by impeachment. Section 2 of Article III describes cases and controversies to which the judicial power extends, and will be covered in detail later.

3.2.2(c)(i) Court Structure

The structure of the federal court system is essentially a pyramid. At the top of the pyramid is the United States Supreme Court which has the power to review all lower federal court decisions. In the middle are the sixteen courts of appeal which have the power to review trial court decisions within their jurisdiction. At the base are the 100+ trial courts where most civil and criminal cases are initiated and resolved. In addition to these three courts, as will be explained below, the federal system also includes a handful of specialty courts exercising jurisdiction over specific kinds of disputes. In this section we will briefly consider each of these courts in the federal judiciary.

Trial Courts

Trial courts are the entry-level courts where cases are initiated and trials are conducted. In the federal system, the primary trial courts are called district courts. Congress has divided the United States and its territories into ninety-four geographic areas called districts. Each state is home to at least one district, and larger states have multiple districts. For example, Nebraska has one district whereas California has four districts. There is one district court in each district. Each district has at least two judges, and the more populous districts have many more. Because each district may cover an entire state or at least a large geographic region, the district court may have a courthouse in several cities. For example, California is divided into the Eastern, Northern, Central and Southern Districts. The Eastern District extends from the Oregon border down to Bakersfield, California, and from the Nevada border almost to the Pacific Ocean. Because of its vast geographic territory, the Eastern District Court has two courthouses, one in Sacramento and one in Fresno.

In the federal system, each case is assigned to a specific district court judge when it is initially filed, and that judge presides over the case from beginning to end. The district court judges do not specialize in any particular type of case but handle a wide range of both civil and criminal actions. In all cases, the judges determine the rules of law which apply to the cases before them. For example, the judge decides which jury instructions should be given at the conclusion of the evidence and arguments. In most civil actions for money damages and felony criminal actions, the litigants may demand a jury to determine questions of fact. For example, when two witnesses offer conflicting testimony over the speed a car was traveling, the jury determines which witness is telling the truth. In cases where a jury is not permitted or where the parties waive their right to a jury, the judge may determine both questions of law and questions of fact.

Two kinds of judges serve in the district courts: district court judges and magistrate judges. District judges are nominated by the President and confirmed by the Senate. To assure their absolute independence, they enjoy life tenure subject only to impeachment by the Senate. Given the significance of the cases they hear and their life tenure, the Senators understandably view the appointment of a district judge in their state as a matter of great importance. For this reason, they are usually actively involved in the selection and appointment process. Magistrate judges, on the other hand, have more limited authority which is delegated to them by the district court judges within restrictions imposed by federal court rules. Typically they hold hearings on pretrial motions and recommend dispositions to the district judges. In addition, with the consent of the parties, they are authorized to conduct trials in civil cases and criminal misdemeanor cases. Unlike district judges, magistrate judges are appointed by the district court judges for fixed terms of eight years with the possibility of reappointment.

In addition to the district courts, Congress has created several other trial-level courts to hear special kinds of cases. Tax Court hears cases brought by taxpayers against the Internal Revenue Service. The Court of Federal Claims hears cases brought to recover money damages from the United States government. The bankruptcy courts hear cases relating to and arising out of bankruptcies. The Court of International Trade hears cases involving disputes relating to customs duties and imports. Finally, the Foreign Intelligence Wiretap Court handles the Attorney General's applications to permit wiretaps for national security purposes.

While these entry-level courts are generally referred to as "trial courts," very few cases actually go to trial. Today, most cases are settled by agreement between the parties without an actual trial. In fact, the number of trials has decreased significantly in the past four decades.[10] One study found that the number of federal civil trials decreased 21% from 1962 to 2002.[11] In that period, the number of cases going to trial dropped from 11.5% to 1.8%.[12] The steepest drop has been in the past two decades. In 1985, federal courts held 12,529 trials; in 2002 the number had dropped 64% to 4,510 trials.[13]

Increasingly, federal judges actively assist the parties in resolving the cases short of trial through affirmative case management. The judge sets a schedule for each case so that it will move efficiently through the system and conducts conferences with the parties to explore the possibility of settlement. Many courts have established alternative dispute resolution procedures (ADR) which also help resolve cases without trials. Given the increasing number of cases in the system, the courts and most experts believe that this active case management is essential to ensure that cases will be resolved without undue delay and expense. Moreover, given the expense and unpredictability of trials, many argue that resolving civil disputes without a trial leaves more money to satisfy the parties.[14] Critics, however, contend that the lack of trials denies the public

---

10. Tyler Cunningham, *Even as U.S. Judicial System Expands, the Number of Trials Has Decreased Dramatically,* Daily Recorder, June 2, 2004.

11. *Id.*

12. *Id.*

13. *Id.*

14. *Id.*

vital information.[15] Settlements and ADR procedures are usually confidential. To many, this secret justice system undermines public accountability.

Appellate Courts

If a party loses in the trial court and wishes to challenge the outcome, the party may appeal. To provide intermediate appellate review of the district courts, Congress has created thirteen judicial circuits. In each circuit, the United States Court of Appeals reviews the decisions of the district courts within the circuit's territory. Eleven of the circuits are numbered and cover designated geographic areas including several states. The Ninth Circuit, for example, is the largest; it includes Alaska, Arizona, California, Guam, Hawaii, Idaho, Nevada, Northern Mariana Islands, Oregon, Montana, and Washington. In contrast to this vast western circuit, the First Circuit consists of Maine, Massachusetts, New Hampshire, Rhode Island, and Puerto Rico. These circuit courts resolve conflicting interpretations of the law in the various district courts. For this reason, it is advantageous to have the circuits cover a somewhat large territory so that the federal law in the region will be uniformly reviewed and applied.

In addition to the eleven numbered circuits, there are two circuits in Washington D.C. which handle a more specialized docket. Specifically, the D.C. Circuit is often called upon to review challenges to federal legislation and regulatory provisions in addition to reviewing the routine appeals from its district court. The United States Court of Appeals for the Federal Circuit reviews cases based on their subject matter including appeals from cases under patent law, claims against the federal government, and claims from the Court of International Trade.

In addition to the circuit courts, Congress has created three appellate courts to hear special kinds of cases. The Court of Military Appeals reviews court-martial convictions of members of the armed forces. The Court of Veterans Appeals reviews decisions of the Veterans Administration denying benefits to claimants. Finally, the Temporary Emergency Court of Appeals hears appeals from district courts involving certain provisions of federal energy regulations.

Like district court judges, appellate judges are nominated by the President and confirmed by the Senate. In contrast to the district court appointment process, the President has more leeway in nominating judges since the circuit courts cover more than one state and no one state Senator has the expectation of deep involvement in the selection.

---

15. *Id.*

Appellate review is limited in scope to correcting errors of law. The court of appeal will review the written record of the trial court to determine whether the court made a legal error so significant that the judgment should be reversed. If the district court, for example, gave the jury a completely erroneous instruction that may have caused the jury to reach the wrong conclusion, then the court of appeal may reverse the judgment. Erroneous legal instructions are mistakes of law which can be grounds for appellate reversal. But the error must be sufficiently serious that the appellate court is convinced the outcome might have been tainted by the error. Trivial errors are ignored on appeal under the doctrine of "harmless error."

While the court of appeal will reverse a judgment where it finds a serious error of law in the record, it does not accept any new evidence and will not review questions of fact. For example, if the testimony of two witnesses conflicted and the jury believed one instead of the other, the losing party cannot claim that the decision should be reversed. Resolving factual disputes is the province of the jury which heard the live testimony and evaluated the witnesses' credibility. The court of appeal accepts the factual determinations of the trier of fact and will not reverse judgments on this basis.

In reviewing lower court decisions, the circuit courts sit in panels of three judges which rotate constantly. When the decisions of these panels conflict and in matters of particular significance, the court may decide to rehear the case *en banc* which usually means that all the active judges will hear the case. In some of the larger circuits, however, en banc review would be extremely unwieldy. For example the Ninth Circuit has nearly thirty active judges. To streamline the en banc process, Congress has authorized a limited en banc review permitting a circuit with more than fifteen judges to sit *en banc* with fewer than all its members. Under this authority, the Ninth Circuit holds en banc hearings with eleven judges.

In recent years, commentators have expressed concern that the crushing caseload in the federal circuit courts is beyond their capacity.[16] As a result, the courts are creating a two-tier system where the complex cases receive careful consideration while the other matters receive only cursory review. To keep up with the work, the courts have increasingly relied on staff attorneys to sort the cases. As Judge Wald explained, "It is a two-track system, and the tracks basically get allocated by non-judges."[17] Moreover, the courts are increasingly

---

16. William Glaberson, *Caseload Forcing Two-Level System for U.S. Appeals*, N.Y. Times, Mar. 14, 1999, at 11.

17. *Id.* at 1.

issuing unpublished decisions and using other procedural short cuts, including one-word decisions, to cope with the burden. According to Professor Baker, "We have so many procedural shortcuts that appeals today are processed in a kind of assembly line and the judges are not paying enough attention to individual cases because they can't."[18] On the other hand, some appellate judges support the two-track system as an efficient method for allocating judicial resources. For example, one circuit court judge stated, "The federal courts have developed sophisticated management techniques that differentiate between cases that are genuinely difficult and challenging and those which are straightforward."[19]

Supreme Court

The United States Supreme Court is established by Article III of the Constitution. Under Article III, Congress determines the number of Justices who sit on the Court. Since the middle of nineteenth century—and despite President Roosevelt's efforts to the contrary[20]—the Court has had nine Justices including one Chief Justice. Like all other Article III judges, the Justices are nominated by the President and confirmed by the Senate for life terms subject only to impeachment by the Senate. Unlike circuit courts which perform their review in small panels, at the Supreme Court all nine Justices participate in every case. The Court opens its annual term on the first Monday in October in its beautiful white marble building inscribed over the entrance with the words "equal justice under law."

The Supreme Court has the power to review all federal court and some state court decisions. The Supreme Court has jurisdiction to review all decisions of the federal appellate courts and, in this sense, it is the top of the pyramid in the federal system. The Court also has the power to review decisions of the highest state courts when questions of federal law are involved. The federal questions may arise either based on the United States Constitution or a federal statute. For example, if the Texas Supreme Court determined that affirmative action programs violate the United States Constitution by denying persons equal protection of the law, then the United States Supreme Court would

---

18. *Id.* at 20.

19. *Id.* at 20.

20. In 1937, President Franklin D. Roosevelt proposed increasing the number of justices up to a maximum of fifteen by adding new justices when older justices failed to retire within six months of reaching their seventieth birthdays. He argued that new blood was needed, but in reality he was frustrated because a bare majority of justices on the Court were invalidating his legislative proposals addressing the economic depression. JOHN E. NOWAK AND RONALD D. ROTUNDA, CONSTITUTIONAL LAW 33 (6th ed. 2000).

have jurisdiction to review that Texas state court decision. On the other hand, the Court has no authority to review questions of purely state law. For example, unless it raises a constitutional problem, the United States Supreme Court has no power to review the Texas Supreme Court's interpretation of a Texas statute; the Texas Supreme Court is the final authority on Texas law.

Obviously, the jurisdiction of the United States Supreme Court is vast. Without even considering review of state court decisions, the nine Justices could not possibly review all the decisions of the federal appellate courts where more than 65,000 cases were filed in 2005.[21] To permit the Court to focus on the cases that truly merit its attention, the Court's review is almost entirely discretionary. A party seeking Supreme Court review files a petition with the court explaining the significance of the issues presented. If four of the nine Justices conclude that they should review the case, they grant a writ of *certiorari* which means that they will hear the case. If fewer than four Justices vote to grant review, the decision of the lower court becomes the final decision in the case. The denial of *certiorari* should not be taken as approval of the lower court's decision. Sometimes the Court finds that its docket is simply too crowded, sometimes the Court defers review so that the law may develop in the lower courts, and sometimes the Court believes that the issues are too idiosyncratic to address. The Court strives to focus on the important questions affecting significant numbers of people.

In determining which cases to review, the Court considers three main factors:

- whether a circuit court has reached a decision that conflicts with decisions of other federal circuit courts or state courts of last resort on an important issue;
- whether a state court of last resort has decided an important federal question in a way that conflicts with a circuit court or other state court of last resort; and
- whether a lower court has decided an important question of federal law that has not been but should be settled by the Court.[22]

While this screening process is necessary, it reflects the unfortunate reality that not every wrong decision will be corrected. Injustice happens.

Recognizing that the Court cannot possibly review every case where a litigant is disappointed (which is every case), and that it must conserve its resources to focus on important questions, how many cases should the Court

---

21. Federal Judicial Caseload Statistics, http://www.uscourts.gov/caseload2005 (last visited Jan. 21, 2006).
22. Supreme Court Rule 10.

resolve each term? Lately, the Court has reviewed fewer and fewer cases. Specifically, in 1981, the Court issued 167 decisions.[23] From 1981 to 1988, the Court averaged about 155 decisions a year.[24] But in the 1990s its docket dropped to fewer than 90 decisions per year.[25] Increasingly, scholars are concerned that the Court's shrinking docket is leaving more inter-circuit conflicts unresolved, more constitutional challenges undetermined, and more injustices uncorrected.[26]

3.2.2(c)(ii) Federal Jurisdiction

Now that we've seen the structure of the federal courts, we'll consider in greater detail the kinds of cases that they decide. Consistent with the Constitution's vision of a limited federal government, the jurisdiction of the federal courts is limited to disputes involving federal questions or interstate or international controversies. Thus, the first issue to be resolved in a federal trial court is whether it has the power to adjudicate the controversy. If the court determines that it lacks jurisdiction, it will refuse to hear the case. Thus, as a threshold matter, the federal court will always determine whether a new case presents a federal question or diversity of citizenship.

Federal question cases are those arising under the federal Constitution, a national treaty, or an act of Congress. For example, cases involving violations of the federal constitutional right to equal protection of the law can be brought in federal courts. Similarly, actions can be brought for violations of statutory rights such as the Americans with Disabilities Act. Federal statutes may also give rights to actions involving labor conditions under the Occupational Safety and Health Act. Federal statutes also apply to voting rights, securities and banking transactions, environmental protection, health insurance coverage, and a host of other matters of national concern. Finally, admiralty has traditionally been viewed as an area of exclusive federal concern. In addition to cases involving rights under the Constitution and federal civil statutes, federal question jurisdiction extends to criminal prosecutions under federal criminal laws. Congress has enacted criminal laws in areas of federal concern including interstate commerce and national security. For example, kidnapping is a federal crime because it often involves transportation of the victim across state lines. Similarly, since drug abuse is a national problem and trafficking crosses state lines, federal criminal statutes apply.

---

23. Erwin Chemerinsky, *What's Up, Docket?*,CAL. LAW., Jan. 1999, at 29.
24. *Id.*
25. *Id.*
26. *Id.*

In addition to federal question cases, the federal courts have jurisdiction to hear diversity cases involving citizens of different states or countries where the matter in controversy exceeds $75,000. Diversity jurisdiction is designed to prevent local prejudice in favor of the state resident from interfering with the impartial administration of justice. For example, assume a California resident and a New York resident have a contract dispute involving a $1 million construction contract. The plaintiff could file the action in federal court because the two parties are residents of different states and the amount in controversy exceeds the $75,000 minimum. Moreover, if the Californian brought suit in a California state court hoping to enjoy a home-field advantage, the New Yorker could have the case transferred to federal court. This transfer from state to federal court is called removal. Thus, even though state law will govern the resolution of the action since it is a basic contract dispute, the federal court will hear the case. In this way, federal courts are frequently called upon to apply state law. While diversity of citizenship is a basis for federal jurisdiction in most disputes, there are two important exceptions where federal courts are generally barred from resolving disputes despite diversity: family law (divorce and child custody) and estates (administration of the property of a deceased person). These cases must be adjudicated in state court.

In short, federal courts are courts of limited jurisdiction. They will only accept actions where federal jurisdictional requirements are satisfied. To proceed in federal court, the litigants must establish either federal question or diversity jurisdiction. The complexities of these issues are covered in depth in a course entitled Federal Jurisdiction.

Now that we've outlined the three branches of the federal government and considered the substantive law areas the federal courts adjudicate, we'll turn to the relationship between these three branches and consider limits on each branch based on the doctrines of judicial review and separation of powers.

3.2.2(c)(iii) Judicial Review

The term "judicial review" has two meanings. The first, and less controversial, is the notion of appellate court review of lower court decisions. By statute in every state and by federal law, a criminal defendant convicted of a crime is entitled to at least one appellate review of the conviction, and this review is considered a part of due process of law under the Fifth and Fourteenth Amendments to the United States Constitution. Although there is no federal constitutional requirement that a litigant in a civil case have a right to appellate review of an adverse trial court action, all states and the federal courts have provided for some right of appeal. Thus, the losing party has an established right to some appellate review of both criminal and civil trial court actions. The federal system and most state systems also provide a second level of (usually) discretionary review in their highest court. With a dual level of review, the first appellate court or intermediate appellate court has responsibility for most error correction. In other words, the intermediate courts of appeal review trial court records for errors of law that affect substantial rights of the parties and require reversal or reconsideration by the trial court. In a dual appellate system, the second level review by the highest court, besides being almost entirely discretionary, is usually a broader, policy-oriented review (sometimes called "institutional review") to rationalize and develop the law.

The second way in which we use the term "judicial review" refers to a more controversial doctrine. The United States Constitution includes provisions that give the executive and legislative branches some control over the judicial branch. The President appoints federal judges; Congress decides whether and which lower federal courts to establish, determines the number of judges on all federal courts including the Supreme Court, confirms judges nominated by the President, and controls the scope of federal judicial power (subject matter jurisdiction). But the Constitution does not expressly provide that the judicial branch has any power to control the executive and legislative branches of the federal government. The principal source of this control was developed (maybe found or, as some argue, created) by the federal courts themselves. This is the second idea of judicial review: that the federal courts, most particularly the Supreme Court, have the power to rule on and declare acts of Congress and the President to be unconstitutional.

This doctrine of judicial review can be traced to the landmark case of *Marbury v. Madison*,[27] a case many of you have already studied as undergraduates. Professor William Burnham stated the reasoning in Marbury v. Madison as follows:

> The Court in *Marbury*, speaking through Chief Justice John Marshall, found judicial review implicit in the nature of a written constitution, in the supremacy clause and in Article III's grant of judicial power. He reasoned as follows. First, the Constitution is law and must be followed; indeed, the supremacy clause makes the Constitution the supreme law of the land. Second, the judges of the judicial branch, being vested by Article III with the "judicial Power of the United States," have the power to say what the law is in cases that come before them. It follows then that, if in a case pending before those judges

---

27. 5 U.S. (1 Cranch) 137 (1803).

both legislation and the Constitution apply to an issue, the judges must follow the hierarchy of law set out in the supremacy clause: they must apply the constitutional provision and disregard the statute.[28]

An example helps illustrate the concept. Assume Congress passed a statute that subjects all high school students to warrantless strip searches in order to locate drugs and that a group of students challenged the statute as violating their Fourth Amendment constitutional right to be free from unreasonable searches. If the Supreme Court agrees that the statute violates the students' constitutional rights, the Supreme Court must follow the Constitution as the supreme law of the land. The Court cannot enforce an unconstitutional statute or the Constitution would be relegated to an inferior status. If the Congress were able to pass laws in defiance of the Constitution, then Congress—not the Constitution— would be supreme. But to enforce the Constitution means the Court must invalidate Congress' legislation. In this way, judicial review gives the Court the power to control Congress when it oversteps constitutional bounds. In other words, the Court serves as the check on congressional excesses.

Critics contend that the democratic process—not the Court—is the proper curb on legislative and executive excesses. If the President or Congress exceeds their proper roles, the voters can correct the abuse at the ballot box. The legitimacy of judicial review and its true source remains a vigorously debated matter to this day, but the doctrine seems firmly established and accepted by all branches of the federal government. Even more hotly debated is whether vigorous judicial review is a good or bad thing, a question that occurs perennially and the answer to which often depends upon the politics of the commentator. After all, the same United States Supreme Court (at different times) declared Congress had no power to end slavery[29] and that segregation of the races in public schools violated the Constitution.[30]

These issues have more than merely historical interest. While from the 1930s to the 1990s the Court rarely struck down statutes on the grounds they exceeded congressional power, more recently the United States Supreme Court has declared several acts of Congress unconstitutional:

United States v. Morrison:[31] By a 5–4 vote, the Court struck down provisions of the Violence Against Women Act. Chief Justice Rehn-

---

28. WILLIAM BURNHAM, INTRODUCTION TO THE LAW AND LEGAL SYSTEM OF THE UNITED STATES 10 (1995).
29. Dred Scott v. Sanford, 60 U.S. (19 How.) 393 (1857).
30. Brown v. Board of Education, 347 U.S. 483 (1954).
31. . 529 U.S. 598 (2000).

quist explained that "The Founders ... reposed in the states the suppression of violent crime and the vindication of its victims.... We accordingly reject the argument that Congress may regulate noneconomic, violent criminal conduct [even though it affects interstate commerce]."

Kimel v. Florida Board of Regents:[32] By another 5–4 vote, the Court held that the Age Discrimination in Employment Act could not be enforced against the states because they have sovereign immunity and the Congress lacked authority to overcome this immunity. Dissenting Justice Stevens wrote, "The kind of judicial activism manifested in [the recent federalism rulings] represents such a radical departure from the proper role of this Court that it should be opposed whenever the opportunity arises."

Board of Trustees of the University of Alabama v. Garrett:[33] The Court held that the Congress exceeded its authority in adopting provisions of the Americans with Disabilities Act requiring states to make special accommodations for the disabled. Again by a margin of 5–4, the Court held such requirements violated state sovereignty since there was no showing of irrational state discrimination against the disabled.

While this line of cases suggested a trend to increased scrutiny by the Court over congressional action, more recent decisions have upheld legislation that had been challenged on the ground that it exceeded congressional authority. Specifically, in 2003, the Court held that the Family and Medical Leave Act was within Congress' power under the Equal Protection Clause to provide prophylactic remedies to counter the well-documented history of gender discrimination in the workplace.[34] And in 2004, the Court upheld provisions of the Americans with Disabilities Act pertaining to access to public buildings in a case where a paraplegic person was required to crawl upstairs in a courthouse that lacked wheelchair accessibility.[35] The Court concluded that the legislation was within congressional power to enforce the Equal Protection Clause.

Today, as this edition is being prepared, the Supreme Court has under consideration the most significant challenge to commerce clause powers since the

---

32. 528 U.S. 62 (2000).
33. 531 U.S. 955 (2001).
34. Nevada Dept. of Human Resources v. Hibbs, 538 U.S. 721 (2003).
35. Tennessee v. Lane, 541 U.S. 509 (2004).

1930s. The constitutionality of the Patient Protection and Affordable Care Act's individual mandate has been challenged by individuals, states, and organizations. They argue that Congress exceeded its power to regulate interstate commerce when it passed the health care law that requires individuals to choose between buying insurance they may not want or paying a penalty. That question about the scope of Congress's power under the Constitution is the heart of the legal battle over the health care law. When you read this book, you will know what the Court decided. What do you think of the Court's recent federalism decisions? Is the Court properly enforcing principles of federalism? Or has it engaged in an undemocratic usurpation of legislative authority? What is the proper relationship between the federal government and the states? What is the proper role of the Court in reviewing democratically adopted legislation supported by the majority of the people? You'll study these questions in Constitutional Law and probably ponder them for the rest of your legal career.

3.2.2(d) Separation of Powers

Because they feared the accumulation of excessive power, the Founding Fathers divided the government's power into three branches—the legislative, the executive and the judiciary. By dividing the power, the framers strove to protect citizens from government abuse which could result from the concentration of too much power in too few hands. Thus, in our system, the "separation of powers" is a fundamental structural safeguard. The Constitution does not contain any explicit mention of "separation of powers," so its meaning has been gradually developed by the three branches themselves, and most notably by the courts. The doctrine today means that each of the three branches has autonomy within its constitutional role. Congress cannot act as the President, or declare laws or acts unconstitutional, as the courts may. The President cannot appropriate money for a war not declared or funded by Congress. Congress and the President cannot reverse a decision of the United States Supreme Court declaring one of their orders or actions in violation of the Constitution (although they may resist the implication of the Court's action and refuse to fund changes the Court may require).

These separation-of-powers issues are frequently raised when the Court considers the constitutionality of actions by the legislative and executive branches under principles of judicial review. In these cases, the legislative or executive action is challenged as unconstitutionally intruding on the power of another branch of government. The Court will then determine whether the action was within or outside constitutional bounds under separation-of-powers principles. This all may seem commonsensical, especially to those of us who have grown up within and been taught about this system all our lives, but it certainly does not appear that way to those outside of the United States. And even for United States lawyers and judges, extraordinarily complex separation-of-powers questions regularly occur. Consider a few examples:

> *Printz v. United States:*[36] The majority held certain provisions of the Brady Handgun Violence Prevention Act to be unconstitutional; the majority concluded that Congress' effort to require state law enforcement officials to execute federal law reduced the executive power of the President, thus undermining the separation of powers;

> *Raines v. Byrd:*[37] The Court denied a challenge to the Line Item Veto Act by members of Congress who voted against the Act on the ground that the members lack standing to sue (the need for a party to have suffered some particularized, concrete and otherwise judicially cognizable personal injury in order to bring an action in federal court), something the majority found "built" on the idea of separation of powers—in this case the need to keep the judiciary's power within its proper constitutional sphere;

> *City of Boerne v. Flores:*[38] The Court held the Religious Freedom Restoration Act of 1993 (RFRA) was unconstitutional; the majority found that RFRA exceeded Congress' powers under §5 of the Fourteenth Amendment because it contradicted principles necessary to maintain separation of powers by limiting the Courts' power to interpret the Constitution; and

> *Clinton v. Jones:*[39] The Court refused to give the president immunity from suit during his time in office; it rejected the separation-of-powers argument that in allowing the suit to go forward the judiciary was imposing a burden on the executive branch that impaired the president's effective performance of his office.

While separation-of-powers questions are frequently resolved in court, the courts can also become involved in the conflicts. When the FBI searched the congressional office of Representative William Jefferson pursuant to a court-

---

36. 521 U.S. 898 (1997).
37. 521 U.S. 811 (1997).
38. 521 U.S. 507 (1997).
39. 525 U.S. 820 (1998).

authorized subpoena, the House leadership responded with a rare demonstration of institutional unity. The Republican Speaker of the House, Dennis Hastert, and the Democratic Leader, Nancy Pelosi, issued a joint statement charging that the executive branch had overstepped its authority and improperly intruded on the legislative branch. Since the legislative branch is responsible for oversight of the executive branch, commentators feared that Congress would be chilled by the threat of having their offices raided by executive officers.

As law students engaged in the process of critical thinking about the law, consider why our federal government is restrained by the principle of separation of powers and what benefits and burdens the principle confers on the government. As a political matter, separation of powers was intended to divide government, diffuse its powers, and provide for checks on each of the three branches. But the idea can also create a sense of entitlement in each of the branches as well, a desire to protect its prerogatives whether good or bad. Certainly for the courts this has been a recurring theme and fundamental to the doctrine of judicial review of legislative and executive conduct.

In addition to limiting the actions of the legislative and executive branches, the federal courts apply separation-of-powers concepts in limiting their own power. In particular, federal courts have always paid strict attention to the limits on their judicial power to resolve cases. Both the constitutional provisions and statutes setting out the limits on federal judicial power have been interpreted narrowly and cautiously to limit interference with both the legislative and executive branches of the federal government as well as state judiciaries and state interests. Separation-of-powers ideas are also at the heart of "justiciability" limits that the federal courts have imposed on themselves. Specifically, federal courts will not render advisory opinions; they insist on injury sufficient to give the parties "standing" to appear before the court. To have standing, a party must show that he or she has a concrete stake in the outcome, not a hypothetical or philosophical objection. Similarly, the federal courts will not resolve political questions which are resolved by the democratic process.

3.3 The State Governments

Like the federal government, each state has a written constitution which establishes the state's three branches of government. In the following sections, we will outline the typical structure of state courts and present some parallels and contrasts to the federal judiciary. The information is simplified; please remember that each of the fifty state governments is somewhat distinct and that they vary in many details. Despite these variations, we can begin our discussion with some useful generalizations.

3.3.1 State Court Structure

Like the federal system, most state judiciaries have three levels of courts: trial courts, intermediate appellate courts, and supreme courts. Beyond this basic structure, there is considerable variation in the state court systems.[40] In this section, we will outline some of the more common features of these systems.

Trial Courts

While the names given to the courts vary from state to state, the entry to the state court system is the trial court where cases are initially filed. For this reason, they are often called courts of original jurisdiction. In many states, these courts are divided into two levels. The lowest level of trial court is typically a court of limited jurisdiction hearing cases involving small claims, traffic violations, and petty offenses. The jurisdiction of these courts is limited to more minor matters and they may be described as courts of limited jurisdiction. Often lawyers are not permitted to represent parties, and the proceedings are conducted quite informally. A dissatisfied party can usually seek a new trial in the next level trial court. The next level of trial court is the trial court of general jurisdiction which hears a wide range of civil and criminal cases. It may be organized into departments or divisions specializing in a particular subject matter such as criminal or family law.

In addition to this pattern of two-tier trial courts, some states have separate courts to hear certain cases. For example, some states have traffic courts with authority only over violations of the vehicle code; some states have drug courts with authority only over violations of the narcotics laws; some states have juvenile courts with authority only over crimes by youthful offenders. These courts may also be described as courts of limited jurisdiction because they are only empowered to handle certain kinds of proceedings. Unlike the lowest level of trial court, though, while these courts have limited jurisdiction, the jurisdiction is limited by subject matter not by the amount of money at stake.

Thus, the state trial courts may have many names and structures. For example, a state could have a two-tiered system and also have some specialized

---

40. The National Center for State Courts has a very informative website, including a page with a map of the United States where you can click on any state to see the structure of its court system. *See* http://www.ncsconline.org, *State Court Structure Charts* (last visited Jan. 29, 2006).

courts of limited jurisdiction. If you wanted to contest a traffic ticket, you might go to traffic court. If you were named administrator of a will, you might go to probate court. If you had a dispute with your landlord about a leaky roof, you might go to small claims court. If you were injured in a traffic accident, you might go to the trial court of general jurisdiction. In many states, the structure is complex and sometimes Byzantine.

In recent years, reformers have launched a movement to simplify and unify state trial courts by consolidating them into a single level to achieve more efficient workload management. In a unified system, cases and judges can be assigned depending on the needs of the docket without numerous restrictions. For example, until recently California had a multi-tiered system (small claims courts of limited jurisdiction, justice courts of limited jurisdiction, municipal courts of limited jurisdiction, and superior courts of general jurisdiction). In an effort to streamline the process, justice courts have been eliminated; municipal and superior courts have been consolidated. The consolidation of these trial courts into a single level should simplify and speed up the administration of the courts' business and reduce unnecessary expense and delay.

Somewhat paradoxically, just as many states are consolidating their trial courts, others are establishing specialized courts to handle commercial cases. According to a report of the ABA Business Law Section's Task Force on Business, "In an era of scarce judicial resources, the inefficiencies that result from a failure to specialize have become less and less tolerable."[41] One general feature of these courts is that one judge is assigned for the life of the case so that the litigants are not required to educate several different judges on complex cases. In this respect, the business courts are following the federal district court system of one judge for all purposes with active case management as the model.[42] Other innovations take advantage of developing technology. For example, Michigan created the nation's first cyber court for business and commercial lawsuits where the amount in controversy exceeds $25,000.[43] All documents are filed electronically and witnesses testify from remote locations via camera.[44] Proponents believe that these specialty courts attract business to the community and relieve the rest of the court's docket.[45] Critics, however, cau-

---

41. 66 U.S.L.W. 2051 (July 22, 1997).
42. Tresa Baldas, *Some Courts Are All Business*, Nat'l L. J., May 17, 2004, at 1.
43. 70 U.S.L.W. 2289 (Nov. 13, 2001).
44. *Id.*
45. Baldas, *supra* note 42, at 1; Victoria Rivkin, *Courting Tech Business*, A.B.A. J., July, 2001, at 39.

tion that these programs may shift the allocation of judicial resources to commercial cases at the expense of the rest of the court's docket.[46]

In addition to business courts, two other specialty courts are increasingly being promoted: health courts and mental health courts. First, the American Medical Association has supported model legislation for the creation of special medical courts composed of judges trained in medical standards "that could render more accurate decisions regarding whether malpractice has actually occurred and, if so, render a judgment as to the amount of monetary damages to be awarded."[47] Senate Majority Leader Bill Frist, a heart surgeon, has supported the concept.[48] Critics argue that the proposed health courts would deprive plaintiffs of their right to a jury trial.[49]

Second, in recent years more than 120 mental health courts have been created across the country.[50] These courts address the special problems the mentally ill encounter in the criminal justice system. According to the Bureau of Justice Administration, the rate of mental illness in our country's jails is 16%, more than three times the average for all Americans, and at least 75% of these people have drug or alcohol abuse problems.[51] Mental health courts attempt to provide alternatives to incarceration by providing supportive services and supervision.[52] While there are some promising trends in terms of decreased recidivism, decreased drug use, and fiscal savings, more study is needed to determine which of these programs are effective and why.[53]

Just as in the federal system, the number of cases actually going to trial in the state courts has dropped dramatically in the past few decades.[54] According to a report by the Bureau of Justice Statistics of the United States Department of Justice, civil trials in state courts in large counties dropped by nearly one-half from 1992 to 2001.[55] According to statistics reported by the National Center for State Courts, although the population in the jurisdiction of twenty-

---

46. Baldas, *supra* note 42, at 1; Wendy N. Davis, *Taking Care of Business,* A.B.A. J. , Feb. 2003, at 35.

47. John Gibeaut, *The Med-Mal Divide,* A.B.A. J., Mar. 2005, at 39.

48. *Id.*

49. Joanne Doroshow, *The Health Courts Facade,* TRIAL, Jan. 2006, at 20.

50. John Koopman, *An Alternative to Incarceration,* S.F. CHRON., Jan. 23, 2006, at A1.

51. *Id.*

52. *Id.*

53. *Id.*

54. Tyler Cunningham, *Even as U.S. Judicial System Expands, the Number of Trials Has Decreased Dramatically,* DAILY RECORDER, June 2, 2004.

55. Bureau of Justice Statistics, *Civil Trial Cases and Verdicts in Large Counties, 2001,* Apr. 2004, at 1.

two general jurisdiction courts grew by 39% from 1976 to 2002, the number of civil trials in these courts fell by 39% in the same time period.[56] As with the decline in federal court trials, commentators disagree over whether this trend reflects desirable efficiency or undermines public accountability.

Intermediate Appellate Courts

In the country's early days, states had only one appellate court, usually named the "supreme court." As litigation increased, intermediate appellate courts were created to ensure that in every dispute the parties had the right to one meaningful appeal. Today, the vast majority of states have intermediate appellate courts to handle the enormous volume of appeals and to enable the states' supreme courts to devote their attention to the most significant matters. Under this system, the dissatisfied litigant is entitled to an initial appeal to the intermediate appellate court but will generally only receive a hearing in the state supreme court in that court's discretion.

From state to state, the structure of these intermediate courts varies significantly. Some are organized geographically. For example, in California, there are six districts which hear appeals from lower courts within their geographic territory. Other intermediate appellate courts are organized by subject matter. For example, Alabama has one court for civil appeals and another for criminal appeals. On the other hand, Pennsylvania has one appellate court for disputes involving government agencies and municipalities and another for all other cases.

While the structure of these intermediate appellate courts varies from state to state, like the federal circuit courts they are limited to reviewing cases for errors of law and do not resolve factual disputes. Like the federal circuit courts, they do not receive live testimony or new evidence. They review the record of the proceedings in the lower courts for significant legal mistakes that might have affected the outcome of the case. And like the federal circuit courts, the state intermediate appellate courts generally sit in three-judge panels.

Supreme Courts

Since the creation of the intermediate appellate courts, the highest court in most states is relieved of the crushing burden of routine matters to turn its attention and resources to the most important legal disputes. In most states, this court is called the supreme court. In New York it is called the Court of Ap-

---

56. National Center for State Courts, Court Statistics Project, Civil Dispositions in Twenty-two General Jurisdiction Courts, 1976–2002, http://www.ncsconline.org (last visited Jan. 29, 2006).

peals. Two states, Texas and Oklahoma, have two courts of last resort, one for criminal matters and another for civil cases. For the sake of simplicity, we will refer to these state courts of last resort as supreme courts.

Often, review by the highest court is largely discretionary. In discretionary matters, these courts will grant review to resolve conflicts between the intermediate appellate courts, to address issues that arise frequently, and to decide significant questions involving the administration of justice. In addition to discretionary jurisdiction, supreme courts are sometimes required to review certain specified matters such as attorney disbarments and death penalty cases. In addition to providing for supreme court review in certain kinds of cases, some states provide for supreme court review of cases where the trial court has held a state or federal law unconstitutional.[57] In some states the intermediate appellate courts have authority to certify cases to the supreme court for resolution.[58] These procedures for review directly in the supreme court may be described as "by-pass" jurisdiction.[59] Also, in some states the supreme court has authority to transfer cases to itself which has been described as "reach-down" jurisdiction.[60] While there are many variations and combinations of these procedures, these procedures are all designed to insure that the supreme courts will hear matters of special significance and urgency and be spared the crushing burden of routine appeals.

3.3.2 Parallels and Contrasts to the Federal System

At this point, let's reflect a moment on some of the key points of similarity and difference between the federal government and the state governments. First, all of these multiple sovereigns are governments established by written constitutions with three branches restricted by separation-of-powers principles. Second, all have adopted the notion of judicial review whereby the courts determine whether the other branches have acted in violation of the constitution or in excess of their power. Third, almost all have court systems divided into trial courts, intermediate appellate courts, and supreme courts. The trial courts are the courts of original jurisdiction where cases are initiated and tried by a single judge with the participation of a jury when authorized. The intermediate appellate courts sit in three-judge panels to review trial court decisions for errors of law. The supreme courts are largely courts of discretionary

---

57. Daniel J. Meador, American Courts 15 (2d. ed. 2000).
58. *Id.*
59. *Id.* at 14.
60. *Id.* at 15.

jurisdiction which reserve their resources for the resolution of important questions of law or policy.

While the parallels are substantial, the points of contrast are also significant. One critical distinction is that federal courts are courts of limited jurisdiction which are only hear certain kinds of cases, whereas state courts include courts of general jurisdiction which hear all kinds of cases. Under our Constitution, the states retained substantially the same legal jurisdiction that they possessed prior to the formation of the United States government, unless that power was taken away by the Constitution or federal legislation. While the role of the federal government has expanded significantly since 1789, state law still governs most of our day-to-day activities. Given the pervasiveness of state law, it is not surprising that most legal disputes are resolved in state courts. According to former Chief Justice Rehnquist "95 percent of the judicial business in the United States is still transacted in state courts."[61]

To help you appreciate the significance of state law in our legal system, some statistics may be helpful:[62]

	50 State Courts	All Federal Courts
Cases filed annually	More than 30,000,000	Fewer than 314,000
Number of judges	More than 29,800	Fewer than 1,500

In other words, there are almost one hundred times as many cases filed each year in state court as in the federal courts. In the next section we will take a look at the nature of all these state court cases.

The method of selecting judges is also an important distinction between the state and federal systems. While federal judges are nominated by the President and confirmed by the Senate for lifetime tenure, most state judges are required to stand some kind of periodic election. In fact, 87% of state judges face some type of election.[63] The elections may be roughly divided into two categories: retention elections where the judges stand for election without competing candidates and contested elections where the judges compete head-to-head for the bench. While most elections are retention-only elections, politicization is increasing.[64]

---

61. W. Rehnquist, *Remarks of the Chief Justice of the United States on the Evolution and Independence of the Federal Courts*, THE JUDGES' JOURNAL, Winter 1997.

62. MEADOR, *supra* note 57, at 8.

63. ABA Task Force Report on Judicial Campaign Finance, Executive Summary, Nov. 1998, at 1.

64. *Id.*

One of the most disturbing problems is the increasing campaign spending and fundraising activities which it compels. Consider the appearance—if not the actuality—of improper influence if a judge is beholden to campaign contributors for her job. For example, in West Virginia, a coal company executive spent $3.5 million to support a candidate for the supreme court bench, roughly $2 for every West Virginian.[65] Moreover, the contests are increasingly politicized since candidates are now free to announce their views on disputed legal or political issues, including tort reform, gay rights, and abortion.[66] What effect does political campaigning and fundraising have on a judge's objectivity and impartiality? What effect does it have on the public's faith in an independent judiciary?

3.3.3 Areas of State Law

As we have seen, the federal courts exercise limited jurisdiction over federal question and diversity cases. In contrast, the state courts exercise general jurisdiction over almost every area of substantive law. This section will briefly outline the major areas of state law:

1. *Criminal prosecutions.* The overwhelming majority of criminal prosecutions in the United States are brought under state statutes. Criminal prosecutions are brought by the state on behalf of the people to punish misconduct. A criminal conviction amounts to a finding of guilt for which punishment—usually a jail or prison sentence—is imposed by the state. The most serious crimes leading to prison sentences are felonies which include murder, manslaughter, rape, arson, robbery, burglary, and larceny. Less serious offenses are misdemeanors or infractions; these crimes carry lesser penalties, usually involving jail terms or monetary fines.

2. *Family law.* The next largest area of state law involves family matters: marriage; divorce; marital property; guardianship and conservatorship; child custody; and adoption. Many states have specialized courts to handle family law matters.

3. *Contract disputes.* Business litigation and consumer actions are governed by contract law which is generally based on state law unless specific federal legislation has superseded the state's authority.

---

65. Terry Carter, *Mud and Money: Judicial Elections Turn to Big Bucks and Nasty Tactics*, ABA J., Feb. 2005, at 40.

66. *Id.*

4. *Real property transactions and disputes.* State law also controls the parties' rights to real property. This category includes laws pertaining to the sale and conveyancing of real property as well as the rights and obligations between landlords and tenants.
5. *Probate law.* State law controls the law of wills, inheritance, intestacy, and trusts. Many states have specialized courts to handle probate matters.
6. *Tort law.* Tort law is the body of law governing the rights of one who has been injured by another to recover for that injury. Tort law recognizes actions for assault, battery, false imprisonment, trespass, nuisance, negligence, malpractice, products liability, and defamation. The same misconduct may be grounds for both a tort action and a criminal prosecution. For example, if someone stole a car and demolished it, the state would prosecute the thief for the criminal violations while the car owner could bring a tort action against the thief to recover the value of the car. State law would govern both actions.

In addition to these vast areas where state law is generally controlling, state courts are often called on to resolve disputes involving federal law. Specifically, under the Supremacy Clause of the United States Constitution, the judges of every state are bound to follow the Constitution as well as federal laws and treaties. In addition, state courts generally have authority to hear disputes arising under federal statutes. For example, cases involving federal civil rights statutes may be filed in either state or federal court. Since state courts are courts of general jurisdiction, they may adjudicate cases brought under federal law unless Congress has specifically prohibited state jurisdiction. Federal law is also brought into state court proceedings in criminal actions where the defendant challenges the prosecution on constitutional grounds. For example, in a state criminal prosecution, a defendant may contend that a police search violated the federal constitutional right to protection from unreasonable searches. Indeed, according to one survey, federal questions were involved in more than 25% of published state supreme court cases.[67]

3.3.4 Continuing Evolution of the Common Law

Except in a few specialized areas, the heart of federal law is constitutional and statutory. Of course, courts are often called upon to enforce and interpret the Constitution and federal legislation, but the starting point for analysis is the Constitution or federal statute itself. In contrast to the federal system, state

---

67. MEADOR, *supra* note 57, at 19.

law includes constitutional and statutory law and also non-statutory, judge-made law having its historical roots in the English common law and chancery courts. To understand the continuing role and development of this judge-made common law, we'll briefly compare civil law and common law systems.

Most western countries have legal systems which may be classified as either common law or civil law systems. The civil law system, having its roots in the Roman Empire, prevails in most of Europe, Japan, Turkey and Latin America. In this system, the primary source of law is legislation which is compiled into comprehensive codes. These codes provide general principles for deciding cases; courts are not bound by prior cases but are bound to follow the codes.

On the other hand, the common law system evolved in medieval England. By colonial times, it was well developed. The common law system prevails, with a few exceptions, in Great Britain, the United States, Canada, Australia, New Zealand, and India. With the exception of Louisiana, all states in the United States adopted the common law of England near the time of their creation. For example, in 1850, California adopted the common law of England insofar as it is neither repugnant to nor inconsistent with the state or federal constitutions.[68] In the common law system, judicial decisions are a primary source of law and are in themselves binding in subsequent similar cases. Through their development of the common law, the state courts establish and refine legal principles which evolve over time in incremental steps, guided by the decisions in prior cases—or "precedents"—but sensitive and responsive to historical and social changes. Each jurisdiction has continued to develop its own common law with numerous substantive variations.

An example may help you understand the basic principles of the development of the common law. In 1348, at the Assizes—one of the King's courts in England—Judge Thorpe heard a case where a woman sued a man after he beat upon the door of her tavern with a hatchet until she stuck her head out of a window to tell him to stop.[69] The defendant argued that since he had not hit her nor caused harm, she had no legal claim or "cause of action." The court upheld the woman's action for assault because the defendant's conduct had caused her apprehension of imminent harm.

Nearly 650 years later, an Indiana court addressed a similar argument:[70] The defendants thought that the plaintiff had been harassing a young woman in their family. They entered the plaintiff's home after he had gone to bed and accused him of misconduct. During this exchange, one of the defendants kept

---

68. Cal. Civ. Code § 22.2 (West 2001).
69. I De S et Ux. v. W De S, Y.B. Lib. Ass. folio 99, placitum 60 (1348).
70. Cullison v. Medley, 570 N.E.2d 27 (Ind. 1991).

grabbing at a gun strapped to his thigh. The defendant argued that since he never removed his gun from the holster, an assault action would not lie. The court held that an action for assault was stated because it protects the right to be free from the apprehension of harmful injuries. Since the plaintiff feared the defendant would draw the gun and shoot him, he had the right to recover for assault. Certainly, Judge Thorpe—although unfamiliar with guns—would agree with the application of his precedent to the Indiana case.

Just as the common law must evolve to meet changing technology, from hatchets to guns, from print to e-mail, it must also evolve to accommodate changing moral, political, and social realities. The judges who are responsible for the upkeep of the common law struggle between maintaining the law's continuity and stability while adapting it to historical and societal change. As Justice Oliver Wendell Holmes, Jr., explained:

> The life of the [common] law has not been logic; it has been experience. The felt necessities of the time, the prevalent moral and political theories, intuitions of public policy, avowed or unconscious, even the prejudices which judges share with their fellow-men, have had a good deal more to do than the syllogism in determining the rules by which men should be governed.... The very considerations which judges most rarely mention, and always with an apology, are the secret root from which the law draws all the juices of life. I mean, of course, consideration of what is expedient for the community concerned.[71]

Our common law heritage and its continuing evolution strongly influence the substance of state law. Virtually all serious criminal felonies can be traced back to the common law, including murder, manslaughter, rape, arson, burglary, robbery, and larceny. While these crimes have been codified (adopted by statute and compiled in codes), courts still look to the common law roots of these crimes to resolve legal disputes. And much of tort law is both grounded in a common law tradition and also currently evolving as a case-by-case, non-statutory, body of law. In short, in our legal system, the state court judges continue to patch and stitch the common law to fit society's needs. In developing the common law, the courts generally reflect society's values and adopt rules supported by our historical traditions and conventional morality. The common law system is dynamic and intensely fact-sensitive. In a later chapter, we will explore the evolution of the common law.

---

71. OLIVER WENDELL HOLMES, JR., THE COMMON LAW 1, 35 (1881).

3.4 Two Features of the United States Judicial Process

We have now outlined the basic relationship between the multiple sovereignties that comprise our legal system and compared their structure and substantive law areas. In your first year of law school, you will learn about our legal system largely by reading appellate decisions. But to most of us, the judiciary and its procedures are unfamiliar and even mysterious. To help you understand the decisions you will be reading, we'll turn now to two key components of judicial process in the United States in both the federal and state systems: (1) the doctrine of *stare decisis* which compels the courts to follow precedent; and (2) the merger of law and equity which enables the courts to offer the litigants complete relief in one judicial proceeding.

3.4.1 The Doctrine of *Stare Decisis*

As we have seen, because of our heritage from the common law of England, prior court decisions represent a significant body of the controlling law. The rules and principles set out in written court opinions, or "cases," are binding in later cases. This is what we mean when we require a court to follow precedent. Today, when written opinions are officially published, they are collected in books which are known as reports or reporters. In addition to being published in books, these cases are also available through electronic retrieval systems.

The function and scope of judicial review are governed in part by the doctrine of *stare decisis*, an abbreviation of the Latin phrase "*stare decisis et non quieta movere*" meaning "to stand by precedents and not to disturb settled points." This doctrine reflects the need for stability and predictability in the law as well as the fundamental principle of fairness that requires similar cases to be treated similarly. It promotes the efficient resolution of disputes and curbs the arbitrary exercise of judicial authority. We will return to this doctrine later in these materials, but for now we will briefly sketch out some restrictions imposed by *stare decisis*.

Under the doctrine of *stare decisis*, courts are generally constrained "to stand by precedents." But what is a precedent? Simply put, a precedent is a prior judicial decision within the same judicial system (or "jurisdiction") resolving a legal dispute involving the same material facts. To illustrate, a decision by the Ninth Circuit Court of Appeals could be precedent in a later case in the Eastern District of California, but would not be a binding precedent in a case brought in Mississippi state court and governed by Mississippi state law. Moreover, a prior decision by the Ninth Circuit resolving a dispute between the Department of the Interior and an Idaho mining company over mineral rights would not necessarily be binding in a later case in the Eastern District of California involving a dispute between a disabled widow and her unscrupulous landlord. If the facts are sufficiently distinguishable, there may be a good reason to reach a different legal conclusion. In other words, although fairness requires similar cases to be decided similarly, fairness may also require different cases to be resolved differently. In short, the operation of a decision as precedent has both territorial and factual limitations.

It may surprise you to learn that you will spend a great deal of time in your first year classes discussing whether a case is precedent or whether it is factually distinguishable. Obviously, no two cases are ever precisely identical, so the question becomes what factual differences matter, what facts are the *material* facts which should influence the legal analysis. A couple of examples may be helpful. Assume in the first case the defendant is convicted of stealing a green Honda. Is that precedent for a later case where the defendant stole a red Buick? Certainly, the factual distinctions—car color and manufacturer—are meaningless in this context and the material fact is that both defendants stole cars. But what if in the first case the defendant committed the crime at gunpoint and in the second the defendant took a parked car without any violence or threat of violence? Do those different facts compel a different outcome in terms of the sentence the defendant should serve? Most of us would probably agree that a car theft involving violence should be treated more harshly than one without violence. In other words, on this point the first case is not precedent and is distinguishable. Discriminating between material and immaterial facts on discrete issues and determining how to handle distinguishing facts is one of the distinctive hallmarks of legal analysis in our common law system.

One limitation on the doctrine of *stare decisis* deserves special mention: a precedent is only binding where the court which issued the prior decision has supervisory authority over the court resolving the later dispute. Thus, decisions of the United States Supreme Court and the Ninth Circuit Court of Appeals are binding on the Eastern District of California, but decisions of the Second Circuit Court of Appeals are not. Nevertheless, under principles of fairness, comity and uniformity, the Eastern District of California may elect to follow decisions of the Second Circuit where there are no Ninth Circuit precedents. In such cases, the non-binding decision which the court elects to follow is described as "persuasive authority."

Since courts are only bound by earlier decisions of courts with supervisory authority over them, no court is bound by its own precedents. This raises the question of how courts should treat their own precedent which brings us to the second part of the doctrine of *stare decisis* providing that courts are generally constrained "not to disturb settled points." This constraint fosters the "evenhanded, consistent, and predictable application of legal rules."[72]

While adherence to *stare decisis* promotes stability and efficiency, it can also perpetuate injustice. Judges make mistakes, and times change. A prior decision may have been wrongly decided or may be antiquated. For these reasons, *stare decisis* is not absolute. The highest court in a jurisdiction retains the right to disturb settled points when justice requires a change in the law. And, while lower courts are bound by precedent of higher courts, on occasion even a lower court will refuse to adhere to a very old and pernicious precedent.

Other pressures also affect the ability of the courts to adhere to the principles of *stare decisis*. Specifically, one of the measures taken by the federal circuit courts to cope with their workload is the practice of publishing fewer opinions; unpublished opinions are not precedent. Currently, they publish only 24% of their decisions.[73] That means that 76% are not published, are not precedent, and are not considered in determining whether the law is being applied consistently and uniformly. While critics are concerned that this level of unpublished cases undermines confidence in our system, many support the current approach as an efficient application of sophisticated management techniques.[74]

The role of unpublished opinions in the decision-making process may be changing. The recently amended Federal Rules of Appellate Procedure provide that a court may not prohibit or restrict the citation of unpublished federal decisions after January 1, 2007. While unpublished decisions may be cited, that does not necessarily mean that they will be given any weight by the courts. For example, the Ninth Circuit—in response to the new federal rule—is considering a rule reaffirming that unpublished decisions are not precedent.

Given the tension between the need for stability and the need for change, and between the need for efficiency and the need for public accountability, you can imagine the difficulty the courts face in deciding which path to follow. As we examine judicial decisions later in these materials, keep this tension in mind and consider how historical, social, and technological changes

---

72. Thomas v. Washington Gas Light Co., 448 U.S. 261, 272 (1980).

73. *Caseload Forcing Two-Level System for U.S. Appeals*, N. Y. TIMES, Mar. 14, 1999, at 20.

74. *Id.*

as well as individual judicial philosophies inform the courts' use of precedent and adherence to or departure from *stare decisis*.

3.4.2 The Merger of Law and Equity

In addition to determining what precedents to follow in a case, the courts must also determine the procedure to apply and the remedy to provide. To help you understand the current practice, this section will briefly review the historical development of the law and equity courts and their subsequent merger.

Our legal system traces its roots to medieval England where two court systems developed, courts of law and courts of equity. Beginning in the reign of Henry II (1154–1189), the royal courts expanded their jurisdiction nationally, displacing the earlier local courts which had applied local customary law.[75] The decisions of these royal courts became the law of the entire kingdom, the "common law."[76] Over time, the common law courts became rigid and formalistic. Dissatisfied litigants petitioned the King seeking the reversal of unfair decisions. To handle the growing flood of petitions, the King created the Court of Chancery which could grant discretionary relief in equity to correct the common law courts and produce a just result.[77] In time the common law courts and the chancery courts of equity developed what became known as the English common law.

While in colonial days the common law system was not formally established, after the American Revolution, it was generally adopted throughout the United States but with limitations. As stated by Judge Story: "The common law of England is not to be taken in all respects to be that of America. Our ancestors brought with them its general principles, and claimed it as their birthright; but they brought with them and adopted only that portion which was applicable to their condition."[78]

In adopting the general principles of the common law system, the United States continued the dual system of law and equity. This dual system was complicated and cumbersome. Suits would be dismissed if they were filed in the

---

75. E. Bodenheimer, J. Oakley, J. Love, An Introduction to the Anglo-American Legal System 23 (1988).

76. G. Bell, *The U.S. Legal Tradition in Western Legal Systems* included in J. Ginsburg, Legal Methods 19 (1996).

77. *Id.* at 20.

78. E. Bodenheimer, et al., *supra* note 75, at 23 (quoting from W. Walsh, A History of Anglo–American Law 85–96 (2d ed. 1932)).

wrong court; often two suits had to be brought to obtain complete relief. Formal or technical mistakes could lead to unjust results.[79] By the mid-nineteenth century, reformers sought the merger of law and equity to simplify litigation procedurally and to administer justice efficiently. As a result, today in both federal and state judicial systems, courts have adopted this reform and act as both courts of law and courts of equity.

While the merger of law and equity has simplified civil procedure, it has not erased all distinctions. Some key distinctions between law and equity remain important today. First, a jury trial is generally available in actions at law while the judge is the exclusive decision-maker in equity. Second, the remedy available in legal actions is generally limited to money damages while the courts in equity have discretion to provide additional relief. For example, in a legal action for breach of contract, the plaintiff is entitled to a jury trial to recover a sum of money to compensate for the loss of the benefit of the bargain or for the out-of-pocket costs incurred. On the other hand, the plaintiff may be better off seeking relief in equity where a judge sitting without a jury may order the breaching party to perform the contract. Thus, while the parties today can seek both legal and equitable remedies in the same courtroom, the procedures for obtaining those remedies differ.

In general, in exercising its equitable authority, a court may fashion remedies as necessary to accomplish a just result. Equitable remedies include the following:

1. *Prohibitory injunctions* are court orders that require a defendant to quit doing something harmful. For example, a court may issue an injunction ordering a defendant to cease discharging toxic chemicals into the ground water.

2. *Mandatory injunctions* are court orders that require a defendant to take affirmative steps to correct its behavior or prevent further harm. For example, a court may order a defendant to install a warning system to warn neighbors of the accidental discharge of toxic chemicals.

3. *Specific performance* is a court order that requires a defendant to perform a contract. Money damages are usually considered to be an adequate remedy for breach of contract, but for unique property, performance may be required. For example, a court may order a breaching seller to transfer a deed for a parcel of real property to the buyer.

4. *Constructive trusts* are court orders that require someone who has a legal title to money or property to convey it to the person having an equi-

---

79. S. MERMIN, LAW AND THE LEGAL SYSTEM 163 (1982).

table right to it. For example, if a lawyer has improperly pressured an elderly and trusting client into naming the lawyer as the main beneficiary on a life insurance policy, the court may order the lawyer to transfer the proceeds to the client's children.[80]

Thus, while law and equity have merged, important distinctions persist. Different rules of pleading may apply, and different remedies may be available depending on whether the action is brought under a legal or equitable theory. Moreover, in one lawsuit a plaintiff may seek both a legal remedy and equitable relief. To illustrate, a plaintiff may claim that the defendant's factory has polluted her land and diminished its market value. She may seek money damages for the lost value and an injunction to prevent future harm. In such cases, a jury would be impaneled to resolve the legal action and assess money damages while the judge alone would determine the right to an injunction. As an attorney, you will need to know when you are entitled to a jury trial, what procedures to follow, and what remedies are available to your clients.

3.5 The Overlap and Complexities

In the preceding sections we've sketched out the major features of our multiple-sovereignty system. But honesty compels us to blur the boundaries we've just drawn. With few exceptions, bright-lines dividing federal and state authority certainly no longer prevail. We are all subject to federal, state, and local laws which may overlap and on occasion even conflict. And since both state courts and federal courts have overlapping jurisdiction, conflicts and a certain amount of confusion can result. Moreover, just as the federal-state dividing line has blurred, so have the boundaries between the different branches of government under separation of powers principles. Beyond that, it is often difficult to determine what is precedent for purposes of *stare decisis* and what remedies are available under applicable law. In this section, we'll illustrate how these questions may and, in fact, do frequently arise. As you read through the next few pages, don't worry about figuring out all the answers to the questions posed, just try to understand how the questions themselves arose.

As a starting point, you are undoubtedly already aware of many areas of federal-state duplication. Many crimes could be prosecuted under either state or federal law. Drug crimes are but one example. Similarly, both state and federal laws regulate civil rights, environmental pollution, and workplace safety.

---

80. Adapted from H. Shapo & M. Shapo, Law School Without Fear 138–41 (1996).

This duplication frequently reflects a congressional conclusion that the matter at issue is one of national interest requiring a federal response. If some states wish to go beyond this national threshold, they may do so as long as they stay within constitutional limits. The federal act imposes restrictions across the country, and the state law is limited geographically to its territory. Proposals for gun control following the Colorado high school shooting tragedy illustrate the point. In the week after the tragedy, President Clinton proposed a ban on importing clips that allow assault weapons to fire more than ten shots.[81] The same day, California Governor Gray Davis supported a bill that would ban all styles of semi-automatic weapons, creating the country's most comprehensive ban on high-powered guns.[82]

Sometimes the overlapping provisions are merely duplicative, sometimes they are supplementary, and sometimes they conflict. Where the federal and state laws conflict, the federal law prevails under the Supremacy Clause of United States Constitution. For example, the tobacco warning labels mandated by federal law have been found to "preempt" the adoption of other labeling requirements by the states. Similarly, if a state law conflicts with a provision of the United States Constitution, that state law will be struck down. So if a local ordinance prohibited certain kinds of adult entertainment which is protected by the First Amendment, that ordinance will be declared unconstitutional. On the other hand, if a state law provides more protection than the United States Constitution and Congress has not pre-empted the area, then the state provision should be enforced in both state and federal court. In other words, states may adopt whatever laws they choose so long as they do not impermissibly intrude on an area taken over by Congress or barred by the United States Constitution.

The tension between federal and state authority is far from academic. For example, two recent Supreme Court decisions considered whether state laws arguably conflicting with the federal Controlled Substances Act had to be struck down. In the first, *Gonzales v. Raich*, the Court concluded that California's medical marijuana law impermissibly conflicted with the federal law.[83] As the Court explained, under the Commerce Clause, Congress has the power to regulate activities that affect interstate commerce and it was rational to con-

---

81. Katerine Q. Seelye, *Terror in Littleton: The President; Clinton's New Gun Proposals Include Charging Parents of Children Who Commit Gun Crimes*, N.Y. Times, Apr. 27, 1999, at A20.

82. Lynda Gledbill, *Davis Backs Assault Gun Ban; Legislation Would Be Nation's Toughest*, S.F. Chron., Apr. 27, 1999, at A15.

83. 545 U.S. 1 (2005).

clude that even the noncommercial, intrastate cultivation of marijuana could affect interstate commerce in this prohibited substance. Where Congress has properly acted within its Commerce Clause power, the federal law will prevail against conflicting state law. The Court did not strike down the California law.

In the second, *Gonzales v. Oregon*, the Court concluded that the federal Controlled Substances Act did not authorize the United States Attorney General to prohibit doctors from prescribing medication for use in physician assisted suicide.[84] In the Court's view, the practice of medicine is an area traditionally governed by state law and the Controlled Substances Act was not intended to displace this state authority. Rather, in areas of traditional state control, the structure and limitations of federalism allow states great latitude to legislate for the protection of the lives, limbs, health, comfort, and quiet of their citizens. In both these cases, we see the Court defining the relative scope of state and federal power.

Now let's consider an example of how a conflict between state and federal law might arise in court. Assume a state prosecutor decided to enforce a local noise ordinance barring airplane landings after 9:00 p.m. The prosecutor filed charges in state court against a charter flight company which regularly lands planes as late as 10:00 p.m. The charter company seeks the dismissal of the charges on the grounds that the federal government through its regulatory agencies has preempted the field of passenger aviation. If federal law in fact preempts the local provision, the state court judge should dismiss the noise ordinance prosecution. Thus, a state court will defer to the higher authority of the federal law because of the Supremacy Clause.

Just as the state judge in the prior example determined that federal law controlled, in many other cases a federal judge may conclude that state law controls an issue. For example, in diversity actions where the parties are from different states, the federal court is often called upon the resolve matters of state law. Assume a California resident booked a flight on a charter to Hawaii. The charter company was incorporated in Delaware (where corporate laws are favorable) and had its principal place of business in Nevada (where taxes are low). Unfortunately, the plane crashed in Hawaii. The passenger's survivors filed suit in federal court claiming diversity jurisdiction. The federal court will have to determine which law to apply—that of California where the contract was made and the flight departed? that of Delaware or Nevada based on the defendant's incorporation or residence? that of Hawaii where the accident occurred? that of the federal government as the primary regulator of passenger

---

84. 546 U.S. 243 (2006).

air travel? In this way, the court is presented with a choice-of-law problem not only between federal and state laws, but also between the laws of several states. If the court determines that California law applies, then the federal court will apply that state's law in the diversity action. You will study choice-of-law problems in your Conflict of Laws course.

As we have just seen, state courts are often required to apply federal laws and federal courts are often required to apply state law. Theoretically, the same determination as to the applicable law should be reached regardless of where the action is initially filed. What happens if the trial court makes a mistake in interpreting the law? When a state court determines a matter of federal law, the issue can be appealed through the state court system. Once the decision of the state's highest court is final, the United States Supreme Court has the power to review the decision in order to correct the state's misapplication of federal law. But when a federal court determines an issue of state law, it is appealed through the federal courts. The highest court of the affected state may never have an opportunity to correct the federal court's misinterpretation of state law. Moreover, it is very unlikely that the United States Supreme Court will grant *certiorari* in such a case (even if it believes that an error was committed) because it would not wish to invest its limited resources in correcting errors of state law. To avoid this gap, many states, including California, have adopted provisions permitting their supreme courts to resolve questions of state law presented, or "certified," to them by federal courts. Once the state supreme court has resolved the state law question, the federal court will continue to resolve the case under this clarified view of the state law.

It doesn't require much imagination to foresee increasing problems in resolving conflicts of law. The federal government, all the states, and all the localities are busily promulgating laws. And the increased mobility of the world's citizens and globalization of its economies will only expand the trend. These problems are magnified because American law is liberal in permitting legal actions to be filed in more than one state.[85] Generally, people and entities can be sued in their home state, in any state where they are physically present (even temporarily), and served with process anywhere they do a substantial amount of business.[86] Since most states are seen as favoring the application of their own law—if only because they are familiar with it—by selecting the most favorable forum the plaintiff may have an opportunity to affect the substantive law governing the dispute. To prevent abuse of this advantage, the defendant

---

85. MEADOR, *supra* note 57, at 39.
86. *Id.*

may challenge the plaintiff's forum selection in a motion for change of venue. And to have a case transferred from state to federal court, a defendant who can make a proper showing of federal jurisdiction can seek removal.

As we've seen, in even relatively simple cases multiple laws may apply and multiple courts may be available. Let's take another example. Assume a California software manufacturer and a New York law firm enter into a contract for software to be provided to all the firm's offices which are located in New York, Washington D.C., Tokyo, and London. Assume that the software fails to perform as promised and the law firm is forced to completely replace it following several weeks of frustration, inconvenience, and expense. If the New York firm wishes to sue the software company, where should the suit be filed? It would have several choices including most clearly New York and California and perhaps the jurisdictions where its other offices are located. Even if we assume that there is no federal law on the issue and narrow the choices down to New York and California, the law firm would still have to choose between the two. If the firm selects California, California law will probably be applied; if the firm selects New York, New York law will probably be applied. So the attorney should research the law of both states to see if one jurisdiction will be more favorable than the other.

Let's say the attorney researches the law of both states and finds no significant differences. At this point, the attorney would probably file in New York because it would be more convenient and less expensive for the firm. Now the attorney has to decide whether to file in state or federal court since diversity jurisdiction would exist. If the firm files in state court, it is quite possible the defendant will remove the action to federal court on the basis of diversity jurisdiction. If the action stays in state court, it is likely that state law will apply and that any appeal would be heard in the state court system. On the other hand, if the firm files in federal court, or the defendant removes the case to federal court, the federal court would apply state law but any appeal would be heard in the federal court system. These factors complicate the forum selection decision. The firm might prefer state judges because presumably they would be more familiar with state law and less likely to make an error applying state law. On the other hand, the backlog in the federal court system is often less than in the state court system and a speedier resolution might be reached by filing in federal court.

This simple problem can easily get even more complicated when both federal statutes and state laws apply to the same dispute. It is fairly common for a legal action to proceed on several distinct theories. For example, assume an employer engaged in sexual harassment of one of his employees by repeatedly engaging in unwelcome physical contact. The employee would have the right to sue based on federal statutes protecting worker's rights. The employee would also be able to sue in most states based on state civil rights statutes. And finally, the employee would probably be able to sue under state common law tort theories including assault, battery, and intentional infliction of emotional distress. Thus, if the employer and the employee were both residents of the same state, the employee could sue in either state court or federal court, and could proceed in either court on all of these theories. And if the employer were an out-of-state company, in addition to the federal statute the employee would have the choice of two states' laws, the law of the employee's state and the law of the employer's state. One state's law might be far more favorable to the employee than the other. Moreover, the employee could select either of the state courts or either of the federal courts in those states, a four-way forum choice. Whichever court is selected would be required to apply both the federal law and the applicable state law to the resolution of the dispute.

Of course, the complications escalate geometrically when we move from these simple fact patterns to truly complex cases. For example, consider the problems with tire-tread separation causing roll-over accidents with sports utility vehicles. There will undoubtedly be hundreds of plaintiffs, multiple defendants, innumerable applicable state and federal laws, and scores of possible forum choices. While a class action might streamline this litigation, it would still create numerous procedural and substantive complications. Similar problems are posed by environmental disasters and airline crashes. Although these massive cases are few in number, they present a serious challenge to the administration of justice because they consume massive resources in a system designed for the traditional two-party lawsuit.[87]

3.6 Discussion Questions

1. The U.S. Minerals Management Service, the federal agency in charge of oil leases, adopted a plan to extend thirty-six leases off the California coast.[88] The California Coastal Commission rejected the agency's proposal and authorized legal proceedings against the federal agency if it continued its plan to renew the leases. According to the Commission, the agency failed to provide sufficient information about the impact drilling would have on the environment and failed to even send a representative to the hearing. The agency con-

---

87. *Id.* at 48.
88. Glen Martin, *Coastal Panel Rejects U.S. Drilling Proposal,* S.F. Chron., Aug. 12, 2005, at A1.

tends that it provided voluminous data about the environmental impact. The Bush administration has taken a strong position on states' rights in the environmental area. For example, the administration argues that drilling should be allowed in the Arctic National Wildlife Refuge because Alaskans support it. On the other hand, a majority of Californians oppose off-shore oil drilling. How should the conflict be resolved? Should federal interests or state interests prevail? Should this question be resolved by the courts or by the political process?

2. Just how important are separation of powers issues? One writer claims that "any power, whatever its nature, necessarily takes its character from the department to which it is assigned by the constitution or the legislature." Thus, whatever proceeds from a court is judicial; whatever proceeds from the Congress is legislative, and whatever actions the President takes are executive. This has a commonsense ring. But does it help? Consider:

a. Following the Watergate scandal, Congress adopted a statute authorizing the appointment of special prosecutors to investigate misconduct by the executive branch. Under this statute, Attorney General Reno recommended the appointment of a special prosecutor to investigate the allegations regarding President Clinton's relationship with Monica Lewinsky. The investigation is supervised by a three-judge panel. Under the statute, the special prosecutor's findings must be reported to Congress. How should this process be classified? Since Congress has permitted the Special Prosecutor law to lapse, we will never know the final answer to this constitutional conundrum.

b. The Supreme Court of Wisconsin issued a decree setting up an integrated (or mandatory) state bar organization. This means that every lawyer in Wisconsin is obligated to become a member of the state bar organization in order to practice law in Wisconsin. Is this action judicial, legislative, or executive in character?

c. In 2004, the voters of California approved an initiative to create the California Institute for Regenerative Medicine to administer a $3 billion research program on human embryonic stem cells. But the program has been tied up in litigation since its passage, on the grounds that it violates the state constitution because it operates outside of normal channels of government and gives researchers too much control over who will financially benefit from tax-payer financed research.[89] Chal-

---

89. Carl T. Hall, *Feb. 27 Court Date for Charter Test of Stem Cell Program,* S.F. CHRON., Dec. 7, 2005, at B1.

lengers contend that the initiative violates separation-of-powers principles because it authorizes the institute to exercise legislative power by determining how to spend public funds. Where does the institute fit within the three branches of government?

3. A, a Davis, California resident, entered into a contract with B, a Texas resident, under which B agreed to construct a house for A in New Mexico. B failed to construct the house as promised.[90]

   a. If A wished to sue B for damages (which you may assume are in excess of $75,000) caused by B's failure to construct the house as promised, in which court or courts, state or federal, can A file suit against B? Could A try filing suit in California Superior Court for Yolo County? How about the United States District Court for the Eastern District of California (Sacramento)? What is B's likely response if A brings suit in California state court?
   b. Which state(s) law will be applied in the A versus B lawsuit? Does the law to be applied depend upon where the suit is brought?

4. The California Supreme Court reviewed the California law requiring a minor seeking an abortion to obtain her parent's consent before she can lawfully have the abortion. It declared that the parental consent provision violates the California constitution's privacy protections. These protections are broader than any the United States Supreme Court has found in the United States Constitution. The United States Supreme Court has decided that states may, but need not, enact parental consent laws. Can the California Attorney General appeal the California Supreme Court decision to the United States Supreme Court?

---

90. Adapted from Meador, *supra* note 57, at 42.

CHAPTER 4

Introduction to Statutes and Statutory Interpretation

Article I, Section 1 of the United States Constitution establishes Congress, the legislative branch of our representative democracy. The structure of the Constitution, as well as history, teach us that the legislature is the cornerstone of our federal system. The same is true for our state governments. These legislatures pass statutes which the courts are bound to apply in resolving cases. But because the meaning of statutory language is often debatable, the courts must interpret and enforce the laws which the legislatures enact. When different interpretations are possible, the courts must determine which interpretation to apply.

A simple example will help you understand the challenge of statutory construction. Tragically, a young woman suffered a brain injury and died after riding on the Indiana Jones amusement ride at Disneyland. The injury was caused by the violent and unpredictable shaking and stresses of the ride. Her heirs sued Disney for her wrongful death arguing that Disney was a common carrier and therefore owed passengers the utmost duty of care.[1] Disney responded that it was not a common carrier and therefore had a lower duty of care. The question before the California Supreme Court was whether the Indiana Jones jeep ride was within the statutory meaning of "common carrier." The outcome depended on the Court's construction of an 1872 statute defining "common carrier." It provided: "Everyone who offers to the public to carry persons, property, or messages ... is a common carrier of whatever he thus offers to carry."[2] After tracing the expansive interpretation given this language in prior decisions – applying it to elevators, sightseeing planes, and ski lifts –

---

1. Gomez v. Superior Court, 35 Cal.4th 1125 (2005).
2. Cal. Civ. Code § 2168.

the Court held that Disney was a common carrier. The dissent concluded, however, that Disney should not be treated as a common carrier since when the legislature enacted the 1872 statute it did not intend that the statute would be applied to theme park thrill rides. This is one of the classic conflicts that statutory construction must resolve: Does the literal text of the statute or the underlying legislative intent determine its proper interpretation?

This chapter will outline some approaches to statutory interpretation, introduce some canons of construction, and consider the use of legislative history to inform statutory construction. It will also briefly explain the rules governing the retroactive application of legislation.

4.1 Approaches to Statutory Interpretation[3]

Before turning to the canons and legislative history used to interpret statutes, we will briefly describe the three basic approaches used by the courts: (1) the literal rule; (2) the golden rule; and (3) the social purpose approach. As you read through the rest of this chapter, consider these views of statutory interpretation.

4.1.1 The Literal Rule

The literal rule holds that the language of a statute must be given its plain meaning. As the United States Supreme Court has stated:

> It is elementary that the meaning of a statute must, in the first instance, be sought in the language in which the act is framed, and if that is plain, and the law is within the constitutional authority of the law-making body which passed it, the sole function of the courts is to enforce it according to its terms....
>
> Where the language is plain and admits of no more than one meaning the duty of interpretation does not arise and the rules which are to aid doubtful meanings need no discussion....
>
> Statutory words are uniformly presumed, unless the contrary appears, to be used in their ordinary and usual sense, and with the meaning commonly attributed to them.

---

3. *Adapted from* EDGAR BODENHEIMER, ET AL., AN INTRODUCTION TO THE ANGLO-AMERICAN LEGAL SYSTEM (2d ed. 1988).

* * *

[T]he name given to an act by way of designation or description, or the report which accompanies it, cannot change the plain import of its words. If the words are plain, they give meaning to the act, and it is neither the duty nor the privilege of the courts to enter speculative fields in search of a different meaning.[4]

Under the literal rule, the courts must enforce the clear language of a statute even "though it should lead to absurd or mischievous results."[5]

4.1.2 The Golden Rule

The golden rule modestly relaxes the literal rule. As one court recently explained:

It is settled law that in construing a statute, the Court must follow the plain meaning rule. The meaning of a statute must, in the first instance, be sought in the language in which the act is framed, and if that is plain, the sole function of the courts is to enforce it according to its terms. The strong presumption that the plain language of the statute expresses congressional intent is rebutted only in rare and exceptional circumstances, when a contrary legislative intent is clearly expressed. This requirement that the Court accept the plain language is tempered only by the admonition that a literal interpretation must be rejected if it would lead to an absurd result.[6]

4.1.3 The Social Purpose Approach

The social purpose approach interprets a statute to further the underlying purpose of the legislature for the good of the public. Under this approach, a court will not apply a statute literally if it would produce a result "at variance with the policy of the legislation as a whole."[7] As one highly-respected jurist observed, statutes "should be construed, not as theorems of Euclid, but with

---

4. Caminnetti v. United States, 242 U.S. 470, 485, 490 (1917).

5. Lord Atkinson in Vacher & Sons, Ltd. v. London Society of Compositors, (1913) A.C. 107, at 121 (House of Lords) as quoted in BODENHEIMER, ET AL., *supra* note 3, at 136.

6. United States v. Revis, 22 F. Supp. 2d 1242, 1250–51 (N.D. Okla. 1998) (citations and internal punctuation omitted); see also BODENHEIMER, ET AL., *supra* note 3, at 136.

7. United States v. Am. Trucking Ass'ns, 310 U.S. 534, 543–44 (1940).

some imagination of the purposes which lie behind them."[8] This elastic approach was adopted by the United States Supreme Court in *Holy Trinity Church v. United States*, 143 U.S. 457, 459, 463 (1892):

> It is a familiar rule, that a thing may be within the letter of the statute and yet not within the statute, because not within its spirit, nor within the intention of its makers....

> Again, another guide to the meaning of a statute is found in the evil which it is designed to remedy; and for this the court properly looks at contemporaneous events, the situation as it existed, and as it was pressed upon the attention of the legislative body....

As Justice Stevens explained, "In determining the meaning of a statute, we look not only to the particular statutory language, but to the design of the statute as a whole and to its object and policy."[9] Under this approach, statutes should be read fully and interpreted judiciously rather than mechanically.[10]

4.2 Canons of Construction

In their quest to develop a principled approach to statutory interpretation, the courts have developed a general set of conventions. These conventions provide some helpful ways to consider statutory language and its interpretation. Although it may give them more dignity than they deserve, these guidelines are usually grouped under the label "canons of construction."

4.2.1 Plain Meaning

The starting point—and often the ending point—for statutory interpretation is the plain meaning of the statute. For example, assume a statute provides: "No dogs are allowed in restaurants except seeing-eye dogs." Under the plain meaning rule, a person bringing a dog into a restaurant will not be permitted to avoid the restriction by arguing that the legislature clearly intended

---

8. Lehigh Valley Coal Co. v. Yensavage, 218 F. 547, 553 (2nd Cir. 1914) (Hand, J.) *quoted in* Connecticut Nat'l Bank v. Germain, 503 U.S. 249, 255 n.1 (1992) (Stevens, J., concurring).

9. Crandon v. United States, 494 U.S. 152, 158 (1990); *see also* BODENHEIMER, ET AL., *supra* note 3, at 137.

10. United States v. Ranger Elec. Commc'ns, Inc., 22 F. Supp. 2d 667, 675 (W.D. Mich. 1998).

to bar only large, disruptive animals, not well-behaved, charming companions. This canon presumes that the legislature meant precisely what it said: no dogs = no dogs (big or small, well-behaved or unruly, *except* seeing-eye dogs). As explained by the United States Supreme Court: "[W]here the act is clear upon its face, and when standing alone it is fairly susceptible of but one construction, that construction must be given to it."[11]

United States v. Locke
471 U.S. 84 (1985)

[In 1960 and 1966, the Locke family purchased mining claims on federal lands in Nevada. These claims were major sources of gravel and building material; they were valued at several million dollars. Indeed, in one assessment year alone, their gross income totaled more than $1 million. Throughout the period during which they owned the claims, the owners complied with annual state-law filing and assessment work requirements.

Unfortunately, the federal approach to managing public lands was in virtual chaos because there was no federal recording system. By 1975, experts estimated that more than half the land in the National Forest System was believed to be covered by claims and more than 6 million claims existed on other public lands. It was nearly impossible for the forest service to effectively manage the public lands for fear that it would be inadvertently interfering with mining claims. But many of these claims had been dormant for decades or were invalid for other reasons.

In 1976, after a decade of studying the problem, Congress enacted a statute to establish a federal recording system to rid the federal lands of stale claims and to provide federal managers with the current information they need to manage the land. The law required claim owners to file an initial recording and then to update the filing every year. For the annual update, the law stated that "prior to December 31" of every year, the claimant must file certain forms with state officials and with the Bureau of Land Management (BLM). It further provided that if a person failed to meet these requirements, the failure "shall be deemed conclusively to constitute an abandonment of the mining claim ... by the owner."

The Locke family filed the initial federal recording properly with BLM, thereby putting their claims on record as the law required. But in 1980, they filed the annual update *on* December 31 — one day too late according to the

---

11. Hamilton v. Rathbone, 175 U.S. 414, 419 (1899).

BLM. Since the filing was late, the government notified the Lockes that their claims had been abandoned. The government declared their mine forfeited.]

Justice Marshall delivered the opinion of the Court.

While we will not allow a literal reading of a statute to produce a result demonstrably at odds with the intentions of its drafters, with respect to filing deadlines a literal reading of Congress' words is generally the only proper reading of those words. To attempt to decide whether some date other than the one set out in the statute is the date actually intended by Congress is to set sail on an aimless journey, for the purpose of a filing deadline would be just as well served by nearly any date a court might choose as by the date Congress has in fact set out in the statute. Actual purpose is sometimes unknown, and such is the case with filing deadlines; as might be expected, nothing in the legislative history suggests why Congress chose December 30 over December 31, or over September 1 (the end of the assessment year for mining claims), as the last day on which the required filings could be made. But deadlines are inherently arbitrary, while fixed dates are often essential to accomplish necessary results. Faced with the inherent arbitrariness of filing deadlines, we must, at least in a civil case, apply by its terms the date fixed by the statute.

Moreover, BLM regulations have made absolutely clear since the enactment of the recording system that "prior to December 31" means what it says. As the current version of the filing regulations states: "The owner of an unpatented mining claim located on Federal lands ... shall have filed or caused to have been filed on or before December 30 of each calendar year ... evidence of annual assessment work performed during the previous assessment year or a notice of intention to hold the mining claim." Leading mining treatises similarly inform claimants that "[i]t is important to note that the filing of a notice of intention or evidence of assessment work must be done prior to December 31 of each year, i.e., on or before December 30." If [the parties in this case], who were businessmen involved in the running of a major mining operation for more than 20 years, had any questions about whether a December 31 filing complied with the statute, it was incumbent upon them, as it is upon other businessmen, to have checked the regulations or to have consulted an attorney for legal advice. Pursuit of either of these courses, rather than the submission of a last-minute filing, would surely have led [them] to the conclusion that December 30 was the last day on which they could file safely.

In so saying, we are not insensitive to the problems posed by congressional reliance on the words "prior to December 31." But the fact that Congress might have acted with greater clarity or foresight does not give courts a carte blanche to redraft statutes in an effort to achieve that which Congress is perceived to have failed to do. There is a basic difference between filling a gap left by Congress' silence and rewriting rules that Congress has affirmatively and specifically enacted. Nor is the Judiciary licensed to attempt to soften the clear import of Congress' chosen words whenever a court believes those words lead to a harsh result. On the contrary, deference to the supremacy of the Legislature, as well as recognition that Congressmen typically vote on the language of a bill, generally requires us to assume that the legislative purpose is expressed by the ordinary meaning of the words used. Going behind the plain language of a statute in search of a possibly contrary congressional intent is a step to be taken cautiously even under the best of circumstances. When even after taking this step nothing in the legislative history remotely suggests a congressional intent contrary to Congress' chosen words, and neither [the parties] nor the dissenters have pointed to anything that so suggests, any further steps take the courts out of the realm of interpretation and place them in the domain of legislation. The phrase "prior to" may be clumsy, but its meaning is clear. Thus, we are obligated to apply the "prior to December 31" language by its terms.

We cannot press statutory construction to the point of disingenuous evasion.[12]

Notes and Questions

1. Which statutory construction approach did Justice Marshall adopt in ruling that the mining claim was forfeited because the renewal notice was filed one day late?

2. Is this result fair and just?

3. If the court follows the plain meaning rule, is it required to confine its analysis to the specific statutory provision at issue or may it consider the context of the entire statute? One court has stated: "Each section of a statute

---

12. We note that the United States Code is sprinkled with provisions that require action "prior to" some date, including at least 14 provisions that contemplate action "prior to December 31." Dozens of state statutes and local ordinances undoubtedly incorporate similar "prior to December 31" deadlines. In addition, legislatures know how to make explicit an intent to allow action on December 31 when they employ a December 31 date in a statute. It is unclear whether the arguments advanced by the dissenters are meant to apply to all of these provisions, or only to some of them; if the latter, we are given little guidance as to how a court is to go about the rather eclectic task of choosing which "prior to December 31" deadlines it can interpret flexibly. Understandably enough, the dissenters seek to disavow any intent to call all these "prior to December 31" deadlines into question and assure us that this is a "unique case," involving a "unique factual matrix." The only thing we can find unique about this particular December 31 deadline is that the dissenters are willing to go through such tortured reasoning to evade it.

should be read in the context of the overall policy of the legislation in order to avoid frustrating legislative intent. *See, e.g., Crandon v. United States*, 494 U.S. 152, 158 (1990) (stating that in determining the meaning of a statute, we look not only to the particular statutory language, but to the design of the statute as a whole and to its object and policy); *Pension Benefit Guar. Corp. v. White Consol. Indus., Inc.*, 998 F.2d 1192, 1198 (3d Cir. 1993) (asserting that the language of a statute must be analyzed against the background of the statute as a whole and its legislative purpose)." Is this approach consistent with the plain meaning rule?

4. If the language is clear, should courts ever consider legislative history to confirm or refute the plain meaning? According to the Seventh Circuit, when a statute is unambiguous, the court need never consider legislative history. *McCoy v. Gilbert*, 270 F.3d 503 (7th Cir. 2001). On the other hand, the Ninth Circuit has concluded that although the plain language is the starting point for statutory construction, the court should consider the entire law, including its object and policy, and should consider legislative history even where the plain language is unambiguous where legislative history clearly indicates that Congress meant something other than what it said. *Carson Harbor Village, Ltd. v. Unocal Corp.* 270 F.3d 863 (9th Cir. 2001). Which approach is better?

5. Why does the Court in a footnote refer to all the other statutes using the "prior to" language? Are these statutes relevant to the interpretation of the statute at issue?

6. Can you draw any practical lessons from this case about drafting legislation and legal documents? About advising clients on how to meet deadlines?

7. Is the Court showing appropriate deference to Congress under separation of powers principles in concluding that the Court is not "licensed to attempt to soften the clear import of Congress' chosen words whenever a court believes those words lead to a harsh result? On the contrary, deference to the supremacy of the Legislature, as well as recognition that Congressmen typically vote on the language of a bill, generally requires us to assume that the legislative purpose is expressed by the ordinary meaning of the words used." Stated differently, is the plain meaning rule required by the separation-of-powers doctrine?

8. Is the Court correct in observing that deadlines are "inherently arbitrary"? Or are some deadlines more arbitrary than others? In criticizing the *Locke* decision, Judge Posner has written, "It is not enough to say that all deadlines are arbitrary and that, if the plaintiffs in *Locke* had won, the next plaintiff would file on January 1 and call it timely. The end of the year is a common deadline and almost certainly what Congress intended, so a claim filed

on January 1 would be too late."[13] To Judge Posner, the problem is that allowing the late filing would require the Court not just to "interpret an ambiguity or plug a gap but to rewrite clear statutory language."[14] Is it ever appropriate for the Court to disregard clear statutory language in favor of reaching a decision reflecting the legislature's intent? In Judge Posner's view, the answer in this case is yes.[15] What approach to statutory interpretation does his conclusion reflect?

9. As we have learned, the Supreme Court limits its docket to cases of national significance involving questions of federal law. Why do you think the Court granted *certiorari* (agreed to hear this case)?

Dissent to United States v. Locke

[Justices Powell, Stevens, and Brennan dissented. Justice Stevens offered several reasons for his disagreement with the majority and Justice Brennan joined his dissent. They concluded that the law's language was ambiguous and created a trap for the unwary that Congress would not have intended. In their view, Congress intended to create a year-end deadline so that any filing before the end of the calendar year would be timely.]

A careful reading of [the law] discloses at least three respects in which its text cannot possibly reflect the actual intent of Congress. First, the description of what must be filed in the initial filing and subsequent annual filings is quite obviously garbled. Read literally, [the law] seems to require that a notice of intent to hold the claim and an affidavit of assessment work performed on the claim must be filed "on a detailed report provided by §28-1 of Title 30." One must substitute the word "or" for the word "on" to make any sense at all out of this provision. This error should cause us to pause before concluding that Congress commanded blind allegiance to the remainder of the literal text.

Second, the express language of the statute is unambiguous in describing the place where the annual filing shall be made. If the statute is read inflexibly, the owner must "file in the office of the Bureau" the required documents. Yet the regulations that the Bureau itself has drafted, quite reasonably, construe the statute to allow filing in a mailbox, provided that the document is actually received by the Bureau before the close of business on January 19 of the year following the year in which the [filing is required]. A notice mailed

---

13. Richard A. Posner, Law and Literature 256 (1988).
14. *Id.*
15. *Id.*

on December 30, 1982, and received by the Bureau on January 19, 1983, was filed "in the office of the Bureau" during 1982 within the meaning of the statute, but one that is hand-delivered to the office on December 31, 1982, cannot be accepted as a 1982 "filing."

The Court finds comfort in the fact that the implementing regulations have eliminated the risk of injustice. But if one must rely on those regulations, it should be apparent that the meaning of the statute itself is not all that obvious. To begin with, the regulations do not use the language "prior to December 31;" instead, they use "on or before December 30 of each year." The Bureau's drafting of the regulations using this latter phrase indicates that the meaning of the statute itself is not quite as "plain," as the Court assumes; if the language were plain, it is doubtful that the Bureau would have found it necessary to change the language at all. Moreover, the Bureau, under the aegis of the Department of the Interior, once issued a pamphlet entitled "Staking a Mining Claim on Federal Lands" that contained the following information:

> Owners of claims or sites located on or before Oct. 21, 1976, have until Oct. 22, 1979, to file evidence of assessment work performed the preceding year or to file a notice of intent to hold the claim or site. Once the claim or site is recorded with BLM, these documents must be filed *on or before* December 31 of each subsequent year. (Emphasis added).

[In other words, the Bureau itself made the same mistake in interpreting the deadline that the Locke family made in filing one day late.] "Plain language," indeed.

There is a more important reason why the implementing regulations cannot be supportive of the result the Court reaches today: the Bureau's own deviation from the statutory language in its mail-filing regulation. If the Bureau had issued regulations expressly stating that a December 31 filing would be considered timely—just as it has stated that a mail filing received on January 19 is timely—it is inconceivable that anyone would question the validity of its regulation. It appears, however, that the Bureau has more power to interpret an awkwardly drafted statute in an enlightened manner consistent with Congress' intent than does this Court.

In light of the foregoing, I cannot believe that Congress intended the words "prior to December 31 of each year" to be given the literal reading the Court adopts today. The statutory scheme requires periodic filings on a calendar-year basis. The end of the calendar year is, of course, correctly described either as "prior to the close of business on December 31," or "on or before December 31," but it is surely understandable that the author of [the law] might inadvertently use the words "prior to December 31" when he meant to refer to the end of the calendar year. As the facts of this case demonstrate, the scrivener's error is one that can be made in good faith. The risk of such an error is, of course, the greatest when the reference is to the end of the calendar year. That it was in fact an error seems rather clear to me because no one has suggested any rational basis for omitting just one day from the period in which an annual filing may be made, and I would not presume that Congress deliberately created a trap for the unwary by such an omission.

It would be fully consistent with Congress' intent to treat any filing received during the 1980 calendar year as a timely filing for that year. Such an interpretation certainly does not interfere with Congress' intent to establish a federal recording system designed to cope with the problem of stale mining claims on federal lands. The system is established, and apparently, functioning.[16] Moreover, the claims here were active; the Bureau was well aware that the Locke family intended to hold and to operate their claims.

Additionally, a sensible construction of the statute does not interfere with Congress' intention to provide "an easy way of discovering which Federal lands are subject to either valid or invalid mining claim locations." The Bureau in this case was well aware of the existence and production of [these] mining claims; only by blinking reality could the Bureau reach the decision that it did. It is undisputed that the [owners] made the first 1980 filing on August 29, 1980, and made the second required filing on December 31, 1980; the Bureau did not declare the mining claims "abandoned and void" until April 4, 1981. Thus, [the owners] lost their entire livelihood for no practical reason, contrary to the intent of Congress, and because of the hypertechnical construction of a poorly drafted statute, which an agency interprets to allow "filings" far beyond December 30 in some circumstances, but then interprets inflexibly in others. The government acknowledges that it may well be that Congress wished to require filing by the end of the calendar year and that the earlier deadline resulted from careless draftsmanship. I have no doubt that Congress would have chosen to adopt a construction of the statute that filing take place by the end of the calendar year if its attention had been focused on this precise issue.

---

16. Several *amici* have filed materials listing numerous cases in which it is asserted that the Bureau is using every technical construction of the statute to suck up active mining claims much as a vacuum cleaner, if not watched closely, will suck up jewelry or loose money.

In my view, this unique factual matrix unequivocally contradicts the statutory presumption of an intent to abandon by reason of a late filing. In sum, this case presents an ambiguous statute, which, if strictly construed, will destroy valuable rights of this family, property owners who have complied with all local and federal statutory filing requirements apart from a 1-day "late" filing caused by the Bureau's own failure to mail a reminder notice necessary because of the statute's ambiguity and caused by the Bureau's information to the owners that the date on which the filing occurred would be acceptable. Further, long before the Bureau declared a technical "abandonment," it was in complete possession of all information necessary to assess the activity, locations, and ownership of [these] mining claims and it possessed all information needed to carry out its statutory functions. Finally, the Bureau has not claimed that the filing is contrary to the congressional purposes behind the statute, that the filing affected the Bureau's land-use planning functions in any manner, or that it interfered in any measurable way with the Bureau's need to obtain information. A showing of substantial compliance necessitates a significant burden of proof; the owners whose active mining claims will be destroyed contrary to Congress' intent have convinced me that they have substantially complied with the statute.

Notes and Questions

1. Which statutory construction approach did Justice Stevens adopt in dissenting on the grounds that Congress did not intend the claim to be lost?

2. Which approach—the majority's or the dissent's—do you think is better? Why?

3. In his dissent, Justice Stevens explained the use of the language "prior to December 31" as "the consequence of a legislative accident, perhaps caused by nothing more than the unfortunate fact that Congress is too busy to do all of its work as carefully as it should." Is it appropriate for the Court to conclude that Congress was sloppy in its drafting? Or should the Court be deferential to the congressional language? Justice Stewart made a similar point in a later case of statutory interpretation where he quoted from a story in the *New York Times:*

> Smoking a big cigar, the Speaker [of the House of Representatives] got angry again over the slap-dash quality of the bill ... with parts of it photocopied from memorandums, other parts handwritten at the last minute, and some final sections hastily crossed out in whorls of pencil marks.

* * *

But then he smiled, too, noting such cryptic and accidental entries in the [budget] bill as the name and phone number—'Ruth Seymour, 225-4844'—standing alone as if it were a special appropriation item.[17]

4. Why do both the majority and the dissent discuss the BLM regulations? What role, if any, should agency regulations play in statutory construction? How can the administrative regulations shed light on the legislative intent when they were adopted after the statute by an administrative agency? Which argument using the regulations is more persuasive? Given that the Court interprets the statute to impose a strict December 30 deadline, how can it be that the BLM accepts mailed filings up to January 19?

5. What happens if the Court interprets a statute contrary to congressional intent? Is there a corrective mechanism?

6. *Epilogue:* Justice Stevens also argued that a phone call from Locke's daughter to the BLM should be considered since the BLM had given her erroneous information about the filing deadline. Responding to this point, Justice Marshall suggested that the district court might have appropriately applied the doctrine of equitable estoppel to bar the government from asserting that the filing was late. Justice O'Connor filed a concurring opinion based entirely on the estoppel issue. As a result, having read the Justices' view of equitable estoppel, the government abandoned its claim and the Lockes got their mine back.[18]

4.2.2 *Ejusdem Generis* ("Of the Same Kind")

The *"ejusdem generis"* canon applies where a string of specific descriptions is followed by a general description. The canon provides that the catch-all description is limited to the class of things which are specifically described. Assume a statute provides: "It is a violation of the law punishable by a fine of $500.00 to import into California without inspection apples, grapes, nectarines, oranges, pears, pomegranates, watermelons, and similar fruits." A prosecutor bringing a case against someone who brought peaches into the state might argue that peaches are very similar to nectarines and that therefore the legislature intended peaches to be included since they are in the same class as the fruits specifically listed. On the other hand, a defendant charged with importing coffee beans could invoke the *ejusdem generis* canon to argue that coffee is outside the class and therefore outside the scope of the statute.

---

17. Sorenson v. Secretary of the Treasury, 475 U.S. 851, 867 n.2 (1986), (Stewart, J., dissenting) (quoting N.Y. Times, July 1, 1981, at A16).

18. Lawrence M. Solan, *Learning Our Limits: The Decline of Textualism in Statutory Cases,* 1997 Wis. L. Rev. 235, 241–42 (1997).

4.2.3 *Noscitur a Sociis* ("It Is Known by Its Companions")

The rule of "*noscitur a sociis*" holds that the meaning of a word, and consequently the intention of the legislature, is to be ascertained from the context and by considering the word in question in light of the surrounding words. Simply put, a word is known by the company it keeps.[19] This canon is often paired with *ejusdem generis* and would apply to our peach and coffee bean examples.

4.2.4 *Expressio Unius* ("The Mention of One Thing Excludes Other Things")

The Latin phrase "*expressio unius est exclusior alterius*" is a canon which presumes that when specific things are expressly included in the statute's coverage, other things are impliedly excluded. Assume a statute states: "It is a violation of the law punishable by a fine of $500.00 to import into California without inspection the following fruits and vegetables: apples, grapes, nectarines, oranges, pears, pomegranates, and watermelons." As above, a prosecutor bringing a case against a peach importer might argue that peaches are similar to nectarines and that therefore the legislature intended peaches to be included as well. But notice how the statute is worded; it does not include a catch-all description after the specific descriptions. The peach importer might well defend on the grounds that peaches fall outside the statute since peaches are not expressly listed in the statute.

4.2.5 Narrow Construction of Penal Statutes

The peach importer could also cite a complementary canon which provides that penal laws are to be strictly construed. This canon is grounded in the basic rule of fairness that a person should only be punished for a crime when the statute provides notice that the conduct is illegal.[20] It is related to the guarantees of due process requiring fair warning and notice of what is prohibited so that one may act accordingly.[21] As the United States Supreme Court has explained, this guarantee provides the public with an understanding of what conduct violates the law and inhibits the police from engaging in arbitrary and discriminatory conduct.[22]

---

19. Gustafson v. Alloyd Co., 513 U.S. 561, 575 (1995).
20. McBoyle v. United States, 283 U.S. 25, 27 (1931).
21. Connally v. Gen. Constr. Co., 269 U.S. 385, 391 (1926).
22. Grayned v. City of Rockford, 408 U.S. 104, 108–09 (1972).

4.2.6 Broad Construction of Remedial Statutes

In contrast to the canon requiring strict construction of penal statutes, another canon provides for the broad construction of remedial statutes. As the United States Supreme Court has explained, "we are guided by the familiar canon of statutory construction that remedial legislation should be construed broadly to effectuate its purposes."[23] For example, in construing the Age Discrimination in Employment Act [ADEA], one court stated:

> The Age Discrimination in Employment Act … prohibits an employer from discriminating against any individual with respect to his or her compensation, terms, conditions, or privileges of employment because of such individual's age. The purpose of the Act is to promote employment of older persons based on their ability rather than age, to prohibit arbitrary age discrimination in employment, and to help employers and workers find ways of meeting problems arising from the impact of age on employment. The ADEA is remedial and humanitarian legislation and should be liberally interpreted to effectuate the congressional purpose of ending age discrimination in employment.[24]

4.2.7 Specific Statutes Take Precedence Over General Statutes

When two or more statutes could be read to govern the same issue, a canon provides that the more specific statute shall be applied. This rule is illustrated by the following case.

Strawberry v. Albright
111 F.3d 943 (D.C. Cir. 1997)

[In 1984, Kenneth Strawberry was required to convert from a Foreign Service Reserve position to a civil service position because he was not available for worldwide assignment. Strawberry had the option of remaining in the Foreign Service retirement program or transferring to the Civil Service retirement program. He chose to remain in the Foreign Service program, which provides a more generous annuity and allows earlier voluntary retirement, but has a

---

23. Tcherepnin v. Knight, 389 U.S. 332, 336 (1967).
24. Whitten v. Farmland Indus., Inc., 759 F. Supp. 1522, 1530–31 (D. Kan. 1991).

mandatory retirement age of 65. Although he wished to continue working, Strawberry was required by Foreign Service policy to retire on July 31, 1995, the last day of the month in which he turned 65.

In October 1995, Strawberry filed suit in district court alleging that the Secretary of State had violated the Age Discrimination in Employment Act (ADEA) by forcing him to retire at 65. Under the ADEA, which applies generally to federal employees, such a mandatory retirement provision is illegal. Strawberry sought backpay, damages, and a jury trial.

The district court dismissed his lawsuit. It held that the more specific provisions of the Foreign Service Act providing for the retirement system which imposed a mandatory retirement age controlled the more general provisions of the ADEA. Strawberry appealed.]

Opinion of the District of Columbia Court of Appeals:

The district court correctly held that the mandatory retirement provisions of the Foreign Service Act do not run afoul of the ADEA. As the district court noted, since the ADEA was adopted and made applicable to federal employees, Congress twice amended the Foreign Service Act. Both times it retained the mandatory retirement provisions for the Foreign Service retirement program. It is well established that where there is no clear intention otherwise, a specific statute will not be controlled or nullified by a general one. Thus, the district court correctly held that the ADEA's general prohibition of age discrimination does not prohibit enforcement of the mandatory retirement provisions. We therefore grant the Secretary's motion for summary affirmance.

Notes and Questions

1. Here the court had to choose between enforcing the Foreign Service Act and the ADEA. If the court had enforced the ADEA, what would the result have been?

2. If you were representing the plaintiff, what canon of construction would you use to support your client's position that the ADEA should control? What authority would you cite to support this argument?

3. If the ADEA is to be liberally construed to prevent age discrimination, why does the court uphold the mandatory retirement provision of the Foreign Service retirement program?

4. How do we know which canon to follow: the canon providing for the liberal construction of remedial statutes, or the canon providing that specific statutes take precedence over general statutes?

5. Does the timing of the statutes influence the court's decision? What would be the outcome if the mandatory retirement provision was adopted be-

fore the ADEA? Should the court conclude that Congress knew of the provision and intended to change it by adopting the ADEA? Or that Congress knew of the provision and intended to retain it as an exception to the ADEA? Or that Congress was not thinking about the Foreign Service retirement system when it adopted the ADEA?

6. As we have learned, federal courts are courts of limited jurisdiction. What is the basis of the court's jurisdiction in this case?

4.2.8 Dueling Canons

In his landmark law review article, Professor Llewellyn compiled a list of canons of construction which exposed the somewhat embarrassing fact that "there are two opposing canons on almost every point."[25] He illustrated the point with a table of thrusts and parries:

Thrust	Parry
Statutes in derogation of the common law are narrowly construed.	**But:** Remedial statutes in derogation of the common law are liberally construed.
Plain and unambiguous language must be given effect.	**But:** Plain language will not be given effect if it would lead to absurd results or thwart the legislature's purpose.
Every word or clause of a statute must be given effect.	**But:** The court may disregard surplus language which has been inadvertently inserted or which is repugnant to the rest of the statute.

Llewellyn's point, that canons are indeterminate and are simply used by judges to justify results reached for other reasons, convinced two generations of scholars that the canons "were not to be taken seriously."[26] But recently the canons have enjoyed a surprising revival across the philosophical spectrum.[27] In the view of the new textualists, adherence to established rules "might make the process of statutory interpretation more predictable, effective, and even

---

25. Karl Llewellyn, *Remarks on the Theory of Appellate Decision and the Rules of Canons About How Statutes Are to Be Construed*, 3 VAND. L. REV. 395, 401 (1950).

26. John F. Manning, *Legal Realism and the Canons' Revival*, 5 GREEN BAG 2D 283, 283 (2002).

27. *Id.*at 284.

legitimate."[28] This revival can be traced in large part to dissatisfaction with the use of legislative history to interpret statutes.[29] As Professor Eskridge explains, "[N]ew textualism posits that once the Court has ascertained a statute's plain meaning, consideration of legislative history becomes irrelevant. Legislative history should not even be consulted to confirm the apparent meaning of a statutory text."[30] Indeed, some members of the Supreme Court have adopted the view that where the meaning of the statute is clear in light of canons of construction, the Court should not resort to legislative history or other extrinsic evidence of the statute's meaning.[31] As we turn to a discussion of the role of legislative history in statutory construction, consider which approach seems to you to be the most useful and legitimate.

4.3 Legislative Intent

While the canons of construction provide some helpful ways to consider statutory language, they provide no magic answers. Where a statute is ambiguous, courts often resort to extrinsic evidence (material outside of the text of the statute itself) to determine its proper interpretation. Most frequently, courts will explore the legislative history of a statute in an attempt to reconstruct the legislative intent behind its enactment. You may wonder what legislative history is. It's the record of the progress of a piece of legislation as it makes its way through the legislature. After a brief outline of the legislative process, we'll take a look at the courts' use of legislative history to determine legislative intent.

4.3.1 The Legislative Process

When a court seeks to look behind the language of the statute to determine the intention of the legislature, it most often turns to the paper trail following a bill from its introduction in the legislature to its signing by the President. The evidence may include sponsors' statements introducing the legislation, committee and subcommittee reports, debates, conference committee reports, presidential signing statements, and post-enactment statements by legislators and administrative agencies responsible for implementing the legislation. Figure 4.1 provides a rough roadmap that should help you follow this trail.

---

28. *Id* at 284.
29. *Id.* at 285.
30. William N. Eskridge, Jr., *The New Textualism*, 37 UCLA L. REV. 621, 623–24 (1989).
31. Circuit City Stores Inc. v. Adams, 532 U.S. 105 (2001).

Figure 4.1   How A Bill Becomes A Law

Most legislation begins as a similar proposal in both houses.

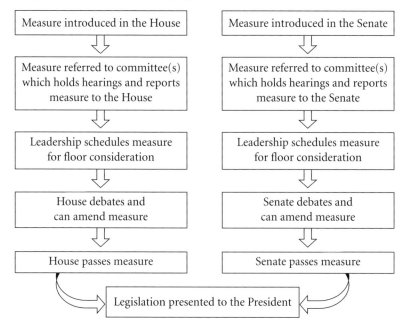

All measures must pass both the House and Senate in identical form before being presented to the President. If they are not identical, the process continues in Congress:

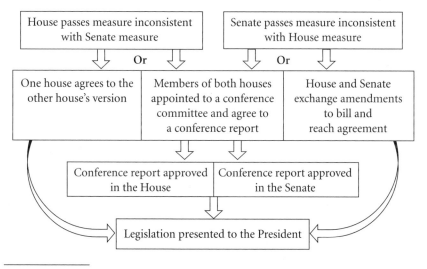

Adapted from "Our American Government," H.R. Doc. No. 102-192, at 32 (1993).

After the legislation is presented, the President may sign it into law. If the President does not sign the measure while Congress is in session, the measure becomes law after ten days. If the Congress is not in session and the President does not sign the measure, it fails to become law (pocket veto). Finally, the President may veto the measure. Congress can override the veto by a two-thirds vote of each house.

4.3.2 Legislative History

As a bill moves from the Capitol to the Rose Garden, its path is documented—perhaps littered—with paper. The sponsors may have introduced it with a press conference and speeches. During the bill's journey, legislative committees may issue reports, debates may be published in the Congressional Record, and proposed amendments may be adopted or rejected. At the signing ceremony, the President and the bill's supporters may crow about its benefits. Long after the statute's enactment, the legislature, individual legislators, and the President may explain their goals and understandings in supporting the law. Administrative agencies enforcing the law may issue regulations reflecting their understanding of the statute's purpose and scope. All of these documents may indicate the intended purpose of the legislation, and the courts may examine them to interpret the statute consistently with the legislative intent.

Wisconsin Public Intervenor v. Mortier
501 U.S. 597 (1991)

[In 1985, the tiny town of Casey, Wisconsin (population 400–500) adopted a local ordinance regulating the use of pesticides. The ordinance required a permit for the application of any pesticide to public lands, to private lands subject to public use, or for the aerial application of any pesticide to private lands. Ralph Mortier applied for a permit for spraying of a portion of his land. The town granted him a permit, but precluded any aerial spraying and restricted the lands on which ground spraying would be allowed.

Mortier, with respondent Wisconsin Forestry/Rights-of-Way/Turf Coalition, sued the town in state court claiming that its ordinance was pre-empted by federal law. The Wisconsin Public Intervenor, an assistant attorney general charged under state law with the protection of the environment, entered into the proceedings as an additional defendant. The lower court ruled that the town's ordinance was pre-empted by federal law, specifically the Federal Insecticide, Fungicide, and Rodenticide Act ("FIFRA" or "the Act"). The Supreme Court of Wisconsin affirmed. The town of Casey and the Wisconsin

Public Intervenor sought review by the United States Supreme Court and it granted *certiorari*.

The Court began by reviewing the history of FIFRA. The Act was adopted in 1947 primarily as a licensing and labeling statute. In 1972, growing environmental and safety concerns led Congress to amend the Act. The 1972 amendments significantly strengthened the Act's registration and labeling standards. To help ensure that pesticides would be applied in accordance with these standards, the revisions "regulated the use, as well as the sale and labeling, of pesticides; regulated pesticides produced and sold in both intrastate and interstate commerce; and provided for review, cancellation, and suspension of registration." The 1972 amendments also granted increased enforcement authority to the Environmental Protection Agency (EPA), which had been charged with federal oversight of pesticides since 1970. Thus, the 1972 amendments "transformed FIFRA from a labeling law into a comprehensive regulatory statute."

As amended, FIFRA specifies several roles for state authorities. The statute, for example, authorizes the EPA Administrator to enter into cooperative agreements with the States to enforce FIFRA provisions. Of particular relevance to this case, one provision specifies that States may regulate the sale or use of pesticides so long as the state regulation does not permit a sale or use prohibited by the Act.

In short, the 1972 amendments increased the federal role in pesticide regulation while expressly preserving a significant role for the States. The question presented by this case is whether FIFRA pre-empted additional regulation of pesticides by local authorities.]

Justice White delivered the opinion of the Court.

Under the Supremacy Clause, state laws that "interfere with, or are contrary to the laws of congress, made in pursuance of the constitution" are invalid. The ways in which federal law may pre-empt state law are well established and in the first instance turn on congressional intent. Congress' intent to supplant state authority in a particular field may be expressed in the terms of the statute. Absent explicit pre-emptive language, Congress' intent to supersede state law may nonetheless be implicit if a scheme of federal regulation is so pervasive as to make reasonable the inference that Congress left no room for the States to supplement it, if the Act of Congress touches a field in which the federal interest is so dominant that the federal system will be assumed to preclude enforcement of state laws on the same subject, or if the goals sought to be obtained and the obligations imposed reveal a purpose to preclude state authority. When considering pre-emption, we start with the assumption that the historic police powers of the States were not to be superseded by the Federal Act unless that was the clear and manifest purpose of Congress.

Even when Congress has not chosen to occupy a particular field, pre-emption may occur to the extent that state and federal law actually conflict. Such a conflict arises when "compliance with both federal and state regulations is a physical impossibility," or when a state law "stands as an obstacle to the accomplishment and execution of the full purposes and objectives of Congress."

Applying these principles, we conclude that FIFRA does not pre-empt the town's ordinance either explicitly or implicitly or by virtue of an actual conflict.

[1. *The Act does not expressly pre-empt local pesticide regulation*]

As the Wisconsin Supreme Court recognized, FIFRA nowhere expressly supersedes local regulation of pesticide use. The court, however, purported to find statutory language "which is indicative" of pre-emptive intent in the statute's provision delineating the "Authority of States." The key portions of that provision state:

(a) A State may regulate the sale or use of any federally registered pesticide or device in the State, but only if and to the extent the regulation does not permit any sale or use prohibited by this subchapter.

(b) Such State shall not impose or continue in effect any requirements for labeling or packaging in addition to or different from those required under this subchapter.

Also significant, in the court's eyes, was FIFRA's failure to specify political subdivisions in defining "State" as "a State, the District of Columbia, the Commonwealth of Puerto Rico, the Virgin Islands, Guam, the Trust Territory of the Pacific Islands, and American Samoa."

[In our reading of the statutory language,] it is wholly inadequate to convey an express pre-emptive intent on its own. The Act plainly authorizes the "States" to regulate pesticides and just as plainly is silent with reference to local governments. Mere silence cannot suffice to establish a "clear and manifest purpose" to pre-empt local authority.

Properly read, the statutory language tilts in favor of local regulation. The principle is well settled that local [governments are political subdivisions of the States. The States can entrust them with whatever powers they find convenient. Thus, since the Act empowers the States to act, they can choose to act through their local political subdivisions.] Indeed, the more plausible reading of the Act's authorization to the States leaves the allocation of regulatory authority to the "absolute discretion" of the States themselves, including the option of leaving local regulation of pesticides in the hands of local authorities.

[2. *The legislative history does not expressly establish a pre-emptive intent*]

Mortier attempts to compensate for the statute's textual inadequacies by stressing the legislative history. The evidence from this source is at best ambiguous. The House Agriculture Committee Report accompanying the proposed FIFRA amendments stated that it had "rejected a proposal which would have permitted political subdivisions to further regulate pesticides on the grounds that the 50 States and the Federal Government should provide an adequate number of regulatory jurisdictions." While this statement indicates an unwillingness by Congress to grant political subdivisions regulatory authority, it does not demonstrate an intent to prevent the States from delegating such authority to its subdivisions, and still less does it show a desire to prohibit local regulation altogether. At least one other statement, however, concededly goes further. The Senate Committee on Agriculture and Forestry Report states outright that it "considered the decision of the House Committee to deprive political subdivisions of States and other local authorities of any authority or jurisdiction over pesticides and concurs with the decision of the House."

But other Members of Congress clearly disagreed. The Senate Commerce Committee, which also had jurisdiction over the bill, observed that "while the Senate Agriculture Committee bill does not specifically prohibit local governments from regulating pesticides, the report of that committee states explicitly that local governments cannot regulate pesticides in any manner. Many local governments now regulate pesticides to meet their own specific needs which they are often better able to perceive than are State and Federal regulators." To counter the language in the Agriculture and Forestry Committee Report, the Commerce Committee proposed an amendment expressly authorizing local regulation among numerous other, unrelated proposals. This amendment was rejected.

As a result, matters were left with the two principal Committees responsible for the bill in disagreement over whether it pre-empted pesticide regulation by political subdivisions. Like FIFRA's text, the legislative history thus falls far short of establishing that pre-emption of local pesticide regulation was the "clear and manifest purpose of Congress." We thus agree with the submission in the amicus brief of the United States expressing the views of the EPA, the agency charged with enforcing FIFRA.

[3. *The Act does not pre-empt local regulation by virtue of actual conflict*]

Finally, like the EPA, we discern no actual conflict either between FIFRA and the ordinance before us or between FIFRA and local regulation generally. Mortier does not rely, nor could he, on the theory that compliance with the ordinance and FIFRA is a "physical impossibility." Instead, he urges that the town's ordinance stands as an obstacle to the statute's goals of promoting pesticide regulation that is coordinated solely on the federal and state levels, that rests upon some degree of technical expertise, and that does not unduly burden interstate commerce. Each one of these assertions rests on little more than snippets of legislative history and policy speculations. None of them is convincing.

To begin with, FIFRA does not suggest a goal of regulatory coordination that sweeps either as exclusively or as broadly as Mortier contends. The statute gives no indication that Congress was sufficiently concerned about this goal to require pre-emption of local use ordinances simply because they were enacted locally. Mortier suggests otherwise, quoting legislative history which states that FIFRA establishes "a coordinated Federal-State administrative system to carry out the new program," and raising the specter of gypsy moth hordes safely navigating through thousands of contradictory and ineffective municipal regulations. As we have made plain, the statute does not expressly or impliedly preclude regulatory action by political subdivisions with regard to local use. To the contrary, FIFRA implies a regulatory partnership between federal, state, and local governments. [One provision] expressly states that the Administrator "shall cooperate with … any appropriate agency of any State or any political subdivision thereof, in carrying out the provisions of this [Act] and in securing uniformity of regulations." Nor does FIFRA suggest that any goal of coordination precludes local use ordinances because they were enacted independently of specific state or federal oversight. As we have also made plain, local use permit regulations—unlike labeling or certification—do not fall within an area that FIFRA pre-empts or even plainly addresses. There is no indication that any coordination which the statute seeks to promote extends beyond the matters with which it deals, or does so strongly enough to compel the conclusion that an independently enacted ordinance that falls outside the statute's reach frustrates its purpose.

FIFRA provides even less indication that local ordinances must yield to statutory purposes of promoting technical expertise or maintaining unfettered interstate commerce. Once more, isolated passages of legislative history that were themselves insufficient to establish a pre-emptive congressional intent do not by themselves establish legislative goals with pre-emptive effect. Mortier nonetheless asserts that local ordinances necessarily rest on insufficient expertise and burden commerce by allowing, among other things, large-scale crop infestation. As with the specter of the gypsy moth, Congress is free to find that local regulation does wreak such havoc and enact legislation with the purpose of preventing it. We are satisfied, however, that Congress has not done so yet.

We hold that FIFRA does not pre-empt the town of Casey's ordinance regulating the use of pesticides. The judgment of the Wisconsin Supreme Court is reversed, and the case is remanded for proceedings not inconsistent with this opinion.

Notes and Questions

1. Apart from the approach to legislative history, what is the significance of the *Mortier* case? Would the preclusion of local regulation of pesticides matter to local governments and environmental groups? Does the continued local regulation of pesticides matter to the agricultural industry? Do these issues matter to us all? If so, why doesn't the Court address the merits of the dispute and underlying policy issues rather than simply debating the language and legislative history of the statute?

2. Consider the analysis historically. As the Court stated, "When considering pre-emption, we start with the assumption that the historic police powers of the States were not to be superseded by the Federal Act unless that was the clear and manifest purpose of Congress." Given the federalism principles that inform our understanding of the relationship between the federal government and the States, is the Court's view of the continued role of state and local government sound?

3. Is this deference to state government outdated in our 21st-century world where global trade cannot function if hindered by the parochial concerns of 500 Wisconsin villagers?

4. Are you persuaded that the Court properly divined Congress' intent? Does the language of the statute support the arguments for continued local regulation? Does the legislative history support this view? Or did Mr. Mortier have the better arguments? If legislative history is evidence of congressional intent, what piece of evidence did you find most persuasive?

5. In addition to considering the statutory language and legislative history, the Court also adopted the views of the EPA, the agency responsible for administering the Act. What is the relevance of the EPA's interpretation of the Act? Should courts consider the interpretation of administrative agencies? The Supreme Court has stated that courts should defer to reasonable interpretations by administrative agencies.[32]

6. As you know, the United States Supreme Court hears a limited number of cases. Why do you think it decided to review this decision by the Wisconsin Supreme Court?

---

32. *See* Chevron U.S.A. Inc. v. Nat'l Res. Def. Council, Inc., 467 U.S. 837, 843–44 (1984); Patricia Wald, *The Sizzling Sleeper: The Use of Legislative History in Construing Statutes in the 1988–1989 Term of the United States Supreme Court*, 39 AM. U. L. REV. 277, 308 (1990) (suggesting that "the executive's interpretation trumps that of the court").

7. Does Congress have the power to prohibit local governments from regulating pesticide use in their communities?

Concurring Opinion in
Wisconsin Public Intervenor v. Mortier

Justice Scalia concurred in the judgment.

I agree with the Court that FIFRA does not pre-empt local regulation, because I agree that the terms of the statute do not alone manifest a pre-emption of the entire field of pesticide regulation.

[T]he Wisconsin justices agreed with me on this point, and would have come out the way that I and the Court do but for the Committee Reports contained in FIFRA's legislative history. I think they were entirely right about the tenor of those Reports. Their only mistake was failing to recognize how unreliable Committee Reports are—not only as a genuine indicator of congressional intent but as a safe predictor of judicial construction. We use them when it is convenient, and ignore them when it is not.

Consider how the case would have been resolved if the Committee Reports were taken seriously: The bill to amend the Act was reported out of the House Committee on Agriculture on September 25, 1971. According to the accompanying Committee Report: "The Committee rejected a proposal which would have permitted political subdivisions to further regulate pesticides on the grounds that the 50 States and the Federal Government should provide an adequate number of regulatory jurisdictions." Had the grounds for the rejection not been specified, it would be possible to entertain the Court's speculation that the Committee might have been opposing only direct conferral upon localities of authority to regulate, in contrast to state delegation of authority to regulate. But once it is specified that an excessive number of regulatory jurisdictions is the problem—that "50 States and the Federal Government" are enough—then it becomes clear that the Committee wanted localities out of the picture, and thought that its bill placed them there.

The House Agriculture Committee's bill was passed by the full House and was referred to the Senate Committee on Agriculture and Forestry. The accompanying Committee Report [endorses the House's rejection of local regulation]: "We have considered the decision of the House Committee to deprive political subdivisions of States and other local authorities of any authority or jurisdiction over pesticides and concur with the decision of the House of Representatives. Clearly, the fifty States and the Federal Government provide sufficient jurisdictions to properly regulate pesticides. Moreover, few, if any, local authorities whether towns, counties, villages, or municipalities have the financial wherewithal to provide necessary expert regulation comparable with that provided by the State and Federal Governments. On this basis and on the basis that permitting such regulation would be an extreme burden on interstate commerce, it is the intent that the section ... by not providing any authority to political subdivisions and other local authorities of or in the States, should be understood as depriving such local authorities and political subdivisions of any and all jurisdiction and authority over pesticides and the regulation of pesticides." Clearer committee language "directing" the courts how to interpret a statute of Congress could not be found, and if such a direction had any binding effect, the interpretation in this case would be no question at all.

But there is still more. After the Senate Agriculture Committee reported the bill to the floor, it was re-referred to the Committee on Commerce. The Report of that Committee reconfirmed the interpretation of the Senate and House Agriculture Committees. The Report said: "While the Agriculture Committee bill does not specifically prohibit local governments from regulating pesticides, the report of that committee states explicitly that local governments cannot regulate pesticides in any manner. Many local governments now regulate pesticides to meet their own specific needs which they are often better able to perceive than are State and Federal regulators." The Court claims that this passage, plus the amendment that it explains, show that "the two principal Committees responsible for the bill were in disagreement over whether it pre-empted pesticide regulation by political subdivisions." I confess that I am less practiced than others in the science of construing legislative history, but it seems to me that quite the opposite is the case. The Senate Commerce Committee Report does not offer a different interpretation of the pre-emptive effect of the bill. To the contrary, it acknowledges that the Report of the originating Committee "states explicitly that local governments cannot regulate pesticides in any manner," and then proceeds to a statement ("Many local governments now regulate pesticides, etc.") which questions not the existence but the desirability of that restriction on local regulatory power. And since it agreed with the interpretation but did not agree with the policy, the Senate Commerce Committee proposed an amendment to the bill, whose purpose, according to its Report, was to "give local governments the authority to regulate the sale or use of a pesticide beyond the requirements imposed by State and Federal authorities." In a supplemental Report, the Senate Agriculture Committee opposed the Commerce Committee's amendment, which it said would "give local governments the authority to regulate the sale or use of a pesticide," thereby "vitiating" the earlier Agriculture Committee Report. This legislative history clearly demonstrates, I think, not (as the Court would have it) that the two principal Senate Committees disagreed about whether the bill pre-empted local regulation, but that they were in accord that it did, and in disagreement over whether it ought to.

Of course that does not necessarily say anything about what Congress as a whole thought. Assuming that all the members of the three Committees in question (as opposed to just the relevant Subcommittees) actually adverted to the interpretive point at issue here—which is probably an unrealistic assumption—and assuming further that they were in unanimous agreement on the point, they would still represent less than two-fifths of the Senate, and less than one-tenth of the House. It is most unlikely that many Members of either Chamber read the pertinent portions of the Committee Reports before voting on the bill—assuming (we cannot be sure) that the Reports were available before the vote. Those pertinent portions, though they dominate our discussion today, constituted less than a quarter-page of the 82-page House Agriculture Committee Report, and less than a half-page each of the 74-page Senate Agriculture Committee Report, the 46-page Senate Commerce Committee Report, and the 73-page Senate Agriculture Committee Supplemental Report. Those Reports in turn were a minuscule portion of the total number of reports that the Members of Congress were receiving (and presumably even writing) during the period in question. In the Senate, at least, there was a vote on an amendment (the Commerce Committee proposal) that would have changed the result of the supposed interpretation. But the full Senate could have rejected that either because a majority of its Members disagreed with the Commerce Committee's proposed policy; or because they disagreed with the Commerce Committee's and the Agriculture Committee's interpretation (and thus thought the amendment superfluous); or because they were blissfully ignorant of the entire dispute and simply thought that the Commerce Committee, by asking for recommittal and proposing 15 amendments, was being a troublemaker; or because three different minorities (enough to make a majority) had each of these respective reasons. We have no way of knowing; indeed, we have no way of knowing that they had any rational motive at all.

All we know for sure is that the full Senate adopted the text that we have before us here, as did the full House, pursuant to the procedures prescribed by the Constitution; and that that text, having been transmitted to the President and approved by him, again pursuant to the procedures prescribed by the Constitution, became law. On the important question before us today, whether that law denies local communities throughout the Nation significant powers of self-protection, we should try to give the text its fair meaning, whatever various committees might have had to say—thereby affirming the proposition that we are a Government of laws, not of committee reports. That is, at least, the way I prefer to proceed.

If I believed, however, that the meaning of a statute is to be determined by committee reports, I would have to conclude that a meaning opposite to our judgment has been commanded three times over—not only by one committee in each House, but by two Committees in one of them. Today's decision reveals that, in their judicial application, Committee reports are a forensic rather than an interpretive device, to be invoked when they support the decision and ignored when they do not. To my mind that is infinitely better than honestly giving them dispositive effect. But it would be better still to stop confusing the Wisconsin Supreme Court, and not to use committee reports at all.

Notes and Questions

1. Which arguments on the legislative intent evidenced in the legislative history are more persuasive, the Court's or Justice Scalia's?

2. Consider the differing interpretations of the report of the Senate Committee on Commerce. According to the Court, that report indicates that the Senate Committee on Commerce disagreed with the House Committee on Agriculture and the Senate Committee on Agriculture about the proposed Act's preclusion of local regulation. According to Justice Scalia, the report shows the Senate Committee on Commerce recognized that the bill would preclude local control (as the House and Senate Committees on Agriculture had stated) and that the Committee therefore attempted (unsuccessfully) to restore local control. In other words, all three committees understood that the bill precluded local regulation. Which interpretation is correct? If Justice Scalia is correct, then the Court's opinion has adopted an interpretation which allows local regulation that the legislature consciously rejected by defeating the Senate Commerce Committee's proposed amendment. And if that is true, why does Justice Scalia concur in the judgment rather than dissenting?

3. Consider the views of Justice Stevens and Justice Scalia as expressed in their concurring opinions in *Bank One Chicago, N.A. v. Midwest Bank & Trust Company*, 516 U.S. 264 (1996):

> A. *Justice Stevens:* Justice Scalia is quite right that it is unlikely that more than a handful of legislators were aware of the Act's drafting history. He is quite wrong, however, to conclude from that observation that the drafting history is not useful to conscientious and disinterested judges trying to understand the statute's meaning.
>
> Legislators, like other busy people, often depend on the judgment of trusted colleagues when discharging their official responsibilities. If a statute ... has bipartisan support and has been carefully consid-

ered by committees familiar with the subject matter, Representatives and Senators may appropriately rely on the views of the committee members in casting their votes. In such circumstances, since most members are content to endorse the views of the responsible committees, the intent of those involved in the drafting process is properly regarded as the intent of the entire Congress.

* * *

I must also take exception to Justice Scalia's psychoanalysis of judges who examine legislative history when construing statutes. He confidently asserts that we use such history as a make-weight after reaching a conclusion on the basis of other factors. I have been performing this type of work for more than 25 years and have never proceeded in the manner Justice Scalia suggests. It is quite true that I have often formed a tentative opinion about the meaning of a statute and thereafter examined the statute's drafting history to see whether the history supported my provisional conclusion or provided a basis for revising it. In my judgment, a reference to history in the Court's opinion in such a case cannot properly be described as a "make-weight." That the history could have altered my opinion is evidenced by the fact that there are significant cases ... in which the study of history did alter my original analysis. In any event, I see no reason why conscientious judges should not feel free to examine all public records that may shed light on the meaning of a statute.

B. *Justice Scalia:* I agree with the Court's opinion, except that portion of it which enters into a discussion of "[t]he drafting history of §4010." ... In my view a law means what its text most appropriately conveys, whatever the Congress that enacted it might have "intended." The law is what the law says, and we should content ourselves with reading it rather than psychoanalyzing those who enacted it. Moreover, even if subjective intent rather than textually expressed intent were the touchstone, it is a fiction of Jack-and-the-Beanstalk proportions to assume that more than a handful of those Senators and Members of the House who voted for the final version of the Expedited Funds Availability Act, and the President who signed it, were, when they took those actions, aware of the drafting evolution that the Court describes; and if they were, that their actions in voting for or signing the final bill show that they had the same "intent" which that evolution suggests was in the minds of the drafters.

Justice Stevens acknowledges that this is so, but asserts that the intent of a few committee members is nonetheless dispositive because legislators are "busy people," and "most members [of Congress] are content to endorse the views of the responsible committees." ... I do not know the factual basis for that assurance. Many congressional committees tend not to be representative of the full house, but are disproportionately populated by Members whose constituents have a particular stake in the subject matter—agriculture, merchant marine and fisheries, science and technology, etc. I think it quite unlikely that the House of Representatives would be "content to endorse the views" that its Agriculture Committee would come up with if that committee knew (as it knows in drafting Committee Reports) that those views need not be moderated to survive a floor vote. And even more unlikely that the Senate would be "content to endorse the views" of the House Agriculture Committee. But assuming Justice Stevens is right about this desire to leave details to the committees, the very first provision of the Constitution forbids it. Article I, Section 1 provides that "[a]ll legislative Powers herein granted shall be vested in a Congress of the United States, which shall consist of a Senate and a House of Representatives." It has always been assumed that these powers are nondelegable—or, as John Locke put it, that legislative power consists of the power "to make laws, ... not to make legislators." ... Thus, if legislation consists of forming an "intent" rather than adopting a text (a proposition with which I do not agree), Congress cannot leave the formation of that intent to a small band of its number, but must, as the Constitution says, form an intent of the Congress. There is no escaping the point: Legislative history that does not represent the intent of the whole Congress is nonprobative; and legislative history that does represent the intent of the whole Congress is fanciful.

Our opinions using legislative history are often curiously casual, sometimes even careless, in their analysis of what "intent" the legislative history shows. Perhaps that is because legislative history is in any event a make-weight; the Court really makes up its mind on the basis of other factors. Or perhaps it is simply hard to maintain a rigorously analytical attitude, when the point of departure for the inquiry is the fairyland in which legislative history reflects what was in "the Congress's mind."

4. As scholars have demonstrated, legislative history is malleable. The Supreme Court justices have shown that it can be used to support any political posture. As one reviewer noted:

Whereas before the 1890's the Supreme Court seldom relied on legislative history, in the ensuing years, the 'progressive judges used legislative history as a weapon against common law assumptions and spurious interpretations, while conservative judges sensitive to charges of anti-democratic activism felt obliged to defend their common law analyses by reference to legislative sources.' Moreover, while New Dealers such as James Landis saw legislative history as a way to protect New Deal legislation and agencies from reactionary federal judges, years later progressives on the Warren Court used it to further the 'progressive evolution of legal policy, not [to] implement the intentions of long-dead politicians.' In short, legislative histories are so wonderfully pliable that they can be used by judges of any political stripe.[33]

The malleability of legislative history has led some critics to compare the use of legislative history to "looking over a crowd and picking out your friends."[34]

5. Another criticism is that legislative history can be manipulated. Lobbyists orchestrate the legislative debate to provide a legislative history favorable to their clients. Opponents of a bill may also tweak the history by floor comments or minority reports.[35]

6. Assuming the courts can productively turn to legislative history for guidance on legislative intent, what parts of the history are useful? Should joint conference committee reports be given more weight than individual committee reports? What about the remarks of individual legislators? Some courts have used the statements of sponsors to reinforce the plain meaning of the statutory language.[36]

7. If statements of sponsors can be used to support an interpretation, can the silence of assumed opponents also be used? In a recent case construing the Food, Drug and Cosmetic Act, the court buttressed its view that Congress did not intend it to cover tobacco products by noting the failure of tobacco states' representatives to oppose the Act.[37] The court pointed out that representatives from North Carolina and Kentucky supported the Act. "Had there been any

---

33. R. Shep Melnick, *Statutory Reconstruction; The Politics of Eskridge's Interpretation*, 84 GEO. L. J. 91, 94–95 (1995) (book review) (footnotes omitted).

34. *Id.* at 95.

35. *See* William S. Moorehead, *A Congressman Looks at the Planned Colloquy and Its Effect in the Interpretation of Statutes*, 45 A.B.A. J. 1314 (1959).

36. *See* North Haven Bd. of Educ. v. Bell, 456 U.S. 512, 526–27 (1982); Bell Atlantic-New Jersey, Inc. v. Tate, 962 F. Supp. 608, 613–14 (D. N.J. 1997).

37. Brown & Williamson Tobacco v. Food & Drug Admin., 153 F.3d 155, 168 n. 15 (4th Cir. 1998).

indication that the Act might apply to tobacco products, we can only assume that such members of Congress would have expressed opposition to the Act."[38] Is this a sensible and reasonable inference? Or an example of Justice Scalia's view that legislative history arguments are simply fairytales?

8. Should courts consider presidential signing statements?[39] President Reagan's Attorney General Edwin Meese arranged for their publication in U.S. Code Congressional and Administrative News hoping that making them available to the courts would "improve statutory interpretation."[40] Some critics have argued that signing statements should be given little, if any, weight because they violate separation of powers principles.[41] But increasingly they are being cited by the courts to confirm the reading of statutory language and support the fundamental purposes of the legislation. For example, the United States Supreme Court supported the conclusion that certain civil rights remedies were to be given prospective application by citing individual legislators' statements, the Equal Employment Opportunity Commission's interpretation, and President Bush's signing statement.[42]

9. What weight, if any, should be given to pronouncements of the legislature after the enactment of a statute?[43] The United States Supreme Court has indicated that later legislation is entitled to significant weight, especially when the precise intent of the enacting Congress is obscure.[44] On the other hand, the Court has stated that legislative pronouncements in later years are in no sense part of the legislative history since it is the intent of the Congress that enacted the original statute that controls its interpretation.[45]

10. What weight, if any, should be given to pronouncements of a legislative committee after the enactment of a statute?[46] While the Supreme Court has been hesitant to give subsequent committee reports much deference, it has

---

38. *Id.*

39. *See* Kristy Carroll, Comment, *Whose Statute Is It Anyway?: Why and How Courts Should Use Presidential Signing Statements When Interpreting Federal Statutes*, 46 Cath. U. L. Rev. 475 (Winter 1997).

40. *Id.* at 491.

41. M. Garber and K. Wimmer, *Presidential Signing Statements As Interpretations of Legislative Intent: An Executive Aggrandizement of Power*, 24 Harv. J. on Legis. 363, 370 (1987).

42. Landgraf v. USI Film Prod., 511 U.S. 244 (1994).

43. Athena Mueller, *Supreme Court's View on Weight to be Accorded to Pronouncements of Legislature, or Members of Legislature, Respecting Meaning or Intent of Previously Enacted Statute*, 56 L. Ed. 2d 918.

44. Loving v. United States, 517 U.S. 748, 770 (1996); Seatrain Shipbuilding Corp. v. Shell Oil Co., 444 U.S. 572, 590–94 (1980).

45. Oscar Mayer & Co. v. Evan, 441 U.S. 750, 758 (1979).

46. *See generally* Mueller, *supra* note 43, at 918.

relied on such committee reports to support interpretations in certain cases. For example, the Court relied on a joint House-Senate conference committee announcement concerning a statutory provision governing veterans' reemployment rights.[47]

11. What weight, if any, should be given to pronouncements of an individual legislator after the enactment of a statute?[48] The Court has been very leery of post-enactment statements by individual legislators. For this reason the Court has rejected affidavits of the author of a statute as reflecting only his personal view.[49]

12. Should post-enactment legislative history be considered to determine whether the interpretation of the regulatory agency should be adopted? The Ninth Circuit has concluded that post-enactment legislative history should be consulted to determine whether Congress acquiesced in an agency's interpretation of a statute of which Congress was aware when it amended the statute.[50]

4.4 The Retroactivity Problem

What happens when a new law imposes new obligations or liabilities? Where a change in the law prejudices a private individual, our tradition condemns the retrospective application of the law. Simple fairness requires this approach so that people have the opportunity to inform themselves of the law and to conform their conduct to its requirements. For this reason, legislation is generally enacted for prospective application only. Moreover, the *ex post facto* clause of the Constitution forbids retroactivity in criminal law.

While statutes are usually enacted for prospective application, does Congress have the power to require the retroactive application of statutes in disputes arising out of events occurring before the statute was enacted? In the criminal context, the *ex post facto* clause would render the statute unconstitutional. However, in the civil context, the constitutional constraints on retroactivity are relaxed since the *ex post facto* clause does not apply. For this reason, while fairness might suggest the prospective application of the new statute, judicial deference to the legislature might require its retroactive application.

This troublesome question arises even when the legislative intent is clear, but is often exacerbated when the legislature fails to clarify its intent. The dif-

---

47. King v. St. Vincent's Hosp., 502 U.S. 215, 222 (1991).
48. *See generally* Mueller, *supra* note 43, at 918.
49. Bread Political Action Comm. v. FEC, 455 U.S. 577, 582 (1982).
50. Stephenson v. Shalala, 87 F.3d 350, 355 (9th Cir. 1996); Dameron Physicians Med. Group, Inc. v. Shalala, 961 F. Supp. 1326, 1332 (N.D. Cal. 1997).

ficulty is manifest in a series of cases where the United States Supreme Court has wrestled with the question of whether a civil statute is to be given prospective or retrospective application.

Nearly two centuries ago, the United States Supreme Court concluded that in matters of national concern, the courts must decide cases according to the statutes in existence at the time of the decision, even when the statutes were adopted after judgment in the lower court. If the law changes while an action is on appeal, the appellate court must apply the new law.[51] In *Schooner Peggy*, the Convention under consideration was entered after the case was pending on appeal and altered the decision reached in the lower court. By its terms it was to apply to pending cases, and the Court gave the Convention that effect. This left open the question of whether a statute would be applied retroactively when such an application was not expressly intended. The Court also recognized that "in mere private cases between individuals" such retrospective application was to be avoided if it would affect the rights of the parties.[52] Over the next two centuries, the Court reaffirmed the view that in matters of public concern statutes should generally be applied retroactively.[53]

An example of this broad retroactivity rule is provided by *Bradley v. School Board of Richmond*, 416 U.S. 696 (1974). In *Bradley*, the plaintiffs in a school desegregation case sought attorneys' fees from the school board for services performed from 1970 to 1971. In 1972, while the case was pending on appeal, Congress passed legislation authorizing attorneys' fees in civil rights cases. The Court held that the fees statute applied to the services performed before its enactment. As the Court explained, "[W]e must reject the contention that a change in the law is to be given effect in a pending case only where that is the clear and stated intention of the legislature."[54] The Court recognized two exceptions to the rule of retroactivity: "[A] court is to apply the law in effect at the time it renders its decision, unless doing so would result in manifest injustice or there is statutory direction or legislative history to the contrary."[55]

The Court revisited the retroactivity issue in deciding whether provisions of the Civil Rights Act of 1991 would be extended to cases pending on appeal when the provisions were adopted.[56] The new provisions created the right to

---

51. United States v. Schooner Peggy, 5 U.S. (1 Cranch) 103, 110 (1801).
52. *Id.*
53. Thorpe v. Hous. Auth., 393 U.S. 268 (1968).
54. Bradley v. School Bd. of Richmond, 416 U.S. 696, 715 (1974).
55. *Id.* at 711.
56. Landgraf v. USI Film Prod., 511 U.S. 244 (1994).

a jury trial and to compensatory and punitive damages in sexual harassment cases. In *Landgraf*, the Court first "concluded that the Civil Rights Act of 1991 does not evince any clear expression of intent" on the provisions' "application to cases arising before the Act's enactment."[57]

The Court recognized that fairness requires a presumption against retroactivity when a statute would impose new burdens on persons after the fact.[58] But the Court also acknowledged that even absent specific legislative authorization, "application of new statutes passed after the events in suit is unquestionably proper in many situations."[59] The key to deciding which approach to apply is whether the statute affects matters which are in some sense collateral to the main cause of action or "whether the new statute would have retroactive effect, i.e., whether it would impair rights a party possessed when he acted, increase a party's liability for past conduct, or impose new duties with respect to transactions already completed. If the statute would operate retroactively, our traditional presumption teaches that it does not govern absent clear congressional intent favoring such a result."[60]

Having set out its approach, the Court applied it to the provisions at issue. The Court held that the jury trial provision might be applied to post-enactment cases as simply a procedural change were it not linked to the damages provisions. However, the Court concluded that the damages provisions substantially increased the party's liability for past conduct and would therefore not be applied to cases pending prior to their enactment in the absence of clear imperative language from Congress.

Justice Blackmun dissented on two grounds. First, he found that Congress intended retroactive application. Second, he pointed out that the presumption against retroactive application did not apply to remedial legislation unless vested rights would be violated. Here the employer's conduct was illegal at the time it was committed and "there is no such thing as a vested right to do wrong."[61] In Blackmun's view, the new provisions simply expanded the remedy for "injuries caused by conduct that has been illegal for almost 30 years."[62] What canon of construction could Justice Blackmun cite to support his view?

The Supreme Court's most recent decision analyzing the retroactivity question is *Martin v. Hadix* decided on June 21, 1999. In *Martin*, the Court granted

---

57. *Id.* at 264.
58. *Id.* at 270.
59. *Id.* at 273.
60. *Id.* at 280.
61. *Id* at 297.
62. *Id.*

certiorari to resolve a conflict in the circuits that had arisen over the proper interpretation of a provision of the Prison Litigation Reform Act (PLRA) that restricted attorneys' fees in civil rights cases challenging the constitutionality of prison conditions. The question was whether the fee restrictions applied to cases which were pending before the statute was adopted.

Martin v. Hadix
527 U.S. 343 (1999)

Justice O'Connor delivered the opinion of the Court.

Section 803(d)(3) of the Prison Litigation Reform Act of 1995 (PLRA or Act) places limits on the fees that may be awarded to attorneys who litigate prisoner lawsuits. We are asked to decide how this section applies to cases that were pending when the PLRA became effective on April 26, 1996. We conclude that §803(d)(3) limits attorney's fees with respect to services performed after the PLRA's effective date but it does not so limit fees for services performed before the effective date.

The fee disputes before us arose out of two class action lawsuits challenging the conditions of confinement in the Michigan prison system. The first case, which we will call Glover, began in 1977 when female prisoners filed a civil rights suit in the United States District Court for the Eastern District of Michigan. The Glover plaintiffs alleged prison officials had violated their rights under the Equal Protection Clause of the Constitution by denying them access to vocational and educational opportunities that were available to male prisoners. They also claimed that the defendants had denied them their right of access to the courts. After a bench trial, the District Court found "significant discrimination against the female prison population" in violation of the Equal Protection Clause, and concluded that the defendants' policies had denied the Glover plaintiffs their right of meaningful access to the courts. In 1981, the District Court entered a Final Order detailing the specific actions to be undertaken by the defendants to remedy the constitutional violations. One year later, the court found that the plaintiffs were prevailing parties and thus entitled to attorney's fees under the civil rights statute providing for fees.

In 1985, the District Court entered an order providing that the plaintiffs were entitled to attorney's fees for monitoring of the defendants' compliance with the court's remedial decrees. This order also established a system for awarding fees that was in place when the present dispute arose. Under this system, the plaintiffs submit their fee requests on a semiannual basis, and the defendants then have 28 days to submit any objections to the requested award. The District Court resolves any disputes. In an appeal from a subsequent dispute over the meaning of this order, the Sixth Circuit affirmed that the plaintiffs were entitled to attorney's fees, at the prevailing market rate. The prevailing market rate has been adjusted over the years, but it is currently set at $150 per hour.

The second case, Hadix, began in 1980. Male prisoners at the State Prison of Southern Michigan, Central Complex sued in the United States District Court for the Eastern District of Michigan claiming that the conditions of their confinement violated the Constitution. Five years later, the Hadix plaintiffs and the defendant prison officials entered into a consent decree to assure the constitutionality of the conditions of confinement. The consent decree addressed a variety of issues, ranging from sanitation and safety to food service, mail, and access to the courts.

In November 1987, the District Court entered an order awarding attorney's fees to the Hadix plaintiffs for monitoring of the defendants' compliance with the consent decree. Subsequently, the Hadix plaintiffs were awarded attorney's fees through a procedure similar to the procedure that had been established for the Glover plaintiffs.

Thus, by 1987, Glover and Hadix were on parallel paths. In both cases, the District Court had concluded that the plaintiffs were entitled to monitoring fees, and the parties had established a system for awarding those fees on a semiannual basis. Moreover, the District Court had established specific market rates for awarding fees. By the time the PLRA was enacted, the prevailing market rate in both cases had been set at $150 per hour.

The fee landscape changed with the passage of the PLRA on April 26, 1996. The PLRA, as its name suggests, contains numerous provisions governing the course of prison litigation in the federal courts. The section of the PLRA at issue here, §803(d)(3), places a cap on attorney's fees that may be awarded in prison litigation suits:

(d) Attorney's fees

(1) In any action brought by a prisoner who is confined to any jail, prison, or other correctional facility, in which attorney's fees are authorized ... such fees shall not be awarded, except to the extent [authorized here].

* * *

(3) No award of attorney's fees in an action described in paragraph (1) shall be based on an hourly rate greater than 150 percent of the hourly rate established ... for payment of court-appointed counsel.

Court-appointed attorneys in the Eastern District of Michigan are compensated at a maximum rate of $75 per hour, and thus, under §803(d)(3), the

PLRA fee cap for attorneys working on prison litigation suits is a maximum hourly rate of $112.50.

Questions involving the PLRA first arose in both Glover and Hadix with respect to fee requests for monitoring performed before the PLRA was enacted. In both cases, in early 1996, the plaintiffs submitted fee requests for work performed during the last half of 1995. These requests were still pending when the PLRA became effective on April 26, 1996. In both cases, the District Court concluded that the PLRA fee cap did not limit attorney's fees for services performed in these cases prior to the effective date of the Act. The Sixth Circuit affirmed this interpretation of the PLRA on appeal.

However the next fee requests covered a time period encompassing work performed both before and after the effective date of the PLRA. In nearly identical orders issued in the two cases, the court reiterated its earlier conclusion that the PLRA does not limit fees for work performed before April 26, 1996, but concluded that the PLRA fee cap does limit fees for services performed after the effective date.

The Court of Appeals for the Sixth Circuit reviewed these orders on appeal. According to the Court of Appeals, the PLRA's fee limitation does not apply to fee requests that relate to cases that were pending on the date of enactment. If it were applied to pending cases, the court held, it would have an impermissible retroactive effect, regardless of when the work was performed.

The Court of Appeals' holding—that the PLRA's attorney's fees provisions do not apply to pending cases—is inconsistent with the holdings of other Circuits. For example, the Courts of Appeals for the Fourth and Ninth Circuits have held that §803(d) caps all fees that are ordered to be paid after the enactment of the PLRA, even when those fees compensate attorneys for work performed prior to the enactment of the PLRA. However, the Second Circuit held that the PLRA does not necessarily limit fees for work performed before its effective date although awarded after its effective date. And the District of Columbia Circuit held that PLRA limits fees for work performed after effective date of Act, and suggested that it does not apply to work performed before the effective date.

Prison officials contend that the PLRA applies to Glover and Hadix, cases that were pending when the PLRA was enacted. This fact pattern presents a recurring question in the law: When should a new federal statute be applied to pending cases? To answer this question, we ask first "whether Congress has expressly prescribed the statute's proper reach." *Landgraf v. USI Film Products*, 511 U.S. 244, 280 (1994). If there is no congressional directive on the temporal reach of a statute, we determine whether the application of the statute to the conduct at issue would result in a retroactive effect. If so, then in keep-

ing with our "traditional presumption" against retroactivity, we presume that
the statute does not apply to that conduct.

[1. *Congress has not expressly mandated retroactive application*]

Congress has not expressly mandated the temporal reach of §803(d)(3)....
[The statutory language] falls short, in other words, of the "unambiguous directive" or "express command" that the statute is to be applied retroactively
[that *Landgraf* requires].

The conclusion that §803(d) does not clearly express congressional intent
that it apply retroactively is strengthened by comparing §803(d) to the language that we suggested in *Landgraf* might qualify as a clear statement that a
statute was to apply retroactively: "[T]he new provisions shall apply to all proceedings pending on or commenced after the date of enactment." This provision, unlike the language of the PLRA, unambiguously addresses the temporal reach of the statute. With no such analogous language making explicit
reference to the statute's temporal reach, it cannot be said that Congress has
"expressly prescribed" §803(d)'s temporal reach.

[2. *The fees limitation would have an impermissible retroactive effect if applied to work performed before its adoption*]

Because we conclude that Congress has not "expressly prescribed" the
proper reach of §803(d)(3) [as required by *Landgraf*], we must determine
whether application of this section in this case would have retroactive effects
inconsistent with the usual rule that legislation is deemed to be prospective.
The inquiry into whether a statute operates retroactively demands a common
sense, functional judgment about "whether the new provision attaches new
legal consequences to events completed before its enactment." *Landgraf.* This
judgment should be informed and guided by "familiar considerations of fair
notice, reasonable reliance, and settled expectations." *Landgraf.*

For monitoring performed before the effective date of the PLRA, the PLRA's
attorney's fees provisions would have a retroactive effect contrary to the usual
assumption that congressional statutes are prospective in operation. The attorneys in both Hadix and Glover had a reasonable expectation that work they
performed prior to enactment of the PLRA in monitoring prisons' compliance
with the court orders would be compensated at the pre-PLRA rates as provided
in the stipulated order. Long before the PLRA was enacted, the plaintiffs were
declared prevailing parties, and the parties agreed to a system for periodically
awarding attorney's fees. The District Court entered orders establishing that
the fees were to be awarded at prevailing market rates, and specifically set those
rates at $150 per hour. The lawyers performed a specific task—monitoring
compliance with the court orders—and they were told that they would be com-

pensated at a rate of $150 per hour. Thus, when the lawyers provided these services before the enactment of the PLRA, they worked in reasonable reliance on this fee schedule. The PLRA, as applied to work performed before its effective date, would alter the fee arrangement post hoc by reducing the rate of compensation. To give effect to the PLRA's fees limitations, after the fact, would "attach new legal consequences" to completed conduct. *Landgraf.*

The prison defendants contest this conclusion. They contend that the application of a new attorney's fees provision is proper because fees questions "are incidental to, and independent from, the underlying substantive cause of action." They do not, in other words, change the substantive obligations of the parties because they are collateral to the main cause of action. Attaching the label "collateral" to attorney's fees questions does not advance the retroactivity inquiry, however. While it may be possible to generalize about types of rules that ordinarily will not raise retroactivity concerns, these generalizations do not end the inquiry. For example, in *Landgraf*, we acknowledged that procedural rules may often be applied to pending suits with no retroactivity problems, but we also cautioned that the mere fact that a new rule is procedural does not mean that it applies to every pending case. We took pains to dispel the suggestion that concerns about retroactivity have no application to procedural rules. When determining whether a new statute operates retroactively, it is not enough to attach a label (e.g., "procedural," "collateral") to the statute; we must ask whether the statute operates retroactively.

Moreover, the prison defendants' reliance on our decision in *Bradley v. School Bd. of Richmond*, 416 U.S. 696 (1974), to support their argument that attorney's fees provisions can be applied retroactively is misplaced. In *Bradley*, the District Court had awarded attorney's fees, based on general equitable principles, to a group of parents who had prevailed in their suit seeking the desegregation of the Richmond schools. While the case was pending on appeal, Congress passed a statute specifically authorizing the award of attorney's fees for prevailing parties in school desegregation cases. The Court of Appeals held that the new statute could not authorize fee awards for work performed before the effective date of the new law, but we reversed, holding that the fee award in that case was proper. Because attorney's fees were available, albeit under different principles, before passage of the statute, and because the District Court had in fact already awarded fees invoking these different principles, there was no manifest injustice in allowing the fee statute to apply in that case. We held that the award of statutory attorney's fees did not upset any reasonable expectations of the parties. In this case, by contrast, from the beginning of these suits, the parties have proceeded on the assumption that [the civil rights attorneys' fees statute] would govern. The PLRA was not passed until well after plaintiffs had been declared prevailing parties and thus entitled to attorney's fees. To impose the new standards now, for work performed before the PLRA became effective, would upset the reasonable expectations of the parties.

[3. *The fees limitation would* not *have an impermissible retroactive effect if applied to work performed after its adoption*]

With respect to services performed after the effective date of the PLRA, by contrast, there is no retroactivity problem. On April 26, 1996, through the PLRA, the plaintiffs' attorneys were on notice that their hourly rate had been adjusted. From that point forward, they would be paid at a rate consistent with the dictates of the law. After April 26, 1996, any expectation of compensation at the pre-PLRA rates was unreasonable. There is no manifest injustice in telling an attorney performing services that, going forward, she will earn a lower hourly rate than she had earned in the past. If the attorney does not wish to perform services at this new, lower, pay rate, she can choose not to work. In other words, as applied to work performed after the effective date of the PLRA, the PLRA has future effect on future work; this does not raise retroactivity concerns.

Plaintiffs contend that the PLRA has retroactive effect in this context because it attaches new legal consequences (a lower pay rate) to conduct completed before enactment. The pre-enactment conduct that they contend is affected is the attorney's initial decision to file suit on behalf of the prisoner clients. Even assuming, *arguendo*, that when the attorneys filed these cases in 1977 and 1980, they had a reasonable expectation that they would be compensated ... based on a particular fee schedule (i.e., the pre-PLRA, "prevailing market rate" schedule), their argument that the PLRA affects pre-PLRA conduct fails because it is based on the assumption that the attorney's initial decision to file a case on behalf of a client is an irrevocable one. In other words, plaintiffs' argument assumes that once an attorney files suit, she must continue working on that case until the decree is terminated. They provide no support for this assumption, however. They allude to ethical constraints on an attorney's ability to withdraw from a case midstream, but they do not seriously contend that the attorneys here were prohibited from withdrawing from the case during the postjudgment monitoring stage. It cannot be said that the PLRA changes the legal consequences of the attorneys' pre-PLRA decision to file the case.

In sum, we conclude that the PLRA contains no express command about its temporal scope. Because we find that the PLRA, if applied to services performed before the effective date of the Act, would have a retroactive effect inconsistent with our assumption that statutes are prospective, in the absence of an express command by Congress to apply the Act retroactively, we decline to do so. *Landgraf.* With respect to services performed after the effective date, by contrast, there is no retroactive effect, and the PLRA fees cap applies to such work. Accordingly, the judgment of the Court of Appeals for the Sixth Circuit is affirmed in part and reversed in part.

Notes and Questions

1. Did the court properly apply the *Landgraf* approach to retroactivity?
2. Is the result fair?
3. What about the plain meaning rule? The statute states:

> No award of attorney's fees ... shall be based on an hourly rate greater than 150 percent of the hourly rate established ... for payment of court-appointed counsel.

Once this statutory limit became effective on April 26, 1996, does the court have any authority to order an award at rates in excess of the statutory rate?

4. Might the legislature's purpose in enacting the PLRA shed light on its proper construction? The Act was adopted to curb frivolous pro se prisoner litigation which imposed a substantial burden on both prisons and the courts. The goal was to discourage prisoners from filing civil rights actions.

5. Clearly, when Congress chooses to expressly indicate that a provision is retroactive it can do so and did in fact do so in other sections of the PLRA. Indeed, in *Landgraf* the Court spelled out exactly what language Congress should use when it wants a statute to apply retroactively. So why didn't Congress adopt language that would clarify its intention and prevent unnecessary confusion and expensive litigation? Does this teach you any lessons about statutory drafting?

6. What do you think of the Court's handling of the defense argument that *Bradley v. School Board of Richmond*, 416 U.S. 696 (1974) supported the retroactive application of the fees provision? The defendants argued that *Bradley* supported their position, and yet the Court used *Bradley* to support the opposite conclusion. Does one side have the right approach? Or are legal precedents completely malleable?

7. Justice Ginsburg, joined by Justice Stevens, dissented in part to this decision. In their view, the prior rates should have been used both for the services performed before the PLRA and after the PLRA. As she explained:

> In my view, [the fee limit] is most soundly read to cover all and only representations undertaken after the PLRA's effective date. Application of §803(d) to representations commenced before the PLRA became law would "attach new legal consequences to an event com-

pleted before the statute's enactment"; hence the application would be retroactive under *Landgraf.* The critical event effected before the PLRA's effective date is the lawyer's undertaking to prosecute the client's civil rights claim. Applying §803(d) to pending matters significantly alters the consequences of the representation on which the lawyer has embarked. Notably, attorneys engaged before passage of the PLRA have little leeway to alter their conduct in response to the new legal regime; an attorney who initiated a prisoner's rights suit before April 26, 1996 remains subject to a professional obligation to see the litigation through to final disposition. See American Bar Association Model Rules of Professional Conduct, Rule 1.3, and Comment [3] (1999) ("A lawyer should carry through to conclusion all matters undertaken for a client."). Counsel's actions before and after that date are thus inextricably part of a course of conduct initiated prior to the law.

While the injustice in applying the fee limitations to pending actions may be more readily apparent regarding work performed before the PLRA's effective date, application of the statute to work performed thereafter in pending cases also frustrates reasonable reliance on prior law and court-approved market rates. Consider, for example, two attorneys who filed similar prison reform lawsuits at the same time, pre-PLRA. Both attorneys initiated their lawsuits in the expectation that, if they prevailed, they would earn the market rate anticipated by pre-PLRA law. In one case, the lawsuit progressed swiftly, and labor-intensive pretrial discovery was completed before April 26, 1996. In the other, the suit lagged through no fault of plaintiff's counsel, pending the court's disposition of threshold motions, and the attorney was unable to pursue discovery until after April 26, 1996. Both attorneys have prosecuted their claims with due diligence; both were obliged, having accepted the representations, to perform the work for which they seek compensation. There is scarcely greater injustice in denying pre-PLRA compensation for pretrial discovery in the one case than the other. Nor is there any reason to think that Congress intended these similarly situated attorneys to be treated differently.

Like the ABA's Model Rules, the Michigan Rules of Professional Conduct, which apply to counsel in both *Hadix* and *Glover* ... provide that absent good cause for terminating a representation, "a lawyer should carry through to conclusion all matters undertaken for a client." ... It is true that withdrawal may be permitted where the representation will result in an unreasonable financial burden on the lawyer, ... but explanatory comments suggest that this exception is designed for situations in which the client refuses to abide by the terms of an agreement relating to the representation, such as an agreement concerning fees.... Consistent with the Michigan Rules, counsel for petitioners affirmed at oral argument their ethical obligation to continue these representations to a natural conclusion.... There is no reason to think counsel ethically could have abandoned these representations in response to the PLRA fee limitation, nor any basis to believe the trial court would have permitted counsel to withdraw. See Rule 1.16(c) ("When ordered to do so by a tribunal, a lawyer shall continue representation."). As I see it, the attorneys' pre-PLRA pursuit of the civil rights claims thus created an obligation, enduring post-PLRA, to continue to provide effective representation.

8. Justice Scalia, concurring in the decision, dismisses Justice Ginsburg's concern as follows: "Like the Court, I do not think it true that an attorney who has signed on cannot terminate his representation; he assuredly can if the client says that he will no longer pay the hourly fee agreed upon." Is this standard appropriate in the case at bar? Two ABA ethics opinions have concluded that where funding cuts result in staffing cuts at legal services offices, the discharged attorneys may be compelled to continue representing clients without payment if necessary to prevent irreparable prejudice to the clients.[63] Compare *Holmes v. Y.J.A. Realty Corp.*, 128 A.D. 2d 982 (N.Y. App. Div. 1987) (a lawyer may withdraw where a client who is able to pay deliberately refuses to pay according to the fee agreement) to *Kriegsman v. Kriegsman*, 150 N.J. Super. 474 (App. Div. 1977) (a lawyer may not withdraw where a client becomes indigent and unable to pay for the lawyer's services, especially where the loss of the lawyer's familiarity and expertise would harm the client).

9. In both *Glover* and *Hadix*, the district courts had established procedures for compensating the attorneys at prevailing market rates. The courts' orders provided that the attorneys would be compensated at $150 per hour. Did the attorneys have a right to rely on these orders in continuing to provide services?

10. Under the "American rule" attorneys' fees are generally borne by the parties themselves, regardless of outcome of the case. Fee-shifting statutes alter this rule. For civil rights cases, Congress has provided for reasonable attor-

---

63. ABA COMM. ON ETHICS AND PROF'L RESPONSIBILITY, Formal Op. 347 (1981) and Formal Op. 96-399 (1996).

ney's fees to be paid to the prevailing party in order to encourage counsel to bring these actions. As the Supreme Court has explained:

> Congress enacted [the attorneys fees provision] specifically because it found that the private market for legal services failed to provide many victims of civil rights violations with effective access to the judicial process. These victims ordinarily cannot afford to purchase legal services at the rates set by the private market. Moreover, the contingent fee arrangements that make legal services available to many victims of personal injuries would often not encourage lawyers to accept civil rights cases, which frequently involve substantial expenditures of time and effort but produce only small monetary recoveries.... Consequently, awarding counsel fees to prevailing plaintiffs in such litigation is particularly important and necessary if federal civil and constitutional rights are to be adequately protected.[64]

11. The reasonable rate is determined by considering a number of factors including: (1) the time and labor expended; (2) the novelty and difficulty of the issues; (3) the skill required to perform the work; (4) the preclusion of employment by the attorney due to acceptance of the case; (5) the customary fee charged for like work; (6) time limitations imposed by the client or circumstances; (7) the amount in controversy and the results obtained; (8) the experience, reputation, and ability of the attorney; (9) the undesirability of the case; (10) the nature and length of the professional relationship between the attorney and client; and (12) attorneys' fees awards in similar cases.[65] The court may not consider the risk or the contingent nature of the recovery.[66]

12. If $150.00 per hour was a reasonable market rate in civil rights cases, why was the rate for court-appointed criminal defense work set at the maximum rate of $75.00 per hour? Does it make a difference that criminal defense attorneys are paid periodically regardless of success while civil rights attorneys are only paid at the end of the case and only if they win? Why is the reasonable rate for attorneys in prisoners' civil rights actions set lower than other civil rights attorneys?

---

64. City of Riverside v. Rivera, 477 U.S. 561, 576–77 (1986).
65. Hensley v. Eckerhart, 461 U.S. 424, 430 (1983).
66. City of Burlington v. Dague, 505 U.S. 557, 566–67 (1992).

CHAPTER 5

INTRODUCTION TO CASES
AND CASE ANALYSIS

In this chapter we will begin to study case analysis, focusing on decisions illustrating the evolution of the common law. We will see how the doctrine of *stare decisis* promotes stability in the law while incremental modifications permit the law to evolve to meet contemporary needs and reflect contemporary values. This chapter will also discuss the rules governing the retrospective application of changes in judge-made law.

Before turning to the cases themselves, we'll outline the structure and main components of a judicial decision. This outline will provide you an approach to briefing cases, which means summarizing in your own words the case components and the court's analysis. In law school, briefing cases is the most useful approach to class preparation.

5.1 Reading Cases

To understand any case, you need to consider the facts of the case, its procedural context, the issue the court is deciding, the substantive law governing the issue, and the rationale the court provides to support its ruling. In this section, we'll briefly consider each of these components.

Facts. First, the facts. Remember that the court is attempting to resolve the parties' specific problem using the applicable law. To accomplish this, the court must understand the problem as it arose between the parties in the real world outside the courtroom. Understanding the facts is critical to determining the applicable law and the soundness of the result.

Eager to explore the legal issues, law students often seem frustrated by their professors' emphasis on factual details. An illustration may help explain why we do this. In a products liability case studied in many first-year classes, the plaintiff claimed an above-ground swimming pool was dangerously defective because its vinyl surface was so slippery that his hands slipped apart so that he collided with the bottom and suffered a tragic spinal injury.[1] He claimed that a different surface would have prevented this injury. When called upon to recite the facts of this case, most law students begin by explaining that the injured plaintiff was a 23-year-old, uninvited intruder who dove into the pool head first from an adjacent garage roof. Did your view of this problem shift as you learned these facts? Aren't they necessary to understanding the court's resolution of the legal dispute?

In evaluating the facts, consider the historical context. For example, assume a court is evaluating the liability of a railroad company for failing to install a barricade to prevent a child from straying onto the tracks. Would a court in rural Kansas in 1871 view the case differently from a 2006 Manhattan court? Why or why not? Similarly, in evaluating the severity of the crime of stealing scrap metal, would a 1944 federal wartime court view the case differently from a 2006 state small claims court? Why or why not?

Procedure. After examining the facts of the case, you need to determine the procedural posture. Again, students are often frustrated with apparently formalistic rigmarole and yearn to reach the legal substance. But a reader cannot evaluate the court's analysis without understanding the procedural constraints any better than a baseball fan can criticize an umpire's calls without bothering to learn the strike zone. Just as in baseball, the even-handed adherence to the established rules is critical to fairness. After all, it would be unfair for the umpire to vary the number and strikes from batter to batter.

To give a legal illustration, assume a jury in a traffic case had heard conflicting testimony from several different witnesses about whether the traffic signal was red or green when the accident occurred. The jury deliberated and concluded that it had been green. The appellate court is bound by this factual finding, even if from reading the transcript the court is convinced that the light was red. The rules require the court to defer to the jurors who heard the live testimony and assessed the credibility of the witnesses; the court cannot substitute its judgment for theirs on questions of fact. In such a case, the court must affirm the result even though it disagrees with the factual findings. If a court disregarded the jury's findings, it would violate the prevailing party's right to a jury trial.

Issue. Next, you need to determine the precise issue the court is deciding. Although many issues may be involved in a case, it is usually included in a law school casebook for one discrete point of law. For example, in a criminal case a court might be required to decide whether the search of the defendant's car was constitutional, whether the admission of certain damaging impeachment

---

1. O'Brien v. Muskin Corp., 463 A.2d 298 (N.J. 1983).

evidence was erroneous, and whether the prison sentence adhered to statutory guidelines. But in deciding to put the case in a casebook, the editor is probably only concerned with one of those issues.

In thinking about each specific issue, the material facts are critical. For example, assume you are reading a case about the constitutionality of an automobile search. If the defendant was driving erratically and the defendant's license was suspended, a warrantless search would probably be constitutional. On the other hand, if the car was parked in the defendant's garage, but the police officer climbed through an unlocked window to search it without a warrant, the search might be unconstitutional. The legal issue (constitutionality of a search) can only be understood in terms of the material facts (erratic driving on a suspended license vs. garaged car at owner's premises). Precisely identifying the issue and material facts bearing on the issue are critical to evaluating the court's decision.

Holding. At last, we come to the substantive law governing the case. The court's "holding" is the result it reaches based on the application of the substantive law to the facts of the case. Just as fairness requires the court to adhere to the procedural rules, the rule of law requires the court to apply the substantive law consistently. In evaluating the law applicable to the problem before the court, consider its source. Is the applicable law constitutional? Is it statutory? Is it common law? Next, consider how clearly it covers the issue. Constitutional provisions are broad and elastic; statutes are sometimes ambiguous; and cases are often factually distinguishable. Most of the cases you will study are interesting precisely because the law is not a perfect fit and reasonable people can disagree about the proper legal analysis. For example, when the Constitution speaks of unreasonable searches, does it mean infrared surveillance cameras? When a statute regulates motor vehicles in public parks, does it apply to motorized wheelchairs? When a prior case determined that a homeowner could shoot an intruder who enters his residence, does it apply when the homeowner installs a spring gun to shoot anyone who enters a boarded-up and abandoned farmhouse?

Rationale. As the court works its way through the legal authorities, it will explain why it is adopting one possible approach over the alternatives. This is the rationale of the decision where the court attempts to demonstrate that its result is well founded in the law and fair to the parties. Consider carefully the court's explanation. How strong are the authorities on which the court relies? Is the law as clear as the court urges? Do you see ambiguities and alternatives that the court discounts? Do you think the result is fair? Does the court's approach further important social policies? Do you think the court's approach should be followed in future cases? How far should the rule be extended? What other factual situations should it govern?

These components of a case—facts, procedure, issue, holding, and rationale—are the elements of a brief. To prepare for class, you should carefully think about each of these elements and summarize them in writing in your own words in a brief. Also include a comment evaluating any concurring or dissenting opinions which are provided. The process of distilling out each of these elements will clarify your understanding of the case and serve you well in class discussions.

5.2 Evolution of the Common Law

As you learned in Chapter 3, in the United States in addition to constitutional and statutory law, we have common law—judge-made law decided on a case-by-case basis following precedent in earlier cases. As long as these decisions do not violate constitutional or statutory restrictions, the courts are entirely free to develop the common law. Indeed, as we have seen, much of state law has common law origins and the courts are responsible for its evolution. Under the doctrine of *stare decisis*, the courts generally adhere to prior precedents to assure fairness and predictability. But over time, the courts must adapt the law to fit society's needs. In the common law tradition, small incremental changes gradually transform legal rules. The question of when, how, and why the law evolves is one of the major themes you will follow in your first-year courses.

In the following series of cases, the courts consider whether a property owner is liable for crimes that occur on the premises. Generally in the United States, state tort law which is derived from the common law of England governs the question of civil liability for wrongs. These cases illustrate how the common law continues to adapt to contemporary conditions and values.

Applebaum v. Kidwell

12 F.2d 846 (D.C. Cir. 1926)

Barber, Acting Associate Justice.

Stripped of verbiage, the declaration alleges: "That defendant leased a room to plaintiffs, which was separated from an adjoining room controlled by defendant by a partition so constructed as to be somewhat unsubstantial, of which latter fact plaintiffs were ignorant, and were not informed by defendant, although he knew how the partition was constructed; that, defendant's room becoming vacant, he permitted the outside doors thereof to become and remain unfastened, and the exposed face of the partition in the vacant room to get into a condition that revealed its character, all without the knowledge of plaintiffs; that thieves, tempted and their action made possible by these conditions, forced an entrance from the vacant room through said partition, and stole and carried away plaintiffs' goods to the value of $1,000, which plaintiffs seek to recover in this action."

It is not claimed that defendant ever agreed to be responsible for any such loss or damage, and it is admitted "that there is no implied warranty in the letting of a house that it is safe and fit for occupation." In effect, plaintiffs contend that defendant was under legal obligation to them to keep in sufficient repair those parts of the premises under his control, and not in the possession or control of the plaintiffs, to prevent burglarizing the same. This doctrine would require a landlord at his peril to always keep his leased premises in such a condition that law-breakers could not enter same and commit crime. It would establish that in leasing property it must always be presumed that a trespass or crime may be committed thereon, and that the landlord owes the duty of protecting his tenant from the same.

As we understand the law, a landlord is not liable to his tenants for interference by third persons with the tenant's possession and business, when no wrongful act of the landlord is shown.

The proximate cause of the injury here complained of was not the condition of the partition, but was the unlawful criminal act of independent moral agencies, over which defendant had no control, with which he was not in collusion, and for whose acts he was not responsible.

The judgment of the court below is affirmed, with costs.

Notes and Questions

1. Is this decision fair and just?

2. The court states that "no wrongful act of the landlord is shown?" Do you agree? Doesn't the landlord have a duty to keep the premises in a safe and secure condition? Didn't the landlord have control over the partition's condition that enabled the trespasser access to the tenant's room? As between the landlord and the tenant, who was in a position to repair the partition to prevent the trespass?

3. Do you rent an apartment? If so, who is responsible for its physical condition and security, you or your landlord?

4. Obviously, if the trespasser is available as a solvent defendant, then the trespasser should pay the tenant for the stolen property. But assuming the trespasser is not available, should the loss fall on the landlord or the tenant? Who is more responsible for the loss?

5. Would imposing liability encourage the landlord to take precautions to improve security? Should the law try to encourage such precautions? Or would liability impose an unjustified economic burden on the landlord and drive up rental rates?

6. Have our views of a landlord's duties changed since 1926 when the *Applebaum* case was decided? If so, should the law change to reflect our current view?

7. In a series of cases beginning in the 1970s, the California courts grappled with the question of a landowner's liability for third-party crimes. In two appellate decisions, the courts held that parking lot operators were required to keep their lots reasonably safe or at least to warn customers of dangerous conditions.[2] Where the parking lots were unsafe and no warnings were posted, the courts held the operators liable to customers who were assaulted by criminals. The courts stressed that these crimes were foreseeable to the defendants because they had allowed conditions to deteriorate and prior crimes had occurred on the premises.

8. In 1984, the California Supreme Court adopted this approach where a community college student was attacked in a parking lot of the City College of San Francisco. *Peterson v. San Francisco Community College District*, 685 P.2d 1193 (1984). The Court imposed liability because the attack was similar to prior attacks in the same parking garage and the defendant has failed to take any steps to protect students or to warn them of the danger. What do you think of this expansion of liability? Can this approach be reconciled with *Applebaum*? How far should liability extend? Should it be limited to parking lots? Should it be limited to cases where there is a special relationship like that of a school to its students? Should it be extended to landlord-tenant cases? Should it be limited to cases where prior similar crimes occurred on the same premises? Should it be limited to violent crimes or extended to property crimes as well?

Isaacs v. Huntington Memorial Hospital

695 P.2d 653 (Cal. 1985)

Bird, Chief Justice.

This court must decide whether a plaintiff, in an action against a landowner for criminal acts of third persons on the landowner's property, may establish foreseeability other than by evidence of prior similar incidents on those premises.

---

2. Campodonico v. State Auto Parks, Inc., 89 Cal. Rptr. 270, 273 (Cal. Ct. App. 1970); Gomez v. Ticor, 193 Cal. Rptr. 600, 607 (Cal. Ct. App. 1983).

I.

Plaintiff, Mervyn Isaacs, is an anesthesiologist affiliated with defendant, Huntington Memorial Hospital, a private hospital located in Pasadena. On March 26, 1978, at approximately 8:30 p.m., Dr. Isaacs arrived at the hospital with his wife. He parked their car in the hospital's research parking lot which was located across the street from the emergency room and the physicians' entrance to the hospital. The lot was open to anyone who wished to park there. While his wife was visiting a friend at the hospital, Dr. Isaacs saw some of his patients who were to undergo surgery.

About 10 p.m., Dr. Isaacs, his wife and a family friend left the building and went to the Isaacs' car. While Dr. Isaacs was moving some belongings from the back seat to the trunk, Ms. Isaacs and the friend got into the car. As he was closing the lid to the trunk, Dr. Isaacs was grabbed from behind by a man who held a gun to the doctor's chest. Dr. Isaacs put up his hands and began to turn around very slowly. At that point, the assailant shot the doctor in the chest. The gunman then fled the scene and was never apprehended.

As a result of the shooting, Dr. Isaacs sustained severe injuries, including the loss of a kidney. [He sued the hospital claiming that the hospital failed to provide adequate security measures to protect him against the criminal acts of third persons on its premises.]

The evidence established that the hospital was in a high crime area and that numerous assaults had occurred on the hospital premises during the three years preceding Dr. Isaacs's shooting. Plaintiff also presented evidence concerning security [including] testimony from two experts in security matters. Both concluded that the hospital's security on the night of the shooting was "totally inadequate." They based their conclusions on (1) the insufficient number of guards, in view of the responsibilities assigned to them and the size of the premises; (2) inadequate administration of the security force; (3) failure to arm the guards with defensive weapons; (4) inadequate television monitoring of the parking lot areas; (5) a lack of any means of communication with the police department on an emergency basis; and (6) an absence of signs warning that the area was guarded. One expert concluded that these aspects rendered the research parking lot "totally devoid of any deterrents or security" on the night of the shooting.

At the close of plaintiff's case in chief, the hospital moved for nonsuit. The trial court granted the motion and entered judgment in the hospital's favor on the ground that there was insufficient evidence to find the hospital liable.

The court concluded that plaintiff failed to introduce evidence essential to prove the following elements of the case:

(a) Notice of prior crimes of the same or similar nature in the same or similar portion of defendant's premises; and

(b) The reasonable foreseeability of the subject crime occurring.

Plaintiff appeals from that judgment.

II.

The primary question presented by this appeal is whether foreseeability, for the purposes of establishing a landowner's liability for the criminal acts of third persons on the landowner's property, may be established other than by evidence of prior similar incidents on those premises. Since foreseeability is of primary importance in establishing the element of duty, it is helpful to review the law in this area.

It is well settled that an owner of land has a duty to take affirmative action to control the wrongful acts of third persons which threaten invitees where the owner has reasonable cause to anticipate such acts and the probability of injury resulting therefrom. This duty is premised on the special relationship between the landowner and the invitee and the general duty to exercise reasonable care in the management of one's property (see Civil Code, §1714, subd. (a);[3] *Peterson v. San Francisco Community College Dist.* 36 Cal.3d 799 (1984) [hereinafter *Peterson*]).

Whether such a duty exists is a question of law to be determined on a case-by-case basis. In considering whether one owes another a duty of care, several factors must be weighed, including: the foreseeability of harm to the plaintiff, the degree of certainty that the plaintiff suffered injury, the closeness of the connection between the defendant's conduct and the injury suffered, the moral blame attached to the defendant's conduct, the policy of preventing future harm, the extent of the burden to the defendant and consequences to the community of imposing a duty to exercise care with resulting liability for breach, and the availability, cost, and prevalence of insurance for the risk involved. (*Peterson*).

It is clear that foreseeability is but one factor to be weighed in determining whether a landowner owes a duty in a particular case. In this balancing process, foreseeability is an elastic factor. The degree of foreseeability necessary to warrant the finding of a duty will thus vary from case to case. For example, in cases where the burden of preventing future harm is great, a high

---

3. Civil Code section 1714, subdivision (a) provides in relevant part: "Every one is responsible, not only for the result of his willful acts, but also for an injury occasioned to another by his want of ordinary care or skill in the management of his property or person, except so far as the latter has, willfully or by want of ordinary care, brought the injury upon himself."

degree of foreseeability may be required. On the other hand, in cases where there are strong policy reasons for preventing the harm, or the harm can be prevented by simple means, a lesser degree of foreseeability may be required. Thus, foreseeability is a somewhat flexible concept.

A recent line of Court of Appeal cases has rigidified the foreseeability concept in situations involving a landowner's liability for the criminal acts of third persons against invitees. Those cases have established the rule that in the absence of prior similar incidents, an owner of land is not bound to anticipate the criminal activities of third persons, particularly where the wrongdoer was a complete stranger to both the landowner and the victim and where the criminal activity leading to the injury came about precipitously.

This rule is fatally flawed in numerous respects. First, the rule leads to results which are contrary to public policy. The rule has the effect of discouraging landowners from taking adequate measures to protect premises which they know are dangerous. This result contravenes the policy of preventing future harm. Moreover, under the rule, the first victim always loses, while subsequent victims are permitted recovery. Such a result is not only unfair, but is inimical to the important policy of compensating injured parties (*Peterson*). Surely, a landowner should not get one free assault before he can be held liable for criminal acts which occur on his property.

Second, a rule which limits evidence of foreseeability to prior similar criminal acts leads to arbitrary results and distinctions. Under this rule, there is uncertainty as to how "similar" the prior incidents must be to satisfy the rule. The rule raises a number of other troubling questions. For example, how close in time do the prior incidents have to be? How near in location must they be? The rule invites different courts to enunciate different standards of foreseeability based on their resolution of these questions.

Third, the rule erroneously equates foreseeability of a particular act with previous occurrences of similar acts. This court has already rejected that notion. The mere fact that a particular kind of an accident has not happened before does not show that such accident is one which might not reasonably have been anticipated. Thus, the fortuitous absence of prior injury does not justify relieving defendant from responsibility for the foreseeable consequences of its acts.

Finally, the "prior similar incidents" rule improperly removes too many cases from the jury's consideration. It is well established that foreseeability is ordinarily a question of fact. It may be decided as a question of law only if, under the undisputed facts there is no room for a reasonable difference of opinion.

Thus, foreseeability is determined in light of all the circumstances and not by a rigid application of a mechanical "prior similars" rule. As this court has held, what is required to be foreseeable is the general character of the event or harm not its precise nature or manner of occurrence. Prior similar incidents are helpful to determine foreseeability but they are not necessary. A rule that limits evidence of foreseeability to prior similar incidents deprives the jury of its role in determining that question.

A number of Courts of Appeal have properly recognized that evidence of prior similar incidents is not the *sine qua non* of a finding of foreseeability. (*Kwaitkowski v. Superior Trading Co.* (1981) 123 Cal.App.3d 324 [hereinafter *Kwaitkowski*] and other citations).

For example, in *Kwaitkowski* the plaintiff was raped and robbed in the lobby of her apartment building. She sued her landlords, alleging that they had notice that (1) the lock of the lobby entrance door was defective at the time of the attack, (2) the apartment building was in a high crime area, and (3) that an assault and robbery had occurred previously in another common area of the building. The trial court sustained the landlord's demurrer without leave to amend.

In reversing the judgment of dismissal, the Court of Appeal noted that foreseeability does not require prior identical or even similar events. The court reasoned that whether a given criminal act is within the class of injuries which is reasonably foreseeable depends on the totality of the circumstances and not on arbitrary distinctions. In concluding that the attack was foreseeable, the court focused on the defective nature of the premises (a broken lock), the easy access that strangers had to the interior of the building, the neighborhood in which the apartment building was located, and the prior assault and robbery.

Two Courts of Appeal have echoed similar concerns [in cases where patrons were injured in a parking garage and a convenience store. The courts analyzed foreseeability in light of all circumstances including the incidence of crime on similar premises. While prior incidents were helpful as evidence establishing foreseeability, such incidents were not required to satisfy this element.] Other types of evidence may also establish foreseeability, such as the nature, condition and location of the defendant's premises. In analyzing foreseeability in this manner, these courts properly followed the well-settled rule that what is required to be foreseeable is the general character of the event or harm not its precise nature or manner of occurrence.

III.

In the present case, this court must determine whether the trial court's invocation of the "prior similar incidents" rule was a proper basis on which to grant defendant's motion for nonsuit.

A judgment of nonsuit removes the case from the trier of fact. For this reason, courts have traditionally taken a very restrictive view of the circumstances under which such a judgment is proper. Thus, it is established that a trial court may not grant a defendant's motion for nonsuit if the plaintiff's evidence would support a jury verdict in the plaintiff's favor.

The totality of the circumstances in this case strongly suggests that the foreseeability of an assault in the research parking lot should have been submitted to the jury. The hospital was located in a high crime area. Several threatened assaults had occurred in the emergency room area directly across from the research parking lot. There had been thefts in the area. The hospital security guard testified that incidents involving harassment were very common. According to one expert witness, emergency room facilities and surrounding areas are inherently dangerous. Parking lots, by their very nature, create an especial temptation and opportunity for criminal misconduct.

Further, two of the lights on the building adjacent to the research parking lot, which normally illuminated that area, were not working on the evening Dr. Isaacs was shot. Two witnesses testified that the research parking lot itself had poor lighting. That a mugger thrives in dark places is a matter of common knowledge. In addition, the research parking lot was devoid of any security at the time of Dr. Isaacs's shooting. This contrasted markedly with the security at another parking lot on the hospital's premises, where a security guard was stationed during shift changes and activity was monitored by a television camera. This information, all of which was known or should have been known to the hospital, was sufficient to provide notice of a risk of an assault in the research parking lot.

Under these circumstances, the trial court erred in concluding as a matter of law that Dr. Isaacs's assault was not foreseeable. Just as we may not rely upon our private judgment on this issue, so the trial court may not impose its private judgment upon a situation, such as this, in which reasonable minds may differ.

It is evident that the hospital had a duty to take precautions to protect Dr. Isaacs from criminal assaults in the parking lot. The foreseeability of an assault was high in comparison to the minimal burden on the hospital to take security measures to ensure the safety of persons using the research parking lot.

The value to the community of imposing such a duty is manifest. That plaintiff suffered serious injury is clear. A jury's affirmative finding on foreseeability would establish not only the foreseeability of harm to plaintiff, but also a sufficiently close connection between the defendants' conduct and the injury suffered. Although defendant's conduct may have been without moral blame, imposition of liability would further the policy of preventing future harm. The evidence clearly indicates that a duty existed.

Once a court finds that the defendant was under a duty to protect the plaintiff, it is for the factfinder to decide whether the security measures were reasonable under the circumstances. The jury must decide whether the security was adequate.

Since the evidence clearly indicates that a duty existed as a matter of law, the trial court erred in removing the case from the jury by granting the hospital's motion for nonsuit.

Mosk, Kaus, Broussard, Reynoso, Grodin, and Lucas, JJ., concur.

Notes and Questions

1. What legal issue was the court addressing in *Isaacs*? Is that issue a question of law for the court to decide or a question of fact for the trier of fact to decide? Is this the same issue that the court addressed in *Applebaum*? Is *Isaacs* consistent with *Applebaum*?

2. What are the key facts of this case? Does it matter that the plaintiff was a doctor who worked at the hospital? What if he had been a visitor? A patient? A vendor? A transient? Does it matter that the crime occurred in the parking lot?

3. What statute did the court cite as governing the problem? Did the court apply the statute correctly? Was the statute helpful in analyzing the case?

4. What cases did the court rely on to support its ruling? Was that authority controlling? Did it require the result the court reached?

5. What policy reasons support the result? Should the court be deciding cases based on public policy rather than on precedent?

6. Is the result fair and just?

7. How far has liability expanded from *Applebaum*? from *Peterson*?

8. *Holding*: The holding of a case is the conclusion reached by the court from applying a rule of law to the facts at issue. What is the holding of the *Isaacs* case?

9. *Dicta*: Statements by a court which are not necessary for the decision are called *dicta* (the singular is *dictum*). Is the following statement by the *Isaacs* court holding or *dictum*? "While prior similar incidents are helpful to determine foreseeability, they are not required to establish it. Other circumstances may also place the landowner on notice of a dangerous condition. A rule which limits proof of foreseeability to evidence of prior similar incidents automatically precludes recovery to first-injured victims. Such a rule is inherently unfair and contrary to public policy."

10. How far does the court's rule extend? Is it limited to parking lots, or would it apply to crimes inside the premises? Is it limited to cases where an employee is injured because of the employer's inadequate security or would it apply to other cases where a landowner maintains premises with inadequate security? Would it apply to customers at the shopping mall? Would it apply to

actions by a resident of an apartment against an apartment owner? Since the court cited the *Kwaitkowski* case with approval, does that suggest that the court would be willing to extend liability to residential landlords?

11. What security precautions does the court require? Will improved lighting be sufficient? Or is the hospital required to install security cameras or hire a guard? How can the hospital determine whether it has met its duty of reasonable care? Who will pay the costs of these increased precautions?

12. What was the law on the issue of landowner liability before this case was decided? How would you have advised a client asking about liability for inadequate security? Were prior crimes required or not? Why did the Supreme Court exercise its discretionary jurisdiction in reviewing this case?

5.3 *Stare Decisis*

As we discussed in Chapter 3, the doctrine of *stare decisis* seeks stability and predictability in the law. The full Latin phrase, "*stare decisis et non quieta movere*," means "to stand by precedents and not to disturb settled points." People need to know what the rules are to get along in society, to raise families, to make plans, to build businesses, to die in peace. The rule of law and basic fairness require that similar cases be treated similarly. The doctrine requiring courts to follow precedent reflects this principle. *Stare decisis* protects us from discrimination, arbitrariness, and chaos. Under the doctrine of *stare decisis*, lower courts are bound to follow the applicable holdings of higher courts. For example, California trial courts and intermediate appellate courts are required to follow the rules announced by the California Supreme Court.

But the law must also be flexible enough to respond to current conditions, developing technology, and evolving social change. The holdings reached by the medieval common law courts do not necessarily fit contemporary circumstances. Courts often struggle to accommodate the tension between the need for stability and the need for flexibility. To provide this needed flexibility, the highest court has some leeway in determining whether to follow its prior decisions. Although fairness generally requires similar cases to be treated similarly, the common law adapts over time through incremental steps. As one court explained:

> We have repeatedly held that the doctrine of *stare decisis* is not an in-flexible rule requiring this court to blindly follow precedents and adhere to prior decisions and that when it appears that public policy and social needs require a departure from prior decisions, it is our

duty as a court of last resort to overrule those decisions and establish a rule consonant with our present day concepts of right and justice.[4]

Ann M. v. Pacific Plaza Shopping Center
863 P.2d 207 (Cal. 1993)

Panelli, Associate Justice.

We granted review in this case to determine whether the scope of the duty owed by the owner of a shopping center to maintain common areas within its possession and control in a reasonably safe condition includes providing security guards in those areas. We conclude that, under the facts of this case, the owner did not owe a duty to provide security guards.

I. *Background*

On June 17, 1985, Ann M. was employed by the Original 60 Minute Photo Company, a photo processing service located in a secluded area of the Pacific Plaza Shopping Center (hereafter shopping center). The shopping center, owned and operated by defendants (hereafter sometimes collectively referred to as Pacific Plaza), is a strip mall located on Garnet Avenue in the Pacific Beach area of San Diego. Approximately 25 commercial tenants occupy the shopping center at any one time.

The lease between the photo store and the shopping center granted the owners of the shopping center the exclusive right to control the common areas. Although the lease gave Pacific Plaza the right to police the common areas, the lease did not purport to impose an obligation to police either the common areas or those areas under the exclusive control and management of the tenants. In fact, Pacific Plaza hired no security guards.

At approximately 8 a.m. on June 17, Ann M. opened the photo store for business. She was the only employee on duty. The door was closed but unlocked. The store was equipped with a "drop gate" that was designed to prevent customer access behind the counter but it had been broken for some period of time. Shortly after Ann M. opened the store, a man she had never seen before walked in "just like a customer." Ann M. greeted the man, told him that she would assist him shortly, and turned her back to the counter. The man, who was armed with a knife, went behind the counter, raped Ann M., robbed the store, and fled. The rapist was not apprehended.

---

4. Molitor v. Kaneland Cmty. Unit Dist. No. 3, 163 N.E.2d 89, 96 (Ill. 1959).

In 1984 and 1985 violent crimes occurred in the census tract in which the shopping center is located. While the record includes some evidence of criminal activity on the shopping center's premises prior to Ann M.'s rape—bank robberies, purse snatchings, and a man pulling down women's pants—there is no evidence that Pacific Plaza had knowledge of these alleged criminal acts. In fact, Pacific Plaza offers uncontroverted evidence that it recorded instances of violent crime and that its records contain no reference to violent criminal acts in the shopping center prior to Ann M.'s rape.

Ann M. presented evidence that the employees and tenants were concerned about their safety prior to her rape. These concerns centered around the presence of persons described as transients, who loitered in the common areas. One of the employees of the photo store called the police on two different occasions prior to the incident involved herein to complain that she felt threatened by persons loitering outside her employer's store. The photo store ultimately granted this employee permission to bring her dog to work for protection. This employee worked a late night shift, while Ann M. worked during the day. During periodic meetings of the merchants' association, an organization to which all tenants belonged, the tenants voiced complaints about a lack of security in the shopping center and the presence of transients. There is no evidence to indicate, however, that Ann M.'s rapist was one of the loitering transients or that the presence of the transients contributed in any way to Ann M.'s attack.

According to Ann M.'s deposition testimony, the merchants' association invited a security company to address the tenants' concerns at one of its meetings. During that meeting, the security company informed the tenants of different security options and recommended that regular walking patrols be instituted. Ann M. stated in her deposition that she was told that the merchants' association decided not to hire the security patrols, because the cost would be prohibitive. Ann M. further testified that she was told at these meetings that the merchants' association requested that the shopping center provide such patrols. No such patrols were provided. According to the lease, if the shopping center had provided the requested patrols, the tenants would have borne the cost in the form of additional rent. Ultimately, the merchants' association hired a security company to drive by the area three or four times a day instead of arranging for foot patrols. Ann M. was raped sometime thereafter.

After the rape, Ann M. filed a civil complaint for damages in the superior court, alleging causes of action for negligence against various defendants. Ann M. alleged that the defendants were negligent in failing to provide adequate security to protect her from an unreasonable risk of harm. This risk specifically was alleged to be the presence of transients and the potential for violent confrontation between transients and employees of the shopping center.

Pacific Plaza filed a motion for summary judgment claiming that it owed no legal duty to Ann M., primarily because Ann M.'s attack was unforeseeable. The trial court granted the motion, finding that Pacific Plaza owed Ann M. no duty of care, and entered judgment in favor of Pacific Plaza.

Ann M. appealed. Following proceedings in the court of appeal, we granted Ann M.'s petition for review.

II. *Discussion*

The existence of a duty is a question of law for the court. (*Isaacs v. Huntington Memorial Hospital* (1985) 38 Cal.3d 112 [hereafter *Isaacs*]). Accordingly, we determine de novo the existence and scope of the duty owed by Pacific Plaza to Ann M.

It is now well established that California law requires landowners to maintain land in their possession and control in a reasonably safe condition. (Civil Code § 1714.) In the case of a landlord, this general duty of maintenance, which is owed to tenants and patrons, has been held to include the duty to take reasonable steps to secure common areas against foreseeable criminal acts of third parties that are likely to occur in the absence of such precautionary measures. (*Isaacs.*)

[The Court rejected defendant's argument that its duty ran only to Ann M.'s employer, the tenant, and not to Ann M. The Court concluded that the duty to the tenant extended to the tenant's employees. The Court also rejected the defendant's argument that it had no duty because the crime occurred in the store rather than the common areas. The Court pointed out the plaintiff's theory was that the inadequate security in the common areas made it possible for the crime to occur in the store.]

Since the existence of a duty on the part of Pacific Plaza to Ann M. is not precluded in this case either by the lack of a direct landlord-tenant relationship or by the lack of control over the premises where the crime occurred, we turn to the heart of the case: whether Pacific Plaza had reasonable cause to anticipate that criminal conduct such as rape would occur in the shopping center premises unless it provided security patrols in the common areas. For, as frequently recognized, a duty to take affirmative action to control the wrongful acts of a third party will be imposed only where such conduct can be reasonably anticipated.

In this, as in other areas of tort law, foreseeability is a crucial factor in determining the existence of duty. (*Isaacs.*) Our most comprehensive analysis to date of the foreseeability required to establish the existence of a business landowner's duty to take reasonable steps to protect its tenants and patrons from third party crime is found in *Isaacs*.

[The Court reviewed the facts and procedure of the *Isaacs* case.] We held that foreseeability, for tort liability purposes, could be established despite the absence of prior similar incidents on the premises. We explained that "foreseeability is determined in light of all the circumstances and not by a rigid application of a mechanical 'prior similars' rule." We also explained that prior similar incidents are "helpful to determine foreseeability but they are not necessary." We further explained that foreseeability should be assessed in light of the "totality of the circumstances," including such factors as the nature, condition and location of the premises. We concluded that the totality of the circumstances in *Isaacs* strongly suggested that the foreseeability of an assault in the parking lot should have been presented to the jury.

Since *Isaacs* was decided, lower court opinions have questioned the wisdom of our apparent abandonment of the "prior similar incidents" rule.

Unfortunately, random, violent crime is endemic in today's society. It is difficult, if not impossible, to envision any locale open to the public where the occurrence of violent crime seems improbable. Upon further reflection and in light of the increase in violent crime, refinement of the rule enunciated in *Isaacs* is required. We are not reluctant to revisit the rule announced in *Isaacs* because it was unnecessary for this court to consider the viability of the "prior similar incidents" rule in order to decide the *Isaacs* case: the record contained evidence of prior, violent, third party attacks on persons on the hospital's premises in close proximity to where the attack at issue in that case occurred.

Moreover, broad language used in *Isaacs* has tended to confuse duty analysis generally in that the opinion can be read to hold that foreseeability in the context of determining duty is normally a question of fact reserved for the jury. Any such reading of *Isaacs* is in error. Foreseeability, when analyzed to determine the existence or scope of a duty, is a question of law to be decided by the court.

Turning to the question of the scope of a landlord's duty to provide protection from foreseeable third party crime, we observe that, before and after our decision in *Isaacs*, we have recognized that the scope of the duty is determined in part by balancing the foreseeability of the harm against the burden of the duty to be imposed. In cases where the burden of preventing future harm is great, a high degree of foreseeability may be required. On the other hand, in cases where there are strong policy reasons for preventing the harm, or the harm can be prevented by simple means, a lesser degree of foreseeability may be required.

While there may be circumstances where the hiring of security guards will be required to satisfy a landowner's duty of care, such action will rarely, if ever, be found to be a minimal burden. The monetary costs of security guards is not insignificant. Moreover, the obligation to provide patrols adequate to deter criminal conduct is not well defined. No one really knows why people commit crime, hence no one really knows what is adequate deterrence in any given situation. Finally, the social costs of imposing a duty on landowners to hire private police forces are also not insignificant. For these reasons, we conclude that a high degree of foreseeability is required in order to find that the scope of a landlord's duty of care includes the hiring of security guards. We further conclude that the requisite degree of foreseeability rarely, if ever, can be proven in the absence of prior similar incidents of violent crime on the landowner's premises.[5] To hold otherwise would be to impose an unfair burden upon landlords and, in effect, would force landlords to become the insurers of public safety, contrary to well established policy in this state.

Turning to the facts of the case before us, we conclude that violent criminal assaults were not sufficiently foreseeable to impose a duty upon Pacific Plaza to provide security guards in the common areas. First, Pacific Plaza did not have notice of prior similar incidents occurring on the premises. Ann M. alleges that previous assaults and robberies had occurred in the shopping center, but she offers no evidence that Pacific Plaza had notice of these incidents. Moreover, even assuming that Pacific Plaza had notice of these incidents, Ann M. concedes that they were not similar in nature to the violent assault that she suffered. Similarly, none of the remaining evidence presented by Ann M. is sufficiently compelling to establish the high degree of foreseeability necessary to impose upon Pacific Plaza a duty to provide security guards in the common areas. Neither the evidence regarding the presence of transients nor the evidence of the statistical crime rate of the surrounding area is of a type sufficient to satisfy this burden.[6]

We, therefore, conclude that Pacific Plaza was entitled to summary judgment on the ground that it owed no duty to Ann M. to provide security guards in the common areas.

---

5. It is possible that some other circumstances such as immediate proximity to a substantially similar business establishment that has experienced violent crime on its premises could provide the requisite degree of foreseeability. Because Ann M. presented no such evidence, we need not further consider this possibility.

6. Ann M. offered no evidence to show that, like a parking garage or an all-night convenience store, a retail store located in a shopping center creates "'an especial temptation and opportunity for criminal misconduct.'" Gomez v. Ticor, 145 Cal. App. 3d 622, 628 (1983) (victim killed returning to car in parking garage); Cohen v. Southland Corp. 157 Cal. App. 3d 130, 141 (1984) (robbery at all-night convenience store). Therefore, we need not consider in this case whether some types of commercial property are so inherently dangerous that, even in the absence of prior similar incidents, providing security guards will fall within the scope of a landowner's duty of care.

Lucas. C.J., Kennard, Arabian, Baxter, and George, JJ., concur.

Mosk, Associate Justice, dissenting.

I dissent.

The "prior similar incidents" test was thoroughly analyzed in *Isaacs v. Huntington Memorial Hospital* [hereafter *Isaacs*], and this court held it to be improper. The opinion by Chief Justice Bird was unanimous, with then-Associate Justice Lucas and me concurring completely in the rationale and result.

Now the majority purport to deal with *Isaacs* by "refinement" and a "revisit," while they in effect revive the rejected "prior similar incidents" test. Indeed, they "conclude that the requisite degree of foreseeability rarely, if ever, can be proven in the absence of prior similar incidents of violent crime on the landowner's premises."

The *Isaacs* decision should be controlling in the instant case, the bottom line being that the issue of liability and what the majority gratuitously describe as "an unfair burden upon landlords" are factual matters that should be decided by a jury, not by summary judgment. [Justice Mosk then quotes at length from the *Isaacs* opinion].

For the foregoing reasons I must dissent from the majority opinion that in effect resurrects an improper test discarded by this court eight years ago.

Notes and Questions

1. What legal issue was the court addressing in *Ann M*? Is that issue a question of law for the court to decide or a questions of fact for the trier of fact to decide? Is this the same issue the court addressed in *Applebaum*? in *Isaacs*?

2. What are the key facts of this case? Does it matter that the crime occurred inside the premises and not in a parking garage? Does it matter that the precaution at issue was the hiring of guards rather than a less expensive security measure or failure to warn?

3. What authority did the court rely on to support its ruling? Was that authority controlling? Did it require the result the court reached?

4. What is the holding of the *Ann M.* case?

5. What policy reasons support the result?

6. Is the result fair?

7. Who has the better view, the majority or the dissent? Why?

8. Has the *Ann M.* case extended or contracted liability? Is the duty to tenants now extended to their employees? Is the duty to maintain safe premises now extended to the entire premises, not just parking garages? Is the duty to maintain safe premises now extended to areas beyond the landlord's control? Are the court's comments on these issues holding or dicta?

9. According to current statistics, the rate of violent crime has declined. Since the court relied on the rising crime rate to explain its conclusion, does the decrease in crime support the opposite result?

10. Was the *Ann M.* court adhering to the doctrine of *stare decisis* or was it departing from prior precedent? What do you think of the court's treatment of *Isaacs*? Is *Ann M.* an unprincipled departure from the rule of law set out in *Isaacs*? Or is it a modest refinement based on the factual distinctions in the two cases? Does it matter that *Isaacs* involved a parking lot? Does it matter that the security precaution at issue in *Ann M.* was the provision of security guards? If the court wants to overturn one of its prior decisions, does it have authority to do so?

11. The United States Supreme Court vigorously debated the role of *stare decisis* in *Payne v. Tennessee*, 501 U. S. 808 (1991). In *Payne*, the Court reconsidered two decisions from 1989 and 1987 barring the admission of "victim impact" evidence as unconstitutional; this time the Court found the evidence admissible. The opinion of the Court by Chief Justice Rehnquist and the dissenting opinion of Justice Marshall put the issue in stark relief.

A. Chief Justice Rehnquist wrote:

Payne and his *amicus* argue that despite these numerous infirmities in the rule created by [our prior decisions], we should adhere to the doctrine of *stare decisis* and stop short of overruling those cases. *Stare decisis* is the preferred course because it promotes the evenhanded, predictable, and consistent development of legal principles, fosters reliance on judicial decisions, and contributes to the actual and perceived integrity of the judicial process. Adhering to precedent is usually the wise policy, because in most matters it is more important that the applicable rule of law be settled than it be settled right. Nevertheless, when governing decisions are unworkable or are badly reasoned, this Court has never felt constrained to follow precedent. *Stare decisis* is not an inexorable command; rather, it is a principle of policy and not a mechanical formula of adherence to the latest decision. This is particularly true in constitutional cases, because in such cases correction through legislative action is practically impossible. Considerations in favor of *stare decisis* are at their acme in cases involving property and contract rights, where reliance interests are involved; the opposite is true in cases such as the present one involving procedural and evidentiary rules.

Applying these general principles, the Court has during the past 20 Terms overruled in whole or in part 33 of its previous constitutional decisions. [The two prior cases on victim impact evidence] were decided by the narrowest of margins, over spirited dissents challenging the basic underpinnings of those decisions. They have been questioned by Members of the Court in later decisions, and have defied consistent application by the lower courts.... Reconsidering these decisions now, we conclude, for the reasons heretofore stated, that they were wrongly decided and should be, and now are, overruled.

B. Justice Marshall wrote:

Power, not reason, is the new currency of this Court's decision-making. Four Terms ago, a five-Justice majority of this Court held that "victim impact" evidence of the type at issue in this case could not constitutionally be introduced during the penalty phase of a capital trial. By another 5–4 vote, a majority of this Court rebuffed an attack upon this ruling just two Terms ago. Nevertheless, having expressly invited respondent to renew the attack, today's majority overrules [those decisions] and credits the dissenting views expressed in those cases. Neither the law nor the facts supporting [those decisions] underwent any change in the last four years. Only the personnel of this Court did.

In dispatching [the prior decisions] to their graves, today's majority ominously suggests that an even more extensive upheaval of this Court's precedents may be in store. Renouncing this Court's historical commitment to a conception of "the judiciary as a source of impersonal and reasoned judgments," the majority declares itself free to discard any principle of constitutional liberty which was recognized or reaffirmed over the dissenting votes of four Justices and with which five or more Justices now disagree. The implications of this radical new exception to the doctrine of *stare decisis* are staggering. The majority today sends a clear signal that scores of established constitutional liberties are now ripe for reconsideration, thereby inviting the very type of open defiance of our precedents that the majority rewards in this case. Because I believe that this Court owes more to its constitutional precedents in general and to [the victim impact cases] in particular, I dissent.

The overruling of one of this Court's precedents ought to be a matter of great moment and consequence. Although the doctrine of *stare decisis* is not an inexorable command, this Court has repeatedly stressed that fidelity to precedent is fundamental to a society governed by the rule of law. It is indisputable that *stare decisis* is a basic self-governing principle within the Judicial Branch, which is entrusted with the sensitive and difficult task of fashioning and preserving a jurisprudential system that is not based upon an arbitrary discretion. The Federalist, No. 78, p. 490 (H. Lodge ed. 1888) (A. Hamilton). *Stare decisis* is essential if case-by-case judicial decision-making is to be reconciled with the principle of the rule of law, for when governing legal standards are open to revision in every case, deciding cases becomes a mere exercise of judicial will, with arbitrary and unpredictable results.

Consequently, this Court has never departed from precedent without "special justification." Such justifications include the advent of subsequent changes or development in the law that undermine a decision's rationale; the need to bring a decision into agreement with experience and with facts newly ascertained; and a showing that a particular precedent has become a detriment to coherence and consistency in the law.

The majority cannot seriously claim that any of these traditional bases for overruling a precedent applies to [the recent victim impact cases]. The majority does not suggest that the legal rationale of these decisions has been undercut by changes or developments in doctrine during the last two years. Nor does the majority claim that experience over that period of time has discredited the principle that any decision to impose the death sentence be, and appear to be, based on reason rather than caprice or emotion, the larger postulate of political morality on which [those cases] rest.

It takes little real detective work to discern just what has changed since this Court decided [the prior cases]: this Court's own personnel. Indeed, the majority candidly explains why this particular contingency, which until now has been almost universally understood not to be sufficient to warrant overruling a precedent, is sufficient to justify overruling [precedent]. "Considerations in favor of *stare decisis* are at their acme," the majority explains, "in cases involving property and contract rights, where reliance interests are involved; the opposite is true in cases such as the present one involving procedural and evidentiary rules." In addition, the majority points out, "[the prior decisions] were decided by the narrowest of margins, over spirited dissents" and thereafter were "questioned by Members of the Court." Taken together, these considerations make it legitimate, in the majority's view, to elevate the position of the dissenters into the law of the land.

This truncation of the Court's duty to stand by its own precedents is astonishing. By limiting full protection of the doctrine of *stare decisis* to "cases involving property and contract rights," the majority sends a clear signal that essentially all decisions implementing the personal liberties protected by the Bill of Rights and the Fourteenth Amendment are open to reexamination. Taking into account the majority's additional criterion for overruling—that a case either was decided or reaffirmed by a 5–4 margin "over spirited dissent,"—the continued vitality of literally scores of decisions must be understood to depend on nothing more than the proclivities of the individuals who now comprise a majority of this Court.

In my view, this impoverished conception of *stare decisis* cannot possibly be reconciled with the values that inform the proper judicial function. Contrary to what the majority suggests, *stare decisis* is important not merely because individuals rely on precedent to structure their commercial activity but because fidelity to precedent is part and parcel of a conception of "the judiciary as a source of impersonal and reasoned judgments." Indeed, this function of *stare decisis* is in many respects even more critical in adjudication involving constitutional liberties than in adjudication involving commercial entitlements. Because enforcement of the Bill of Rights and the Fourteenth Amendment frequently requires this Court to rein in the forces of democratic politics, this Court can legitimately lay claim to compliance with its directives only if the public understands the Court to be implementing "principles founded in the law rather than in the proclivities of individuals."

Today's decision charts an unmistakable course. If the majority's radical reconstruction of the rules for overturning this Court's decisions is to be taken at face value—and the majority offers us no reason why it should not—then the overruling of [the victim impact decisions] is but a preview of an even broader and more far-reaching assault upon this Court's precedents. Cast aside today are those condemned to face society's ultimate penalty. Tomorrow's victims may be minorities, women, or the indigent. Inevitably, this campaign to resurrect yesterday's "spirited dissents" will squander the authority and the legitimacy of this Court as a protector of the powerless.

What do you think about these two views of the role of *stare decisis* and its limitations?

12. *Ann M.* indicates that foreseeability sometimes depends on a showing of prior crimes on the premises. Is this a clear rule for future courts to apply or does it open up a new set of questions? How similar must the prior crime be? How close geographically? How close in time? Would a prior purse snatching in the parking lot of the Pacific Plaza have been sufficient to meet the requirement? Or a series of robberies at a convenience store at the far end of the Pacific Plaza?

13. Does *Ann M.* stand for the proposition that foreseeability can *never* be established without a showing of prior similar crimes on the premises?

14. In a 1999 decision, *Sharon P.*, the California Supreme Court reviewed a case where the plaintiff was attacked in a subterranean parking garage in the office building where she worked.[7] The evidence showed that the garage was in a high crime area, that security had deteriorated, that several lights were out, and that the security cameras had not been working for months. Expert testimony established that underground garages are dangerous because they provide locations where criminals can lie in wait. Moreover, although no crimes had occurred in the garage, several robberies had taken place at the bank directly above the garage. The trial court granted summary judgment for the defendant because no prior similar crimes had occurred in the parking garage and therefore the plaintiff failed to meet the requirement of establishing foreseeability.

The Supreme Court affirmed. It held that the evidence failed to support the view that underground parking garages are inherently dangerous. It rejected the argument that the bank robberies satisfied the prior similar crimes requirement: "[T]he prior robberies, which all specifically targeted a bank elsewhere on the premises and did not involve violent attacks against anyone, were not sufficiently similar to the sexual assault inflicted upon plaintiff to establish a high degree of foreseeability that would justify the imposition of [a duty to provide security guards.]"[8] It also concluded that the evidence of foreseeability was insufficient to impose other security obligations such as improved lighting and reconnection of the security camera. In conclusion, Justice Baxter stated: "Absent any prior similar incidents *or other indications of a reasonably foreseeable risk* of violent criminal assaults in that location, we cannot conclude defendants were required to secure the area against such crime"[9] (emphasis added).

In a concurring and dissenting opinion, Justice Werdegar agreed that parking garages are not inherently dangerous. But she added that the garage in question might have some duty to prevent crime if there were "other indications of a reasonably foreseeable risk of violent criminal assaults in that location."[10] As she explained, "Emphatically, the landlord is not, as the prior similar incidents rule would have it, entitled to one free assault before the failure to take appropriate security measures subjects him or her to the risk of civil liability."[11]

As commentators have observed the "other indications" language used by Justices Baxter and Werdegar re-opens the question of whether prior similar

---

7. Sharon P. v. Arman, Ltd., 989 P.2d 121 (1999).
8. *Id.* at 127.
9. *Id.* at 133.
10. *Id.* at 134.
11. *Id.* at 134–35.

crimes are a necessary criterion for establishing foreseeability.[12] What advice would you give to a client who owned a parking lot and wanted to know what kind of security precautions she was required to install?

15. Most recently, the California Supreme Court has taken up the issue in four cases:

- *Wiener v. Southcoast Childcare Centers, Inc.*, 32 Cal. 4th 1138 (2004): A driver intentionally drove through a chain-link fence at childcare center and killed two children. The Court held that under *Ann M.* the child-care center had no duty to the parents to prevent this third-party crime since there had been no prior crimes on the premises. It rejected the claim that prior traffic accidents at the site created a duty to prevent wholly unforeseeable criminal misconduct.

- *Delgado v. Trax Bar & Grill*, 36 Cal. 4th 224 (2005) and *Morris v. De La Torre*, 36 Cal. 4th 260 (2005): In these companion cases, the Court held that business proprietors have a duty to take nonburdensome precautions to protect business invitees from criminal misconduct, even where no prior similar crimes had occurred on the premises. In *Delgado*, the bar's bouncer had recognized that the plaintiff might be attacked by several bar patrons and asked him to leave to avoid a confrontation, but failed to escort him to his car. In *Morris*, restaurant employees failed to call 911 after a patron had been attacked in the parking lot with a knife seized in the kitchen. In both cases, the Court ruled that while prior similar crimes are required before the very burdensome precaution of providing security guards would be imposed, a lesser showing of foreseeability will support the requirement of taking lesser, reasonable precautions. Are these decisions consistent with *Ann M.?* with *Sharon P.?* with *Isaacs?*

- *Castaneda v. Olsher*, 41 Cal. 4th 405 (2007): In *Castaneda,* a mobile home park resident was shot by a stray bullet in a gang fight on the premises. The resident sued the landlord for failing to provide adequate precautions against gang violence. The evidence showed that the landlord was aware of gang activity in the park and that on two prior occasions bullets shot from outside the park had entered the same area of the park where the plaintiff was shot. Based on these facts, the plaintiff argued that gang violence in the park was foreseeable, unlike the random unpredictable crimes in *Ann M.* and *Sharon P.* The plaintiff contended

---

12. David Kravets, *High Court: Parking Lots Not Liable in Assault,* DAILY RECORDER, Dec. 20, 1999, at 1.

that the defendant should have refused to rent to people with gang affiliations, should have evicted people if gang affiliations were discovered, and should have provided better lighting or security guards. The appellate court concluded that these facts were sufficient to go to the jury. The California Supreme Court reversed, holding that landlords, including mobile home park owners, ordinarily have no duty to reject prospective tenants they believe, or have reason to believe, are gang members. The Court said that "to recognize such a duty would tend to encourage arbitrary housing discrimination and would place landlords in the untenable situation of facing potential liability whichever choice they make about a prospective tenant." The Court acknowledged that in some situations, a tenant's behavior and known criminal associations may create such a high level of foreseeable danger to others that the landlord is obliged to take measures to remove the tenant from the premises or bear a portion of the legal responsibility for injuries the tenant subsequently causes. However, the Court concluded that the facts known to Olsher did not make a violent gang confrontation so highly foreseeable as to justify imposition of a duty to undertake eviction proceedings.

5.4 Continuing Evolution of the Common Law

After the state supreme court establishes a common law rule, the lower courts are required to follow it. But, as we have seen, the task is delicate for each new case presents its own factual details which must be considered in determining how the law applies. As you read through the next case, consider how the court is applying the rules laid down by the California Supreme Court in *Isaacs v. Huntington Memorial Hospital* and *Ann M. v. Pacific Plaza Shopping Center.*

Rosenbaum v. Security Pacific Corporation

50 Cal. Rptr. 2d 917 (Cal. Ct. App. 1996)
(Review denied with three justices dissenting)

Woods, J.

The issue in this case is whether a landlord can be held liable for a tenant's injuries caused by the criminal activities of third persons off the premises. For the reasons discussed below, we conclude that under the circumstances of this case the landlord had no duty to protect plaintiff from an attack on a public street and therefore affirm the judgment for defendant.

Facts and Proceedings Below

Plaintiff, Debra Rosenbaum, brought this negligence action against her landlord, Security Pacific Corporation, after she was robbed and severely injured on the street in front of her apartment building. We state the facts in the light most favorable to the verdict for plaintiff.

In 1985, plaintiff moved into the Plymouth Apartments located at the intersection of 8th Street and Plymouth Boulevard in Los Angeles. The premises consist of two apartment buildings, two garage buildings in the rear and a central courtyard between the buildings. A hallway provides access from the courtyard to the rear driveway and garages. Plaintiff lived in the front corner apartment facing Plymouth Boulevard. Her garage door faced 8th Street. The shortest route from her garage to her apartment was to walk up 8th Street to a driveway behind the apartment buildings, down the driveway to a hallway that led to the courtyard and through the courtyard to the front door of her apartment.

Plaintiff testified the 8th Street garage area was very dark at night. The only lighting was from two 100-watt floodlights which provided little illumination. There was no direct lighting in the hallway linking the courtyard to the driveway and garage area. In addition, the courtyard was always very dark. The only lighting was supplied by the porch lights of the individual apartment units. If the tenants did not manually turn on their porch lights, the courtyard was "pitch black." Even so, only four of the porchlights worked and the courtyard was very dark even if all four lights were on.

Plaintiff never used her garage because she did not believe it was safe to do so. The lack of lighting in the hallway and the courtyard also influenced her decision not to park in the garage. Instead she would park on Plymouth as close to the apartment building and her front door as she could.

Prior to the attack on plaintiff which led to this lawsuit there had been numerous robberies and assaults on the tenants of the Plymouth Apartments in the garage area and the courtyard. One tenant's apartment had been burglarized twice. Plaintiff herself had been assaulted on the street two years earlier while getting out of her car. Defendant was aware of these crimes and the tenants' complaints about the inadequacy of lighting on the premises. Defendant promised to add additional lighting but never did so.

On an evening in December 1989, plaintiff returned home from school and parked her car on Plymouth across the street from her apartment, near, but not directly under, a street light. As plaintiff was removing some of her things from her car she saw a car come down 8th Street and turn onto Plymouth. The car stopped along side hers. One of the men in the car grabbed plaintiff and forced her into the back seat where there were two other men. Plaintiff was robbed and shot in the head, then released. She suffered devastating injuries, including permanent brain damage.

The evidence showed the attack on plaintiff was part of a crime spree in which the same men who assaulted her had committed another robbery earlier that night on a street nearby and, immediately after robbing and shooting plaintiff, proceeded to rob a man and his wife on another street in the same vicinity.

Plaintiff's expert testified the insufficient lighting at the Plymouth Apartments posed a dangerous condition because it created an opportunity for an attacker to conceal himself in the darkness of the garage area, hallway and courtyard. This dangerous condition, the expert testified, could have been eliminated easily and inexpensively by the installation of high-density mercury vapor lights in the courtyard, hallway and garage area.

The jury returned a special verdict finding defendant was negligent and that its negligence was a legal cause of plaintiff's injury. It further found plaintiff suffered economic and noneconomic damages totaling approximately $3.5 million. The jury then apportioned fault, finding the assailants to be responsible for 90 percent of plaintiff's injuries, defendant responsible for 9 percent and plaintiff responsible for 1 percent.

[Defendant moved for judgment notwithstanding the verdict and the trial court granted the motion. Plaintiff appealed.]

I. *Standard of Review Applicable to Judgment Notwithstanding the Verdict*

In reviewing a judgment notwithstanding the verdict we accept as true the evidence in support of the verdict and view all the evidence in the light most favorable to the verdict. The question of whether a duty exists is a question of law which we review de novo on appeal. (*Ann M. v. Pacific Plaza Shopping Center*, 6 Cal. 4th 66 (1993) [hereinafter *Ann M.*].)

II. *Under the Circumstances of this Case, the Landlord Owed the Tenant No Duty to Protect her from Criminal Activity off the Premises*

A landlord's duty to protect tenants from injuries caused by the criminal acts of third parties is a recent development....

This duty to take reasonable steps to secure common areas of the premises against foreseeable criminal acts of third parties has become well-established law in California. (*Ann M.*)

Given the precedents, it is fair to say that under California law the location of the crime does not necessarily determine the landowner's liability for injuries resulting from criminal acts. (*Ann M.*) However, no case in California, nor any other jurisdiction so far as we can determine, has extended the landlord's liability for the criminal acts of third persons to injuries suffered by the tenant off the premises.

California cases which have considered a property owner's duty in the context of injuries occurring off the property have imposed liability only if the harm was foreseeable and the owner controlled the site of the injury, or affirmatively created a dangerous condition on the site or if there was a functional connection between the owner's conduct and the injury suffered. None of these factors are present in the case before us. Clearly, Security Pacific did not control the public street on which plaintiff's injury occurred, nor did it create the dangerous condition of a band of marauding thugs using the street to seek out victims to attack. Nor do we find a close connection between the defendant's conduct in failing to adequately light the common areas of the apartment building and the injury suffered by plaintiff when she was attacked on a public street.

As previous cases have made clear, the duty of a landlord to protect the tenant from criminal activity is not a general one but arises only where the landlord's negligence facilitates the criminal act. The landlord is not the insurer of his tenant's safety. Rather, the landlord's duty to provide adequate lighting in common areas arises because failure to do so may facilitate a criminal attack on the tenant in the common areas or the tenant's apartment. In other words, a duty is imposed on the landlord where there is a close, or functional, connection between the landlord's conduct and the harm suffered.

Plaintiff attempts to establish liability in this case by arguing Security Pacific had a duty to secure its premises against criminal acts of third parties and her injury was a foreseeable result of its failure to do so. Her argument is as follows. Security Pacific had a duty of care to adequately light the entire premises, including the garage area, courtyard and walkways, given the numerous tenant complaints regarding the darkness of the premises and the repeated instances of criminal attacks on and near the premises. Security Pacific breached this duty of care by failing to adequately light the premises thereby causing plaintiff to decide not to use her assigned garage out of fear for her safety and to park on the street instead. If plaintiff had been in her garage on the night in question she would not have been attacked. Therefore, it was the dangerous condition of the apartment premises which caused plaintiff to park on the street and thereby become vulnerable to the attack which was perpetrated on her.

Under this theory, a plaintiff establishes a landowner's liability by establishing the existence of a dangerous condition on the property and letting the doctrines of foreseeability and proximate cause do the rest. Such a theory was rejected in *Medina v. Hillshore Partners*, 40 Cal. App. 4th 477 (1995). In *Med-*

ina, gang members mistook Mr. Medina for a member of a rival gang. They attacked and killed him as he was walking near an apartment complex owned by defendants. The plaintiffs alleged defendants were liable for Mr. Medina's death because they allowed the gang, which included tenants and non-tenants, to congregate in and around the apartment complex thereby creating a dangerous condition on the premises. The Court of Appeal affirmed dismissal of the action on the ground that under the facts pled in the complaint the defendant landowners owed no duty to protect members of the public from gang members who congregate around an apartment complex and assault individuals on adjacent public streets. The court reasoned: "The negligence and premises liability causes of action fail because no facts are alleged that the decedent entered the apartment complex or was assaulted on property controlled by landowner. No court has extended liability to a situation where a tenant leaves the premises and shoots a pedestrian on an adjacent street." Thus, even assuming that allowing the gang to congregate on the premises constituted a dangerous condition, there was an insufficient causal nexus between this condition and the independent, intentional killing of Mr. Medina off the premises.

The theory of liability in the present case is even more attenuated than the one rejected in *Medina* because here it cannot be argued the dangerous condition the defendant created on the premises spilled over into the public streets causing plaintiff's injury. Unlike the apartment building in *Medina*, which provided a meeting point for the gang and a launching pad for its attack on the victim, the inadequate lighting on the premises of the Plymouth Apartments played no role in facilitating the attack on Ms. Rosenbaum. This case has nothing to do with the landlord's creation of an opportunity to commit crime by providing the perpetrator a place of concealment. Plaintiff's assailants were not lurking in the shadows of her garage or the passageway to her apartment nor did they originate their street attack from a dark area of the apartment building. Furthermore, the function of adequate lighting on the premises was to protect the tenants against the risk of an attack on the premises, not to protect them against an attack on a public street. Such an attack was as likely to occur whether or not the common areas of plaintiff's apartment building were secure.

Were we to accept plaintiff's reasoning, there would be no way to prevent the connection between the landlord's conduct and the tenant's injury from becoming more and more tangential until it virtually disappeared. Suppose, for example, a tenant decides the building's laundry facility is unsafe due to inadequate lighting and no lock on the door. He therefore takes his clothes to a local Laundromat where he is assaulted and robbed. Under plaintiff's theory of liability the landlord would be liable for the tenant's injury. Or, to take a more extreme example, suppose a tenant decides the entire building including her apartment is unsafe at night due to inadequate lighting, lack of a security patrol and similar causes. Therefore, she takes a job working nights in order to be away from her apartment in the nighttime. Leaving work one morning she is mugged in the company parking lot. Her landlord is liable for her injuries according to the plaintiff's reasoning.

Furthermore, we reject the plaintiff's theory of liability in the present case because it ignores the underlying rationale for imposing a duty on landlords to protect their tenants from criminal attack.

The duty to secure the common areas with adequate lighting, locks and other appropriate security measures is imposed to protect the tenants against "the risk of unauthorized entrance into the apartment house by intruders bent upon some crime of violence or theft." Because "only the landlord is in the position to secure common areas, he has a duty to protect against types of crimes of which he has notice and which are likely to recur if the common areas are not secure." Patently, muggings on public streets are not the foreseeable result of the landlord's negligence in maintaining adequate lighting in the apartment building's common areas. Indeed, one would think just the opposite to be true: that crimes of violence would be more likely to occur in the dimly lit passageway of an apartment building than on a well lit public thoroughfare.

To adopt plaintiff's theory of liability would, in our view, impose an unfair burden on landlords and, in effect, force them to become the insurers of their tenants' safety, contrary to the well-established policy of this state. (Cf. *Ann M.*) While recognizing the modern landlord has a duty to take reasonable precautions against foreseeable criminal acts, courts have been careful to avoid imposing standards of conduct which would effectively hold the landlord liable for all crimes committed on the premises. For example, recent decisions have linked the level of security the landlord must provide to the degree of foreseeability of the harm. (*Ann M.*) The goal of imposing a duty on landlords to protect their tenants should be to promote tenant safety without touching off skyrocketing inflation in the rental housing market which, ironically, would have the greatest impact on low-income tenants in high-crime neighborhoods who are most in need of protection. This goal is not achieved by extending the duty of landlords to protect their tenants off the premises, at least not under the circumstances of this case. Thus, although we sympathize with the plaintiff's plight, as did the trial court, we must conclude, as did the trial court, that liability cannot be imposed on the defendant under the circumstances of this case.

Johnson, Associate Justice, Dissenting.

I respectfully dissent in what I acknowledge is a very close, difficult case.

I do not quarrel with the majority's careful exposition of the present state of the law as to a landlord's responsibility for third party crime on its premises. Instead I am convinced the facts of this case illustrate the need for a logical, narrowly drawn extension of that duty. Otherwise the law creates a wrong set of incentives. Landlords who fall a bit short in the lighting and other security measures they provide in common areas risk liability for injuries their tenants suffer at the hands of third party criminals. But those who leave their common areas in the most dangerous possible condition, thus denying their tenants any use of those common areas and compelling them to substitute dangerous alternatives, get off scot-free.

I would limit the scope of the expanded duty I propose in four ways. First, it would require actual, not merely constructive, knowledge about the danger the plaintiff faced if forced to use the alternative off-premises area. Second, there would have to be a high risk of serious harm from criminal activity at the alternative location. Third, the victim would have to be a member of a class, such as a tenant, to whom the landowner owes a heightened responsibility. Fourth, it would have to be foreseeable the landlord's failure to provide proper security measures against criminal activity on its own premises would cause the plaintiff to use the alternative, dangerous site on which she suffered the injury. (With respect to the causation rather than the duty question, I would require a close and direct causal link between the landlord's negligence and the criminal acts which injured the tenant off the premises.)

The evidence in this case supports the existence of all of these conditions. There is no dispute appellant is a member of a class to whom the landlord owed a heightened duty of care. She was a tenant who was paying rent to the landlord for an apartment and a garage and use of common areas. The evidence supports a finding that people parking on the street in the area of this apartment house ran a great risk of serious harm at the hands of street criminals. Furthermore, the landlord was more than aware of the risk its tenants faced if forced to park on the streets in this neighborhood. The landlord's agents possessed actual knowledge of serious assaultive crimes against people parking their cars and walking on the streets near its apartment building. So this is not a case where the landlord could reasonably believe the alternative site its tenants might use for parking was relatively safe.

The landlord also had actual notice of several serious criminal attacks on tenants in the unlighted garages and other unlighted common areas of its own property, including an assault against this tenant's roommate in a garage.... Indeed in this case the tenants informed the landlord's agents in detail about the crimes against them, and demanded adequate lighting in the common areas and other security measures. The landlord even promised to cure the problem and take those measures. Yet it still failed to do so.

* * *

A high degree of "moral blame attache[s] to the defendant's conduct" in this case.... This landlord had received specific complaints about these facts from its tenants and even promised to remedy the conditions. Yet it had failed to act. Indeed the breach here was so blatant and persistent as to approach if not reach the level of "reckless disregard of the safety of" this landlord's tenants. So there can be no question but that moral blame attaches to landlords that behave as this one did.

There also can be no serious question but that we would advance "the policy of preventing future harm" by imposing liability on landlords that breach their duty to provide reasonably secure premises in high crime areas and thus cause tenants to resort to the equally or nearly equally dangerous alternative of street parking. Indeed to allow them to escape liability in these circumstances encourages rather than discourages future harm.... Conversely, if we impose liability in these circumstances we increase the landlord's incentive to provide adequate security arrangements and thereby discourage criminal assaults on future tenants.

Expanding the landlord's duty along the lines suggested would not impose an additional "burden" on landlords beyond those they already bear. That is because they already owe the duty and "bear the burden" of providing adequate security measures on their own premises. The duty I propose does not require them to supply any greater security on their own premises or to extend their security measures to the streets. By satisfying the duty they already owe on their own premises, they meet the duty to avoid causing their tenants to substitute street parking for onsite parking. If a tenant elects to use the streets despite the availability of secure onsite parking, the landlord would not be liable. So the burden of this expanded duty is the same as the burden of the duty already owed.

The "consequences to the community" of this expanded duty appear entirely positive. Landlords would have an added incentive to fulfill their existing duty to supply tenants with reasonably secure onsite parking, thus reducing the level of criminal attacks and injuries to tenants. The impact on rents and insurance rates should be minimal. After all, we would only be increasing the consequences for conduct that constitutes a breach of a duty landlords already owe tenants, and then only when the breach is so blatant it is foreseeable those tenants will reasonably feel the streets are safer than the landlord's common areas. This is a risk landlords should have no trouble ensuring under policies presently available. On the other hand, it would be more difficult for tenant drivers to ensure against the risk they will be criminally assaulted in or near automobiles they park on the streets—and especially the special case where they are compelled to park there because their landlord failed to supply reasonably secure parking on the premises.

[Plaintiff] was robbed and nearly killed while doing the very thing, parking her car, which the unlit parking lot prevented her from doing in safety. It is as if, after appellant paid rent for secure parking on the premises, the landlord stood in the driveway and told her, "you can't park here, go park on the street." ... In essence, respondent's deliberate refusal to provide its tenants with safe on premises parking left appellant with no choice but to park in a location only somewhat safer than respondent's unlit garage.

For these reasons, I consider it is feasible and proper to expand slightly the liability landlords face when they breach their duty to take reasonable security measures against reasonably foreseeable criminal activity.... Logic and sound policy both dictate landlords should be held liable when their clearly blameworthy conduct has these predictable and serious consequences.

Notes and Questions

1. What legal issue was the court addressing in *Rosenbaum*? Is that issue a question of law for the court to decide or a question of fact for the trier of fact to decide? Was that the same issue as in *Applebaum*? in *Isaacs*? in *Ann M.*?

2. What are the key facts of this case? Does it matter that the crime occurred on the street and not in the tenant's garage? that the plaintiff was a renter, not a visitor? that the landlord had promised to improve the lighting? that improved lighting is a relatively inexpensive measure compared to the provision of security guards at issue in *Ann M*?

3. What authority did the court rely on to support its ruling? Was that authority controlling precedent under the doctrine of *stare decisis*? Did it require the result the court reached? Or are the prior precedents fairly distinguishable?

4. What is the holding of the *Rosenbaum* case?

5. What policy reasons support the result?

6. Is the result fair?

7. In support of its decision, the court sketches two hypothetical cases where the plaintiff goes off the premises out of fear of crime on the premises and is then injured. In the first, he goes to a laundromat instead of the apartment facility. In the second, she takes a night job and is injured in the company parking lot. According to the court, the plaintiff's argument in *Rosenbaum* would also support liability in these hypothetical cases. Is that true or are the facts fairly distinguishable? Are these hypotheticals helpful in analyz-

ing the problem? Or should judges confine their analysis to the facts properly before them?

8. Who has the better view, the majority or the dissent? Why?

9. What about the economic consequences of imposing liability on the landlord? Is it proper for the court to consider these consequences? The majority expresses concern about "skyrocketing inflation in the rental housing market" while the dissent concludes that the "impact on rents and insurance rates should be minimal." What evidence supports these conclusions? One jurisprudential school of thought is "law and economics" which holds that law-makers, including both legislatures and courts, should (1) evaluate legal questions in terms of costs and benefits and (2) select the alternative which promotes economic efficiency. How would this approach apply to the *Rosenbaum* case?

10. Might men and women view this problem differently? Would that be relevant to the legal analysis? Feminist jurisprudence is a field of study evaluating the influence of gender differences on the development of the law. How would this approach apply to the *Rosenbaum* case?

11. Might landlords and tenants view this problem differently? Does economic class make a difference? The "critical legal studies" movement, or CLS, considers legal decisions from the perspectives of politics and ideology, especially taking into account the influences of race and class. How would this approach apply to the *Rosenbaum* case? Consider the California Supreme Court's observations in evaluating a landlord's liability for negligently maintained premises.[13] The Court recognized that while the law generally holds that people are liable for the injuries caused by their negligence, landowners were historically immune from liability. As the Court explained, "It has been suggested that the special rules regarding the liability of the possessor of land are due to historical considerations stemming from the high place which land has traditionally held in English and American thought, the dominance and prestige of the landowning class in England during the formative period of the rules governing the possessor's liability, and the heritage of feudalism." To what extent does this feudal heritage influence contemporary judicial decisions? Does the doctrine of *stare decisis* perpetuate entrenched class powers and prerogatives?

12. Might people of different races and ethnicities view this problem differently? Critical Race Theory (CRT) analyzes the effect of race in the evolution of the law, especially with respect to African Americans. This has been refined by Latino/a Critical Theory (Lat/Crit) which brings into the analysis the special issues affecting the Latino community including immigration is-

---

13. Rowland v. Christian, 443 P.2d 561(1968).

sues. The *Rosenbaum* case involved a residential tenant at an apartment in South Central Los Angeles, historically a minority neighborhood. Does the racial and ethnic makeup of the community affect the decision? Are minorities more likely to live in neighborhoods having high-crime rates and unsafe rental housing? Might these groups be especially vulnerable to unscrupulous landlords?

5.5 The Retroactivity Problem

As we have seen, the common law evolves in response to our changing society. If these changes were to occur too rapidly and unpredictably, the rule of law would collapse and chaos would reign. As reflected in the doctrine of *stare decisis,* courts are sensitive to the tension between the need for change and the need for stability. The common law generally evolves in small increments signaled in advance by *dicta* to alert the public to an anticipated change to minimize the disruption of settled expectations.

However, despite the courts' caution, there is a fairness problem in applying a change in the law retroactively. For example, assume two people entered into a contract a year ago and a dispute arose. Assume further that while the dispute was being litigated, the law applicable to that contract was revised by a court decision. In fairness, which law should the court apply to the dispute, the law in effect when the contract was formed and the dispute arose? or the law in effect when the case comes to trial? Shouldn't liability be based on the rules in effect at the time of the parties' conduct, the rules they played by? But if the old rule has been rejected because it is unfair, ill-founded, and outdated, then isn't it unfair to continue to apply it to anyone? And what about the administration of justice? If the new law does not apply, then the law applied in one courtroom will be different from that applied down the hall. How is the court to keep track of which law to apply? On the other hand, if the new law is to be applied retroactively, then consider the burden of relitigating cases already well underway under the former law.

Courts have struggled to accommodate the need for stability, fairness, and evolution. Whichever approach the court adopts, the new law will almost always be applied to the parties before the court. As one court explained, if the party advocating the change in the law is not benefited by the change there would be no incentive to appeal the application of an unjust precedent and the common law would be frozen in time.[14]

---

14. Molitor v. Kaneland Comm. Unit Dist. No. 302, 163 N.E. 2d 89 (Ill. 1959).

While there are several variations, the following four approaches are applied in most cases:

1. Retroactive only as to the parties before the court and cases that have not yet arisen. This approach is the most protective of the possible reliance interests and allows for people to adjust their conduct to comply with the new law.
2. Retroactive only as to the parties and cases filed after the date of decision. This approach is less protective for it applies to events and transactions occurring before the change in the law. It minimizes disruption of on-going litigation by continuing to apply the former law to cases already being litigated.
3. Retroactive only as to the parties and in cases where a final judgment has not been entered. This approach is less protective of reliance interests for it applies to events and transactions occurring before the change in the law and to cases which may have been litigated for many years under the prior law.
4. Retroactive as to all cases, even those arising well before the decision was announced and where final judgments have been entered in the trial court. This is the broadest approach to retroactivity and permits the application of the new law even to those cases which have proceeded through the trial court and are pending in the courts of appeal or being litigated in the trial court on remand from the appellate courts. It requires the relitigation of cases and has the potential for imposing a significant burden on the administration of the courts.

The approach taken usually depends on how the application of the new law might affect settled expectations. Generally, the more of a surprise the new rule is, the less retroactive effect it will have. Conversely, if the change in the law is predictable and obvious, it will be given a greater retroactive effect. For example, assume an 1875 state decision had concluded that women were not qualified to serve as trustees because they lacked business experience and the facility to work with numbers. Although the matter had not been litigated for decades, every other jurisdiction which had considered similar rules had overruled them. In 2006, a woman who is appointed to serve as a trustee is challenged by her opponent based on the 1875 decision. A court would have no difficulty overruling the prior decision and giving its new rule full retroactive effect. A good-faith argument of reliance on the prior law would simply not be credible.

On the other hand, assume that historically charitable institutions had enjoyed immunity from civil actions and that the state courts had repeatedly reaffirmed this immunity. In reliance on the immunity, charities would not invest in insurance policies to protect their assets in the event of litigation. If the courts eliminate this immunity, should the rule be applied retroactively with the effect of wiping out the charities' assets? To protect the charities' expectations and allow time for necessary adjustments to the new rule, the court might adopt a narrow approach to retroactivity.[15]

The retroactivity issue is especially sensitive in criminal cases. Under the Constitution's *ex post facto* clause, legislation regarding criminal law cannot be applied retroactively. However, that provision does not expressly apply to changes in the common law. The United States Supreme Court recently examined the issue of retroactivity of changes in judge-made criminal law.[16] In *Rogers,* the Tennessee Supreme Court abolished its common law rule that a defendant could only be convicted of murder if the victim died within one year and one day of the defendant's act. The court applied its new rule to defendant Rogers who claimed that the retroactive application of the new rule violated his right to due process. The United States Supreme Court held that the restrictions on retroactive applications of judicial decisions are not as stringent as those the *ex post facto* clause imposes on legislation. According the Justice O'Connor, a court may give an interpretation of common law or criminal statute retroactive effect unless the interpretation is "unexpected and indefensible" in light of previously expressed law.[17] She emphasized that the basic question was whether the defendant had fair warning. Under this approach, the Court concluded that the abrogation of the year-and-a-day rule was hardly unexpected and that therefore there was nothing unfair about applying it to the defendant.[18] The dissenters argued that due process prohibited a court from giving retroactive effect to a decision changing the criminal law.

Douglas v. Ostermeier

2 Cal. Rptr. 2d 594 (Cal. Ct. App. 1991)

Appellants, Anton Ostermeier and West Coast Car Sales, appeal from a judgment entered on a jury verdict awarding respondents rescission on a car sales contract of $24,354 and awarding compensatory damages of $10,624 on

---

15. See Dupuis v. General Casualty Co., 152 N.W.2d 884 (Wis. 1967).
16. Rogers v. Tennessee, 532 U.S. 451 (2001).
17. *Id.* at 461–62.
18. *Id.*

the fraud cause of action as well as $187,000 in punitive damages. Appellants attack the amount of punitive damages as excessive as a matter of law.

During the pendency of this appeal, the California Supreme Court decided *Adams v. Murakami*(1991) 54 Cal 3d 105, which determined a plaintiff must present evidence of a defendant's financial condition as a prerequisite to an award of punitive damages. We conclude principles of fairness and public policy do not compel the conclusion the decision should be given only prospective effect and apply this new requirement to the case at bar. However, we further conclude adequate evidence of appellants' financial condition was presented at trial to substantiate the jury's award of punitive damages. We consequently affirm the judgment.

Facts and Proceedings Below

In July 1983 respondents, Patricia and Michael Douglas, decided to buy a new car. They originally intended to purchase a new diesel automobile but a friend suggested looking at used Mercedes automobiles at West Coast Car Sales. This friend had purchased a used Mercedes from appellants for what she believed was a reasonable price.

Patricia Douglas visited West Coast Car Sales, a business wholly owned by Ostermeier. She saw a diesel Mercedes for sale but also saw a 450 SLC model Mercedes which interested her more because of its style and sportiness. Each time she visited West Coast Car Sales there were about ten cars with for sale signs on the parking lot.

Approximately one week later, respondents again visited West Coast Car Sales and met with Ostermeier to discuss purchasing the 450 SLC. Ostermeier stated the car was a 1978 model worth $29,000. The parties negotiated price and extras and respondents ultimately agreed to purchase the car for $22,500 plus tax, registration and license fees with upgraded wheels and a general three-month warranty on the car.

The Douglases returned the next day to pay for the car and to sign documents. The following day the car would not start and it had to be towed for repairs.

On May 1, 1984, representatives of the California Highway Patrol (CHP) went to the Douglas' residence and impounded the car. A CHP officer showed Patricia a photograph of a totally wrecked car with the fatally injured driver still in the driver's seat. The officer explained he had reason to believe her car was the same as depicted in the photograph and was concerned her car might be stolen. The car remained impounded for approximately a month. The CHP determined the car had not been stolen but when it was returned to the Douglases the CHP required it be re-registered as a 1973 vehicle. Sometime after the CHP returned the car, the front frame of the car broke off and the car had to be towed and repaired. At some point Patricia Douglas permanently parked the car in their garage at home.

Apparently, Ostermeier had purchased two totally wrecked, "salvage" cars. He purchased the 1978 450 SLC Mercedes which had been in a car accident. From another auto wrecking facility he purchased the frame of a 1973 Mercedes which had been gutted by fire. From these two cars Ostermeier created the composite 450 SLC sold to the Douglases.

When Ostermeier purchased the two wrecks he received "pink slips" indicating their respective vehicle identification numbers (VIN). He re-registered these two cars with the Department of Motor Vehicles (DMV) as "salvage" automobiles. This re-registration triggered the attention of the CHP who regularly monitor the switching or disguising of VIN numbers for the purpose of switching high priced vehicles for salvage. In this case the re-registration led the CHP to investigate the Douglases' car.

The CHP investigation revealed VIN numbers of the 1973 Mercedes frame had either been filed off or had been covered over by a new VIN plate indicating a year and model of a 1978 Mercedes. Alteration of any VIN number is a criminal offense. The officer testified he had personally warned Ostermeier on a prior occasion to cease tampering with official identifications of cars he restored. In this case Ostermeier claimed he received the 1973 frame with the VIN numbers already obliterated. He testified that because he could no longer read the numbers and, because he could not be sure of the correct VIN number for the 1973, he covered the old 1973 VIN numbers with new 1978 numbers. On cross-examination, however, Ostermeier admitted the "pink slip" he received when purchasing the 1973 frame recorded the proper VIN number.

Appellant was not prosecuted in this instance but the Douglases were required to re-register their car as a 1973. Based on expert testimony concerning the relative values of used, new and composite 1978 and 1973 cars, the composite car Ostermeier sold the Douglases was worth less than half its purchase price of $24,354.

Appellant testified the Douglases knew the car was a composite because he personally told them it was. Based on contradictory evidence, the jury found appellant did not tell them the truth about the car. Both Michael and Patricia Douglas testified Ostermeier never told them the car was a composite nor that it was comprised of parts from salvaged cars. The sales invoice did not mention the word "salvage." The registration forms did not bear the word "salvage."

The Douglases retained counsel to negotiate a rescission of the contract. When these negotiations failed the Douglases brought suit for rescission of the contract alleging fraudulent misrepresentation and requesting compensatory and punitive damages.

The case was tried before a jury. The jury awarded the Douglases rescission of the contract and restitution of the sales price of $24,354.25 with return of the car to appellants. The jury also awarded compensatory damages in the amount of $10,624 and punitive damages of $187,000.

Alleging the punitive damage award was excessive, appellants filed post-trial motions for judgment notwithstanding the verdict and for a new trial. Appellants' motions were denied and this appeal followed.

Discussion
The Award of Punitive Damages Is Appropriate in this Case

During the pendency of this appeal the California Supreme Court rendered its opinion in *Adams v. Murakami,* holding that as a prerequisite to an award of punitive damages, a plaintiff must present evidence of a defendant's financial condition. We requested briefing from the parties on the issues of whether this decision should be applied retroactively to this case; and, if so, whether sufficient evidence of the defendants' financial condition was presented at trial to satisfy the requirements of *Adams.*

The general rule is that an overruling decision of a court of supreme jurisdiction is retrospective in its application. There are exceptions, however, and this new rule announced by the Supreme Court presents an extraordinarily close case on the issue of retroactivity.

Exceptions to the general rule of retroactivity are recognized when considerations of fairness, foreseeability and public policy preclude full retroactivity. For example, where a constitutional provision or statute has received a given construction by a court of last resort, and contracts have been made or property rights acquired in accordance with the prior decision, neither will the contracts be invalidated nor will vested rights be impaired by applying the new rule retroactively. [According to the California Supreme Court, considerations of fairness and public policy dictate that parties who had already embarked on litigation should receive the benefit of the highest court's express prior ruling on which they had relied. Moreover, in addition to the parties' reliance on prior law, the Court will consider the impact full retroactivity would have on the administration of justice where large numbers of cases would be required to have new trials].

[As the California Supreme Court explained:] "Public policy considerations include the purpose to be served by the new rule, and the effect on the administration of justice of retroactive application. Considerations of fairness would measure the reliance on the old standards by the parties or others similarly affected, as well as 'the ability of litigants to foresee the coming change in the law....'"

* * *

[Several factors in the case at bar] point to retroactive application of the high court's decision in *Adams v. Murakami.*...

First, considerations of fairness—reliance on the old standards and foreseeability of a change in the law—on balance weigh in favor of retroactive application. Retroactive application of the rule will not deprive a plaintiff of a property or contract right. Nor will a plaintiff be denied any remedy whatsoever. A plaintiff is still entitled to punitive damages, although proof of entitlement will be much more burdensome. The *Adams* decision did not overrule a prior decision of the state's highest court. The California Supreme Court had never before spoken on the issue. Nor did the *Adams* decision overrule a series of unanimous and consistent Court of Appeal decisions on the issue....

[Moreover, h]ere, there was disagreement among the Courts of Appeal, albeit minor, as to a requirement of evidence of a defendant's financial condition as a prerequisite to an award of punitive damages. The majority rule in California was a plaintiff could, but was not required to, present evidence of a defendant's financial condition. However, [one court] concluded meaningful appellate review of an award of punitive damages was impossible in the absence of evidence of a defendant's financial condition. The decision, while criticized by many courts, generated considerable attention, and ultimately the Supreme Court granted review in *Adams v. Murakami* to resolve the issue.[19] Thus, because of the lack of unanimity in Court of Appeal decisions on such an important and controversial matter, it was foreseeable the state's highest court would at some point need to address the issue directly. What was not particularly foreseeable, however, was that the Supreme Court would

---

19. The general rule a plaintiff was not required to present evidence of a defendant's worth to sustain an award of punitive damages was first expressly recognized in *Hanley v. Lund* (1963) 218 Cal. App. 2d 633, 645–646, a Court of Appeal decision from the Second Appellate District. This rule has been followed exclusively in the Second Appellate District and has been the controlling rule in other districts as well. (The court provides numerous citations.) On September 11, 1989, a panel of the Fourth Appellate District decided *Dumas v. Stocker*, 213 Cal. App. 3d 1262, which held an award of punitive damages could not stand in the absence of evidence of a defendant's net worth. This decision broke with longstanding practice and was considered an aberration in California jurisprudence. *See, e.g.,* Liberty Transport, Inc. v. Harry W. Gorst Co., 229 Cal. App. 3d 417, 438; Fenlon v. Brock, 216 Cal. App. 3d 1174 (another Fourth District panel refused to follow the *Dumas* analysis as erroneously decided). At the time of the Supreme Court's decision in *Adams v. Murakami*, only one other court had adopted the analysis of *Dumas*.

adopt the conclusion and rationale of the minority position among the Courts of Appeal that had considered the question. [But because there was disagreement between the lower courts, reliance on the majority rule] became a somewhat more risky proposition once contrary authority appeared.

Thus, since at least 1989 there has been some question whether absolute reliance on the old rule was warranted. And as noted, while the new rule was not particularly foreseeable, it was expected the Supreme Court would in time definitively resolve the question of whether evidence of a defendant's financial condition was a prerequisite for an award of punitive damages. We conclude, on balance, considerations of fairness in terms of parties' reliance on the old rule and the foreseeability of the new rule do not compel the conclusion an exception to the general rule of retroactivity is warranted in this case.

Public policy considerations include the purpose to be served by the new rule and the effect of the new rule on the administration of justice. The purposes enunciated in *Adams v. Murakami* for evidence of a defendant's wealth as a prerequisite for punitive damages are two-fold. First, evidence of financial condition in the record will assist an appellate court in determining whether the amount of an award of punitive damages is appropriate in a given case. Second, evidence of a defendant's wealth will assist the jury in determining what amount of damages, in light of the defendant's wealth, it will require to punish past misconduct and deter this defendant's misconduct in the future.

If evidence of financial condition was presented at trial, the purposes of the new rule have been served even without retroactive application of the *Adams* decision. But where there was insufficient evidence presented at trial to support the award of punitive damages, retroactive application of the *Adams* decision would further the purpose of meaningful appellate review and assure the punishment meted out to the defendant is neither inadequate nor excessive to fulfill the dual purposes of punishment and deterrence.

We first consider the potential effects on the administration of justice from retroactive application of the decision in *Adams v. Murakami*.

It is very likely plaintiffs in many cases not yet final presented sufficient evidence of the defendant's financial condition to satisfy the new requirements of *Adams v. Murakami*. These cases, of course, would be unaffected by this decision, as would cases not yet brought to trial. There also might be cases in which the defendant presented evidence of his or her financial condition. Although the burden is now on the plaintiff to present such evidence, there is no principled reason to require re-trial of those cases. Nor do we believe it would be necessary, except perhaps in the most extraordinary case, to require re-trial of liability for compensatory damages or entitlement to punitive damages where insufficient evidence of a defendant's financial condition was presented at trial to support the amount of the award.

In this case, the jury used a special verdict form which first inquired as to appellant's liability for and the amount of compensatory damages to be awarded on each cause of action. The jury was separately asked whether appellant was liable for punitive damages and, if so, in what amount. Because the amount of punitive damages awarded was segregated from the question of entitlement to punitive damages, the amount of the award may be excised and re-tried without disturbing the jury's other findings. This will be true of the vast majority of cases involving punitive damages which are not yet final.

Nevertheless, re-trial of even the limited issue of the appropriate amount of punitive damages in light of the defendant's financial condition will place a heavy burden on the administration of justice. First, before re-trial of the amount of punitive damages, it will be necessary to conduct extensive discovery of the defendant's finances [which will require extensive court supervision].

Secondly, in most, if not all, of the cases requiring re-trial the parties will request a jury trial. Jury trials are, of course, time consuming, expensive and taxing on a superior court system which already is overburdened with pending civil and criminal matters.

Thirdly, in order to demonstrate the reprehensibility of the defendant's conduct, witnesses will need to testify and evidence will need to be presented, presumably as extensively as would be required to prove entitlement to punitive damages in the first instance. It would be the rare plaintiff who would consent to a stipulation the defendant acted fraudulently, with malice or oppression and forego the opportunity to have the jury hear the precise factual details of the defendant's reprehensible conduct. The practical effect of a plaintiff wanting to re-establish entitlement to punitive damages will be lengthy re-trials, possibly consuming as many court days as it took to try the matter originally. Re-trials will require duplication of efforts by counsel, higher costs to litigants and an increased demand on court personnel and resources. Thus, retroactive application of the *Adams* decision will have a definite negative impact on judicial resources in terms of adding to an already overburdened justice system which is currently suffering from an excessive work load and severe budgetary restraints.

On the other hand, while it is impossible to be certain precisely how many cases currently pending in the court system will require re-trial, it appears the actual numbers may be fewer than media accounts of the incidence of punitive damages might suggest. A somewhat dated study prepared by the Rand Corporation indicates retroactive application of the requirement of evidence of a defendant's financial condition might only affect two or three hundred cases and possibly fewer.[20] Under these circumstances, the effect of retroactive application of the *Adams v. Murakami* decision on the administration of justice, while not negligible, is not of the magnitude [of other more sweeping decisions].

On balance and by a narrow margin, fairness and public policy concerns, as defined and explained in decisions of our highest court indicate retroactive application of its decision in *Adams v. Murakami* is appropriate. Accordingly, we apply that decision to the instant case.

In *Neal v. Farmers Ins. Exchange* (1978) 21 Cal. 3d 910, the Supreme Court cited three factors the jury must consider in awarding punitive damages: the nature of the defendant's wrongdoing, the amount of compensatory damages and the wealth of the particular defendant. Because one of the purposes of a punitive damage award is to deter future misconduct, "It follows that, the wealthier the wrongdoing defendant, the larger the award of exemplary damages need be in order to accomplish the statutory objective." On the other hand, the award should not be so excessive it "exceeds the level necessary to properly punish and deter."

Our finding the decision in *Adams v. Murakami* should be given full retroactive effect, however, does not require retrial of the punitive damage award in this case. In the case at bar, sufficient evidence was presented at trial to support the jury's award of $187,000 in punitive damages.

---

20. According to a study conducted by the Rand Corporation's Institute for Civil Justice of tort cases in California, punitive damages were awarded in approximately one of every ten trials in which plaintiffs won compensatory damages during the period 1980 to 1984. (Peterson, Sarma, Shanley, Punitive Damages Empirical Findings, RAND Corporation, R-3311-ICJ (1987) p. 33.) The study broke down the frequency of awards by jurisdiction as follows:

	Punitive Damage Awards 1981–1984	Punitive Damage Awards Percentage of Trials in Which Compensatory Damages Awarded
Los Angeles County	149	10.1%
San Francisco County	51	13.6%
Major urban counties	120	11.0%
Other urban counties	86	6.8%
Rural counties	12	5.2%
Total California	418	9.4%

Many of the cases awarding punitive damages during this period were actions involving bad faith in the business or contract context. Presumably, the *Foley* and *Moradi-Shalal* decisions have since had some effect on the incidence of punitive damage awards in insurance and employment cases.

There was testimony from both sides. Ostermeier operated several wholly owned businesses. Appellant's main business property was located in a prime area near all major freeways and the San Pedro Harbor. According to Patricia Douglas' expert testimony on the market value of this business property, the land alone was worth between $5 and $6 million.

Ostermeier testified his business property was worth approximately $1 million but was encumbered with an $850,000 mortgage. He also testified his car restoration business was worth $100,000 and his home equity was $80,000. According to Ostermeier his 4,000 square foot restaurant had no value and he lost money building gull wing vehicles despite an average sales price of $60,000 per vehicle. While there was evidence of other business tenants who occupied his business property, there was no evidence of precisely how much income Ostermeier derived from these tenants.

Thus, evidence of appellant's financial condition was presented at trial for the jury's, and this court's, evaluation.

If the jury believed only Ostermeier's testimony and rejected Patricia Douglas' testimony in its entirety, the punitive damage award of $187,000 would be nearly half the admitted value of Ostermeier's business property. However, if the jury believed Patricia Douglas that the value of the land occupied by Ostermeier's business property alone was worth between $5 and $6 million, the punitive damage award of $187,000 was a small fraction of appellant's worth and cannot be viewed as excessive. This is especially true in light of appellant's egregious conduct. Even if the jury believed Ostermeier's testimony the property was encumbered with an $850,000 mortgage, the net value of the land would still be over $4 million. If the jury believed this version of the facts, the award could still not be viewed as excessive.

It is an important principle of appellate law that "All issues of credibility are within the province of the trier of fact. In reviewing the evidence all conflicts must be resolved in favor of the respondent, and all legitimate and reasonable inferences indulged in to uphold the verdict if possible. It is an elementary principle of law, that when a verdict is attacked as being unsupported, the power of the appellate court begins and ends with a determination as to whether there is any substantial evidence, contradicted or uncontradicted, which will support the conclusion reached by the jury. Here the jury clearly resolved the issue of credibility of the testimony against appellants.

Nor after a review of the entire record can we say the punitive damage award was a result of passion and prejudice. It is not so grossly disproportionate to the award of compensatory damages as to raise the presumption it was the result of passion and prejudice....

* * *

Also a critical factor for consideration is the egregiousness of the defendant's conduct. Here, the nature of appellant's acts, quite possibly criminal in nature, were at a minimum fraudulent and despicable. Ostermeier's acts demonstrated he was a menace to society and presented a public nuisance. This is a particularly fitting case for an award of punitive damages to punish misconduct and to deter similar acts in the future.

Notes and Questions

1. The *Douglas* court had to decide whether a California Supreme Court decision imposing a new requirement would be applied to cases already on appeal when the requirement was announced. What factors did the court consider in deciding the requirement applied?

2. Is the result fair in this case? Would it be fair if evidence of the defendant's financial condition had not been presented at trial? In addition to concerns about the administration of justice, consider the burden on the parties in terms of legal expense and delay of having to discover additional evidence and retry their case.

3. Since the court concluded that the plaintiffs had introduced sufficient evidence of defendant's financial condition to satisfy the new requirement, why did the court bother to address the issue of retroactivity? Is this discussion holding or dicta?

4. Is the court correct in suggesting that plaintiffs will want to retry defendant's liability as well as financial condition? Why would plaintiffs want to incur the additional expense of more protracted proceedings? Consider the issue of the defendant's credibility in this case. Wouldn't the plaintiffs want to introduce evidence of the defendant's testimony denying liability in order to undermine his testimony about his financial condition?

5. Should the law allow punitive damages in civil cases? If the general goal of tort law is to compensate for injuries, what goal do punitive damages serve? Should the plaintiff be entitled to this windfall? Why? Should cases involving punitive damages be treated under the rules governing retroactivity in civil or criminal law?

6. The court relies on a study by the Rand Corporation's Institute for Civil Justice to support the conclusion that retroactive application of the rule will affect only 200–300 cases. Is this proper evidence for the court to consider? How did the study come to the court's attention?

7. While the Rand study covered the period from 1980 to 1984, the number of punitive damage awards has remained relatively constant. For example, a 1995 study by the National Center for State Courts found that nationwide punitive damages were awarded in 6% of tort verdicts. And a study of civil

cases tried in large counties in 2001 found that punitive damages were awarded in 6% of the cases where plaintiffs prevailed.[21] The median punitive damage award was $50,000.[22]

Before reading these figures, did you think punitive damages were common or rare?

8. The decline in punitive damage awards mirrors the decline in tort filings. According to the California State Judicial Council,[23] filings have declined as follows:

Year	Motor Vehicle Cases	Other Tort Cases*	Total
1988–89	91,450	40,869	132,319
1989–90	82,866	39,167	122,033
1990–91	80,208	37,100	117,308
1991–92	70,680	38,575	109,255
1992–93	55,487	35,224	90,711
1993–94	49,495	34,036	83,531
1994–95	47,493	31,997	79,490

*Includes claims for personal injury, death and property damage.

The trend has continued. In 1996, according to the National Center for State Courts, personal injury actions had dropped 39 percent since 1987. More specifically, in California motor vehicle personal-injury cases dropped from 91,450 in 1988–1989 to 43,908 in 1996–1997.[24] State wide, the total number of civil damage suits for $25,000 or more decreased from 203,710 in fiscal year 1994–95 to 178,716 in fiscal year 1998–1999.[25] Another report found that the number of civil suits by consumers dropped 20 percent between 1996 and 2000.[26] And all tort filings dropped 4 percent from 1993 to 2002, despite population growth.[27]

Most recently, a 2005 study by the Bureau of Justice Statistics of the U.S. Department of Justice found that the number of tort cases tried in federal court

---

21. Thomas H. Cohen, et al., *Civil Trial Cases and Verdicts in Large Counties, 2001*, Bureau of Justice Statistics, Apr. 2004, at 1.

22. *Id.*

23. Richard C. Reuben, *Putting Breaks on Torts*, A.B.A. J., Jan. 1997, at 39.

24. Dick Goldberg, *PI Cases, Counsel Are Dwindling*, Daily Recorder, Mar. 17, 1999, at 1.

25. Quentin L. Kopp, *California Courts Are Putting Themselves Out of Business*, The Recorder, Feb. 7, 2001, at 5.

26. Alfred P. Carlton, Jr., *Standing Up for Lawyers*, Part II, ABA J., Dec. 2002, at 8.

27. Myron Levin, *Coverage of Big Awards for Plaintiffs Helps Distort View of Legal System*, L.A. Times, Aug. 15, 2005.

dropped by almost 80 percent in the past two decades.[28] Specifically, the number of tort trials declined from 3,600 in 1985 to 800 in 2003.[29] Researchers at the National Center for State Courts reported that the decline in tort cases in federal courts has been mirrored, although less dramatically, in state courts.[30] Consider the following information from the Bureau of Justice Statistics:

Trends in Civil Trials in State Courts in the Nation's 75 Largest Counties, 1992–2001:[31]

Case Type	1992	1996	2001	Percent change 1992–2001
All tort cases	11,660	10,278	7,948	−31.8%
Automobile	4,980	4,994	4,235	−15.0%
Premises liability	2,648	2,232	1,268	−52.1%
Product liability	657	421	158	−76.0%
Medical malpractice	1,347	1,201	1,156	−14.2%

9. The decline in tort filings is also reflected in the decline in the liability costs for American businesses. According to a study by Ernst & Young and Risk & Insurance Management Society, Inc., liability costs for U.S. companies decreased by 37 percent between 1994 and 1999.[32]

10. Before reading these figures, did you think tort filings and liability costs were increasing or decreasing? Do these figures surprise you?

11. *The McDonald's Case:* Most of you have probably heard of the notorious McDonald's coffee case which is frequently offered as an example of our runaway tort system. Did you know that the plaintiff, Ms. Liebeck, was a 79-year-old woman who was seated in her grandson's parked car when she removed the lid from her coffee to add cream and sugar? The coffee spilled on her lap. The coffee was 180–190 degrees Fahrenheit, in accordance with McDonald's policy. This temperature is about 40 degrees hotter than is fit for human consumption and hot enough to cause second- and third-degree burns within two seconds after it touches skin. In the decade before this accident, McDonald's had received more than 700 complaints of burns, but never consulted a doctor to assess the risks. Ms. Liebeck went immediately to the hos-

---

28. Lawrence Hurley, *Study Shows Sharp Decline in Tort Cases,* DAILY RECORDER, Aug. 19, 2005, at 1.

29. *Id.*

30. *Id.*

31. Thomas H. Cohen, et al., *Civil Trial Cases and Verdicts in Large Counties, 2001,* BUREAU OF JUSTICE STATISTICS, Apr. 2004, at 9.

32. Russell E. Nordstrom, *Anti-Plaintiff Propaganda Mocks Real Human Tragedies,* DAILY RECORDER, May 20, 1999, at 2.

pital; she had third-degree burns over six percent of her body including her inner thighs, buttocks, and genital area. She was hospitalized for eight days and underwent painful skin grafts. Do these facts change your perspective on the case?

Ms. Liebeck sought compensation for her injuries. Her hospital bill was more than $10,000. Although McDonald's had previously settled coffee burn claims for as much as $500,000, it offered Ms. Liebeck $800. She retained a lawyer and offered to settle the case before trial for $20,000. McDonald's rejected this offer. During the trial, McDonald's witnesses testified that they would not lower the temperature of their coffee despite the history of serious burns. The jury awarded Ms. Liebeck $200,000 for her medical expenses, pain and suffering, but reduced this sum to $160,000 because it found her to be 20 percent at fault. The jury also awarded $2.7 million in punitive damages because McDonald's had clear knowledge of the danger but refused to change its policy. The next day, McDonald's lowered its coffee temperature by 30 degrees. The trial judge reduced the punitive damages to $480,000. On appeal, the court affirmed this reduced award. The case eventually was settled.[33]

---

33. *Id.*; Bruce L. Braley, *Trust Common Sense in Awarding Damages,* Des Moines Reg., July 29, 1998, *available at* 1998 WL 3218333; Timothy Castle & Carl Peel, *A Hot Issue,* 167 Tea & Coffee Trade J., Sept. 1, 1995, *available at* 1995 WL 12575356; Craig Crawford, *Hot Coffee Lawsuit Drew Scorn,* Orlando Sentinel, May 8, 1995, at A4; *available at* 1995 WL 6437376; Terry D. Edwards, *Don't Let the Courts Shut Out the Injured,* Charleston Gazette & Daily Mail, Apr. 6, 1995, at 4A, *available at* 1995 WL 11634752; Ann Landers, *Plaintiff's Lawyer Rebuts Spilled-Hot Coffee Stories,* Chi. Trib., Jan. 16, 1995, *available at* 1995 WL 6170276; Anthony Marshall, *Costly Cup of Coffee Stirs Legal Question,* 210 Hotel & Motel Mgmt., July 5, 1995, at 13, *available at* 1995 WL 12303768.

CHAPTER 6

PUTTING IT ALL TOGETHER

Throughout this book, we've been introducing ways to think about and understand the law. We've looked at the structure of our legal system and seen how it determines the law-making powers of each branch of government. We've considered the hierarchy of legal authorities—from constitutional provisions to statutes to case law. To help you understand statutory construction, we've presented canons of construction and discussed legislative history. In explaining how the common law works, we've selected judicial decisions to illustrate the tension between adhering to *stare decisis* to ensure that the law is even-handed and predictable and departing from precedent to permit the law to evolve to meet new needs and to reflect contemporary values.

To help you understand our legal system, we have presented these concepts in isolation with one chapter illustrating statutory construction and another tracing the evolution of caselaw. But, as you have surely guessed, the law is multifaceted and an individual case may raise any number of interrelated issues. In this chapter, we will present a case illustrating the complex interplay of legal principles and rich texture of the law. In *Lockyer v. San Francisco*, the California Supreme Court considered whether an individual local official, Mayor Gavin Newsom of San Francisco, could refuse to enforce a statutory ban on same-sex marriage that he believed to be unconstitutional. In analyzing this question, the court tackled a number of issues including the rule of law, separation of powers, statutory construction, federalism, and equitable remedies.

Lockyer v. City and County of San Francisco
33 Cal. 4th 1055, 95 P.3d 459 (2004)

We assumed jurisdiction in these original writ proceedings to address an important but relatively narrow legal issue—whether a local executive official who is charged with the ministerial duty of enforcing a state statute exceeds his or her authority when, without any court having determined that the statute is unconstitutional, the official deliberately declines to enforce the statute because he or she determines or is of the opinion that the statute is unconstitutional.

In the present case, this legal issue arises out of the refusal of local officials in the City and County of San Francisco to enforce the provisions of California's marriage statutes that limit the granting of a marriage license and marriage certificate only to a couple comprised of a man and a woman.

The same legal issue and the same applicable legal principles could come into play, however, in a multitude of situations. For example, we would face the same legal issue if the statute in question were among those that restrict the possession or require the registration of assault weapons, and a local official, charged with the ministerial duty of enforcing those statutes, refused to apply their provisions because of the official's view that they violate the Second Amendment of the federal Constitution. In like manner, the same legal issue would be presented if the statute were one of the environmental measures that impose restrictions upon a property owner's ability to obtain a building permit for a development that interferes with the public's access to the California coastline, and a local official, charged with the ministerial duty of issuing building permits, refused to apply the statutory limitations because of his or her belief that they effect an uncompensated "taking" of property in violation of the just compensation clause of the state or federal Constitution.

Indeed, another example might illustrate the point even more clearly: the same legal issue would arise if the statute at the center of the controversy were the recently enacted provision (operative January 1, 2005) that imposes a ministerial duty upon local officials to accord the same rights and benefits to registered domestic partners as are granted to spouses and a local official—perhaps an officeholder in a locale where domestic partnership rights are unpopular—adopted a policy of refusing to recognize or accord to registered domestic partners the equal treatment mandated by statute, based solely upon the official's view (unsupported by any judicial determination) that the statutory provisions granting such rights to registered domestic partners are unconstitutional because they improperly amend or repeal the provisions of the voter-enacted initiative measure commonly known as the California Defense of Marriage Act without a confirming vote of the electorate, in violation of the California Constitution.

As these various examples demonstrate, although the present proceeding may be viewed by some as presenting primarily a question of the substantive legal rights of same-sex couples, in actuality the legal issue before us implicates the interest of all individuals in ensuring that public officials execute their official duties in a manner that respects the limits of the authority granted to them as officeholders. In short, the legal question at issue—the scope of the authority entrusted to our public officials—involves the determination of a fundamental question that lies at the heart of our political system: the role of the rule of law in a society that justly prides itself on being "a government of laws, and not of men" (or women).[1]

As indicated above, that issue—phrased in the narrow terms presented by this case—is whether a local executive official, charged with the ministerial duty of enforcing a statute, has the authority to disregard the terms of the statute in the absence of a judicial determination that it is unconstitutional, based solely upon the official's opinion that the governing statute is unconstitutional. As we shall see, it is well established, both in California and elsewhere, that—subject to a few narrow exceptions that clearly are inapplicable here—a local executive official does *not* possess such authority.

This conclusion is consistent with the classic understanding of the separation of powers doctrine—that the legislative power is the power to enact statutes, the executive power is the power to execute or enforce statutes, and the judicial power is the power to interpret statutes and to determine their constitutionality. It is true, of course, that the separation of powers doctrine does not create an absolute or rigid division of functions. Furthermore, legislators and executive officials may take into account constitutional considerations in making discretionary decisions within their authorized sphere of action—such as whether to enact or veto proposed legislation or exercise prosecutorial discretion. When, however, a duly enacted statute imposes a ministerial duty upon an executive official to follow the dictates of the statute in performing a mandated act, the official generally has no authority to disregard the statutory mandate based on the official's own determination that the statute is unconstitutional.

Accordingly, for the reasons that follow, we agree with petitioners that local officials in San Francisco exceeded their authority by taking official action in violation of applicable statutory provisions. We therefore shall issue a writ of mandate directing the officials to enforce those provisions unless and until they are judicially determined to be unconstitutional and to take all necessary remedial steps to undo the continuing effects of the officials' past unautho-

---

1. The phrase "a government of laws, and not of men" was authored by John Adams (Adams, Novanglus Papers, No. 7 (1774), reprinted in 4 WORKS OF JOHN ADAMS (Charles Francis Adams ed. 1851) p. 106), and was included as part of the separation of powers provision of the initial Massachusetts Constitution adopted in 1780. (Mass. Const. (1780) Part The First, art. XXX.) The separation of powers provision of that state's Constitution remains unchanged to this day, and reads in full: "In the government of this commonwealth, the legislative department shall never exercise the executive and judicial powers or either of them; the executive shall never exercise the legislative and judicial powers, or either of them; the judicial shall never exercise the legislative and executive powers, or either of them: *to the end it may be a government of laws and not of men.*" (Emphasis added by the Court.)

rized actions, including making appropriate corrections to all relevant official records and notifying all affected same-sex couples that the same-sex marriages authorized by the officials are void and of no legal effect.

To avoid any misunderstanding, we emphasize that the substantive question of the constitutional validity of California's statutory provisions limiting marriage to a union between a man and a woman is not before our court in this proceeding, and our decision in this case is not intended, and should not be interpreted, to reflect any view on that issue. We hold only that in the absence of a judicial determination that such statutory provisions are unconstitutional, local executive officials lacked authority to issue marriage licenses to, solemnize marriages of, or register certificates of marriage for same-sex couples, and marriages conducted between same-sex couples in violation of the applicable statutes are void and of no legal effect. Should the applicable statutes be judicially determined to be unconstitutional in the future, same-sex couples then would be free to obtain valid marriage licenses and enter into valid marriages.

I

The events that gave rise to this proceeding began on February 10, 2004, when Gavin Newsom, the Mayor of the City and County of San Francisco and a respondent in one of the consolidated cases before us,[2] sent a letter to Nancy Alfaro, identified in the letter as the San Francisco County Clerk, requesting that she "determine what changes should be made to the forms and documents used to apply for and issue marriage licenses in order to provide marriage licenses on a non-discriminatory basis, without regard to gender or sexual orientation." The mayor stated in his letter that "[t]he Supreme Courts in other states have held that equal protection provisions in their state constitutions prohibit discrimination against gay men and lesbians with respect to the rights and obligations flowing from marriage," and explained that it is his "belief that these decisions are persuasive and that the California Constitution similarly prohibits such discrimination." The mayor indicated that the request to the county clerk was made "[p]ursuant to [his] sworn duty to uphold the California Constitution, including specifically its equal protection clause."[3]

---

2. [Petitioner in the *Lockyer* matter is Bill Lockyer, the Attorney General of California, who named as respondents the City and County of San Francisco, Mayor Newsom, and other city officials. The other petitioners are individual residents and taxpayers of San Francisco. In both cases the petitioners sought a writ of mandate to require San Francisco to stop issuing marriage licenses to same-sex couples. The cases were consolidated to be heard together by the California Supreme Court.]

3. The letter read in full: "Upon taking the Oath of Office, becoming the Mayor of the City and County of San Francisco, I swore to uphold the Constitution of the State of Cal-

In response to the mayor's letter, the county clerk designed what she describes as "a gender-neutral application for public marriage licenses, and a gender-neutral marriage license," to be used by same-sex couples. The newly designed form altered the official state-prescribed form for the "Application for Marriage License" and the "License and Certificate of Marriage" by eliminating the terms "bride," "groom," and "unmarried man and unmarried woman," and by replacing them with the terms "first applicant," "second applicant," and "unmarried individuals." The revised form also contained a new warning at the top of the form, advising applicants that "[b]y entering into marriage you may lose some or all of the rights, protections and benefits you enjoy as a domestic partner" and that "marriage of gay and lesbian couples may not be recognized as valid by any jurisdiction other than San Francisco, and may not be recognized as valid by any employer," and encouraging same-sex couples "to seek legal advice regarding the effect of entering into marriage."[4]

The county clerk, using the altered forms, began issuing marriage licenses to same-sex couples on February 12, 2004, and the county recorder thereafter

---

ifornia. Article I, Section 7, subdivision (a) of the California Constitution provides that '[a] person may not be ... denied equal protection of the laws.' The California courts have interpreted the equal protection clause of the California Constitution to apply to lesbians and gay men and have suggested that laws that treat homosexuals differently from heterosexuals are suspect. The California courts have also stated that discrimination against gay men and lesbians is invidious. The California courts have held that gender discrimination is suspect and invidious as well. The Supreme Courts in other states have held that equal protection provisions in their state constitutions prohibit discrimination against gay men and lesbians with respect to the rights and obligations flowing from marriage. It is my belief that these decisions are persuasive and that the California Constitution similarly prohibits such discrimination.

Pursuant to my sworn duty to uphold the California Constitution, including specifically its equal protection clause, I request that you determine what changes should be made to the forms and documents used to apply for and issue marriage licenses in order to provide marriage licenses on a non-discriminatory basis, without regard to gender or sexual orientation."

4. The warning reads in full: "Please read this carefully prior to completing the application: [¶] By entering into marriage you may lose some or all of the rights, protections, and benefits you enjoy as a domestic partner, including, but not limited to those rights, protections, and benefits afforded by State and local government, and by your employer. If you are currently in a domestic partnership, you are urged to seek legal advice regarding the potential loss of your rights, protections, and benefits before entering into marriage. [¶] Marriage of gay and lesbian couples may not be recognized as valid by any jurisdiction other than San Francisco, and may not be recognized as valid by any employer. If you are a same-gender couple, you are encouraged to seek legal advice regarding the effect of entering into marriage."

registered marriage certificates submitted on behalf of same-sex couples who had received licenses from the city and had participated in marriage ceremonies. The declaration of the county clerk, filed in this court on March 5, 2004, indicates that as of that date, the clerk had issued more that 3,500 marriage licenses to same-sex couples. In more recent filings, the city has indicated that approximately 4,000 same-sex marriages have been performed under licenses issued by the County Clerk of the City and County of San Francisco.

On February 13, 2004, two separate actions were filed in San Francisco County Superior Court seeking to halt the city's issuance of marriage licenses to same-sex couples and the solemnization and registration of marriages of such couples. In each case, a request for an immediate stay of the city's actions was denied by the superior court after a hearing.

On February 27, 2004, the Attorney General filed in this court a petition for an original writ of mandate, prohibition, certiorari, and/or other relief, and a request for an immediate stay. The petition asserted that the actions of the city officials in issuing marriage licenses to same-sex couples and solemnizing and registering the marriages of such couples are unlawful, and that the problems and uncertainty created by the growing number of these marriages justify intervention by this court. The petition pointed out that despite a directive issued by the state Registrar of Vital Statistics, the San Francisco County Recorder had not ceased the practice of registering marriage certificates submitted by same-sex couples on forms other than those approved by the State of California, and that officials of the federal Social Security Administration had raised questions regarding that agency's processing of name-change applications resulting from California marriages— not confined to single-sex marriages—because of the uncertainty as to whether certain marriage certificates issued in California are valid under state law. Noting that "[t]he Attorney General has the constitutional duty to see that the laws of the state are uniformly and adequately enforced" (see Cal. Const., art. V, §13), the petition maintained that the existing "conflict and uncertainty, and the potential for future ambiguity, instability, and inconsistent administration among various jurisdictions and levels of government, present a legal issue of statewide importance that warrants immediate intervention by this Court." The petition requested that this court issue an order (1) directing the local officials to comply with the applicable statutes in issuing marriage licenses and certificates, (2) declaring invalid the same-sex marriage licenses and certificates that have been issued, and (3) directing the city to refund any fees collected in connection with such licenses and certificates.

Anticipating that the respondent city officials likely would oppose the petition by arguing that the applicable state laws are unconstitutional, the petition maintained that such a claim could not justify the officials' issuance of same-sex marriage licenses in violation of state law "because article III, section 3.5 of the California Constitution prohibits administrative agencies from declaring state laws unconstitutional in the absence of an appellate court determination." The petition asserted that "[t]he county is a political subdivision of the state charged with administering state government, and local registrars of vital statistics act as state officers. The state's agents at the local level simply cannot refuse to enforce state law."

Although the Attorney General's petition acknowledged that the court could grant the relief requested in the petition without reaching the substantive question of the constitutionality of the California statutes limiting marriage to a man and a woman, the petition urged that we also resolve the substantive constitutional issue at this time, arguing that "[a]s the issues presented are pure legal issues, and there is no need for the development of a factual record, these issues are ready for this Court's review."

On February 25, 2004, two days prior to the filing of the petition in *Lockyer,* the petition in *Lewis* was filed in this court. In *Lewis,* three residents and taxpayers in the City and County of San Francisco sought a writ of mandate to compel the county clerk to cease and desist issuing marriage licenses to couples other than those who meet state law marriage requirements and on forms that do not comply with state law license requirements, and also sought an immediate stay pending the court's determination of the petition.

After receiving the petitions in *Lockyer* and *Lewis,* we requested that the city file an opposition to the petition in each case. The city filed its opposition to the petitions arguing that the provisions of article III, section 3.5 of the California Constitution do not apply to local officials and that, in any event, under the supremacy clause of the United States Constitution, California Constitution article III, section 3.5 could not properly be applied to preclude a local official from refusing to enforce a statute that the official believes violates the federal Constitution. With regard to the question of the constitutionality of California's statutory ban on same-sex marriages, the opposition maintained that "the issue is one best left to the lower courts in the first instance to undertake the extensive fact-finding that will be necessary."

On March 11, 2004, we issued an order in both *Lockyer* and *Lewis* directing the city officials to show cause why a writ of mandate should not issue requiring the officials to apply and abide by the current California marriage statutes in the absence of a judicial determination that the statutory provisions are unconstitutional. Pending our determination of these matters, we directed the officials to enforce the existing marriage statutes and refrain from issuing marriage licenses or certificates not authorized by such provisions.

II

It is well settled in California that "the Legislature has full control of the subject of marriage and may fix the conditions under which the marital status may be created or terminated...." "The regulation of marriage and divorce is solely within the province of the Legislature, except as the same may be restricted by the Constitution." In view of the primacy of the Legislature's role in this area, we begin by setting forth the relevant statutes relating to marriage that have some bearing on the issue before us. As we shall see, the Legislature has dealt with the subject of marriage in considerable detail.

The provisions regarding the validity of marriage are set forth in the Family Code. Section 300 provides in full: "*Marriage is a personal relation arising out of a civil contract between a man and a woman,* to which the consent of the parties capable of making that contract is necessary...." (emphasis added by the Court).

[The Court set out numerous other statutes pertaining to marriage, including those prescribing in detail the content of official state marriage forms and the responsibilities of county officials to issue licenses and register certificates.]

III

In light of several questions raised by the briefs filed by the city in this court, we begin with a brief discussion of the respective roles of state and local officials with regard to the enforcement of the marriage statutes (in particular, the issuance of marriage licenses and the registering of marriage certificates), and of the nature of the duties of local officials under the applicable statutes.

A

[T]he Legislature has enacted a comprehensive scheme regulating marriage in California, establishing the substantive standards for eligibility for marriage and setting forth in detail the procedures to be followed and the public officials who are entrusted with carrying out these procedures. In light of both the historical understanding reflected in this statutory scheme and the statutes' repeated emphasis on the importance of having uniform rules and procedures apply throughout the state to the subject of marriage, there can be no question but that marriage is a matter of "statewide concern" rather than a "municipal affair" and that state statutes dealing with marriage prevail over any conflicting local charter provision, ordinance, or practice.

Furthermore, the relevant statutes also reveal that the only local officials to whom the state has granted authority to act with regard to marriage licenses and marriage certificates are *the county clerk* and *the county recorder*. The statutes do not authorize the mayor of a city (or city and county, as is San Francisco) or any other comparable local official to take any action with regard to the process of issuing marriage licenses or registering marriage certificates. Although a mayor may have authority under a local charter to supervise and control the actions of a county clerk or county recorder with regard to other subjects, a mayor has no authority to expand or vary the authority of a county clerk or county recorder to grant marriage licenses or register marriage certificates under the governing state statutes, or to direct those officials to act in contravention of those statutes. [When a state statute requires local officials to discharge state duties, the local official acts as a state officer.]

Accordingly, to the extent the mayor purported to "direct" or "instruct" the county clerk and the county recorder to take specific actions with regard to the issuance of marriage licenses or the registering of marriage certificates, we conclude he exceeded the scope of his authority. Furthermore, if the county clerk or the county recorder acted in this case in contravention of the applicable statutes solely at the behest of the mayor and not on the basis of the official's own determination that the statutes are unconstitutional, such official also would appear to have acted improperly by abdicating the statutory responsibility imposed directly on him or her as a state officer.

The city maintains that when, as here, a public official has asserted in a mandate proceeding that a statutory provision that the official has refused to enforce is unconstitutional, a court may not issue a writ of mandate to compel the official to perform a ministerial duty prescribed by the statute unless the court first determines that the statute is constitutional. If, however, the controlling rule of law requires such an official to carry out a ministerial duty dictated by statute unless and until the statute has been judicially determined to be unconstitutional, it follows that such an official cannot *compel* a court to rule on the constitutional issue by refusing to apply the statute and that a writ of mandate properly may issue, without a judicial determination of the statute's constitutionality, directing the official to comply with the statute unless and until the statute has been judicially determined to be unconstitutional. Accordingly, in deciding whether a writ of mandate should issue, it is appropriate to determine whether the city officials were obligated to comply with the ministerial duty prescribed by statute without regard to their view of the constitutionality of the statute.

B

In addition, we believe it is appropriate to clarify at the outset that, under the statutes reviewed above, the duties of the county clerk and the county recorder at issue in this case properly are characterized as *ministerial* rather than discretionary. When the substantive and procedural requirements established by the state marriage statutes are satisfied, the county clerk and the county recorder each has the respective mandatory duty to issue a marriage license and record a certificate of registry of marriage; in that circumstance, the officials have no discretion to withhold a marriage license or refuse to record a marriage certificate. By the same token, when the statutory requirements have not been met, the county clerk and the county recorder are not granted any discretion under the statutes to issue a marriage license or register a certificate of registry of marriage. As we stated recently: " 'A ministerial act is an act that a public officer is required to perform in a prescribed manner in obedience to the mandate of legal authority and without regard to his own judgment or opinion concerning such act's propriety or impropriety, when a given state of facts exists.' "

Thus, the issue before us is whether under California law the authority of a local executive official, charged with the ministerial duty of enforcing a state statute, includes the authority to disregard the statutory requirements when the official is of the opinion the provision is unconstitutional but there has been no judicial determination of unconstitutionality.

IV

[T]he city maintains that a local executive official's general duty and authority to apply the law includes the authority to refuse to apply a statute whenever the official believes it to be unconstitutional, even in the absence of a judicial determination of unconstitutionality and even when the duty prescribed by the statute is ministerial. The city asserts that such authority flows from every public official's duty "to conform [his or her] acts to constitutional norms." The Attorney General argues, by contrast, that it is well established that a duly enacted statute is presumed to be constitutional, and he maintains that "the prospect of local governmental officials unilaterally defying state laws with which they disagree is untenable and inconsistent with the precepts of our legal system."

As we shall explain, we conclude that a local public official, charged with the ministerial duty of enforcing a statute, generally does not have the authority, in

---

5. As indicated, the issue presented in this case is purely whether a local official may refuse to apply a statute solely on the basis of the official's view that the statute is uncon-

the absence of a judicial determination of unconstitutionality, to refuse to enforce the statute on the basis of the official's view that it is unconstitutional.[5]

A

In the initial petitions filed in this matter, petitioners relied primarily on the provisions of article III, section 3.5 of the California Constitution (hereafter generally referred to as article III, section 3.5) in maintaining that the challenged actions of the local officials were improper.

Article III, section 3.5 provides in full:

> An administrative agency, including an administrative agency created by the Constitution or an initiative statute, has no power:
>
> (a) To declare a statute unenforceable, or refuse to enforce a statute, on the basis of its being unconstitutional unless an appellate court has made a determination that such statute is unconstitutional.
>
> (b) To declare a statute unconstitutional.
>
> (c) To declare a statute unenforceable, or to refuse to enforce a statute on the basis that federal law or federal regulations prohibit the enforcement of such statute unless an appellate court has made a determination that the enforcement of such statute is prohibited by federal law or federal regulations."

[The Attorney General argued that Article III, section 3.5 applies to both state and local agencies; the city argued that it only applies to state agencies, not local agencies.]

As we shall explain, we have determined that we need not (and thus do not) decide in this case whether the actions of the local executive officials here at issue fall within the scope or reach of article III, section 3.5, because we conclude that prior to the adoption of article III, section 3.5, it already was established under California law—as in the overwhelming majority of other states—that a local executive official, charged with a ministerial duty, generally lacks authority to determine that a statute is unconstitutional and on that basis refuse to apply the statute. Because the adoption of article III, section 3.5 plainly *did not grant or expand* the authority of local executive officials to

_____

stitutional. There is no claim here that the officials acted as they did because of questions regarding the proper interpretation of the applicable statutes or because of doubts as to which of two or more competing statutory provisions to apply. Here, the officials acknowledge that the current California statutes limit marriage to a union between a man and a woman, and concede that they refused to apply the relevant statutory provisions solely because of a belief that this statutory requirement is unconstitutional.

determine that a statute is unconstitutional and to act in contravention of the statute's terms on the basis of such a determination, we conclude that the city officials do not possess this authority and that the actions challenged in the present case were unauthorized and invalid.

B

We begin with a few basic legal principles that were well established prior to the adoption of article III, section 3.5 in 1978.

First, one of the fundamental principles of our constitutional system of government is that a statute, once duly enacted, "is presumed to be constitutional. Unconstitutionality must be clearly shown, and doubts will be resolved in favor of its validity." [Citations to treatises and cases omitted.]

Second, it is equally well established that when, as here, a public official's authority to act in a particular area derives wholly from statute, the scope of that authority is measured by the terms of the governing statute. "It is well settled in this state and elsewhere, that when a statute prescribes the particular method in which a public officer, acting under a special authority, shall perform his duties, the mode is the measure of the power." [Citations to cases omitted.]

The city has not identified any provision in the California Constitution or in the applicable statutes that purports to grant the county clerk or the county recorder (or any other local official) the authority to determine the constitutionality of the statutes each public official has a ministerial duty to enforce. Instead, the city's position appears to be that a public executive official's duty to follow the law (including the Constitution) includes the implied or inherent authority to refuse to follow an applicable statute whenever the official personally believes the statute to be unconstitutional, even though there has been no judicial determination of the statute's unconstitutionality and despite the existence of the rule that a duly enacted statute is presumed to be constitutional.

As we shall see, the California authorities that were in place prior to the adoption of article III, section 3.5, do not support the city's position.

C

Although in this case we need not determine the scope of article III, section 3.5, the historical background that led to the proposal and adoption of that constitutional provision in 1978 nonetheless provides a useful starting point for our analysis. As this court explained, "[a]rticle III, section 3.5, was placed on the ballot by a unanimous vote of the Legislature in apparent response to this court's decision in *Southern Pac. Transportation v. Public Utilities Com.* (1976) 18 Cal.3d 308 (hereafter *Southern Pacific*), in which the majority held that the Public Utilities Commission had the power to declare a state statute unconstitutional." Accordingly, the decision in *Southern Pacific* is an appropriate place to begin. [In *Southern Pacific*, the Public Utilities Commission (PUC) concluded that a state statute dealing with railroad crossings was an unconstitutional delegation of state police power to private interests and refused to enforce it. The California Supreme Court unanimously disagreed with this conclusion. But the court recognized that the PUC had the authority to rule on the constitutionality of the statute since the California Constitution gave the PUC broad judicial powers in conducting administrative hearings. Some language in a footnote suggested that all public officials have the duty to obey the Constitution and therefore must determine the constitutional validity of statutes they are required to enforce. Article III, section 3.5 was placed on the ballot by a unanimous vote of the Legislature apparently in response to this expansive footnote language and with the purpose of overruling it. But no case – either before or after *Southern Pacific* – suggested that "*a local executive official such as a county clerk,* who is charged with the *ministerial* duty to enforce a statute, has the authority to exercise judicial power by determining whether a statute is constitutional." In *Southern Pacific*, the PUC's authority was broader than local officials charged with ministerial duties because it had quasi-judicial authority under the California Constitution to determine the constitutionality of statutes in administrative hearings. The Court reviews other decisions relevant to this point.]

In light of the foregoing review of the relevant case law, we believe that after this court's decision in *Southern Pacific* the state of the law in this area was clear: administrative agencies that had been granted judicial or quasi-judicial power by the California Constitution possessed the authority, in the exercise of their administrative functions, to determine the constitutionality of statutes, but agencies that had not been granted such power under the California Constitution lacked such authority. Accordingly, these decisions recognize that, under California law, the determination whether a statute is unconstitutional and need not be obeyed is an exercise of judicial power and thus is reserved to those officials or entities that have been granted such power by the California Constitution.[6]

Given the foregoing decisions and their reasoning, it appears evident that under California law as it existed prior to the adoption of article III, section 3.5 of the California Constitution, *a local executive official,* such as a county

---

6. In this regard it is worth noting that article III, section 3 of the California Constitution explicitly provides: "The powers of State government are legislative, executive, and judicial. Persons charged with the exercise of one power may not exercise either of the others *except as permitted by this Constitution.*" (Italics added by the Court.)

clerk or county recorder, possessed no authority to determine the constitutionality of a statute that the official had a ministerial duty to enforce. If, in the absence of a grant of judicial authority from the California Constitution, an administrative agency that was required by law to reach its decisions only after conducting court-like quasi-judicial proceedings did not generally possess the authority to pass on the constitutionality of a statute that the agency was required to enforce, it follows even more so that a local executive official who is charged simply with the ministerial duty of enforcing a statute, and who generally acts without any quasi-judicial authority or procedure whatsoever, did not possess such authority. As indicated above, we are unaware of any California case that suggests such a public official has been granted judicial or quasi-judicial power by the California Constitution.

Accordingly, we conclude that at the time article III, section 3.5 was adopted, it was clear under California law that a local executive official did not have the authority to determine that a statute is unconstitutional or to refuse to enforce a statute in the absence of a judicial determination that the statute is unconstitutional.

The adoption of article III, section 3.5, of course, effectively overruled the majority's holding in *Southern Pacific* and amended the California Constitution to provide that "[a]n administrative agency, *including an administrative agency created by the Constitution or an initiative statute, has no power ... [t]o ...* refuse to enforce a statute on the basis of its being unconstitutional unless an appellate court has made a determination that such statute is unconstitutional." (Italics added.) As we already have noted, we need not and do not decide in this case what effect the adoption of article III, section 3.5 has on the authority of local executive officials, because it is abundantly clear that this constitutional amendment did not *expand* the authority of such officials so as to permit them to refuse to enforce a statute solely on the basis of their view that the statute is unconstitutional. Accordingly, we conclude that under California law a local executive official generally lacks such authority.

E

Some academic commentators, while confirming that as a general rule executive officials must comply with duly enacted statutes even when the officials believe the provisions are unconstitutional, have suggested that there may be room to recognize an exception to this general rule in instances in which a public official's refusal to apply the statute would provide the most practical

---

7. A number of law review articles suggest that the federal Constitution should be interpreted as permitting the President of the United States to refuse to enforce a statute that

or reasonable means of enabling the question of the statute's constitutionality to be brought before a court.[7]

Although it may be appropriate in some circumstances for a public entity or public official to refuse or decline to enforce a statute as a means of bringing the constitutionality of the statute before a court for judicial resolution, it is nonetheless clear that such an exception does not justify the actions of the local officials at issue in the present case. Here, there existed a clear and readily available means, other than the officials' wholesale defiance of the applicable statutes, to ensure that the constitutionality of the current marriage statutes would be decided by a court. If the local officials charged with the ministerial duty of issuing marriage licenses and registering marriage certificates believed the state's current marriage statutes are unconstitutional and should be tested in court, they could have denied a same-sex couple's request for a marriage license and advised the couple to challenge the denial in superior court. *That* procedure—a lawsuit brought by a couple who have been denied a license under existing statutes—is the procedure that was utilized to challenge the constitutionality of California's antimiscegenation statute, and the procedure apparently utilized in all of the other same-sex marriage cases that have been litigated recently in other states. The city cannot plausibly claim that the desire to obtain a judicial ruling on the constitutional issue justified the wholesale defiance of the applicable statutes that occurred here.

Accordingly, the city cannot defend the challenged actions on the ground that such actions were necessary to obtain a judicial determination of the constitutionality of California's marriage statutes.

F

The city also relies on the circumstance that each of the city officials in question took an oath of office to "support and defend" the state and federal Constitutions, suggesting that a public official would violate his or her oath of office were the official to perform a ministerial act under a statute that the

---

the President believes is unconstitutional. Other scholars, however, have made a strong argument that the history of the proceedings of the constitutional convention that drafted the federal Constitution, and in particular the Founders' explicit rejection of a proposal for an absolute presidential veto, refutes such an interpretation. To date, no court has accepted the contention that the President possesses such authority. (See, e.g., *Ameron, Inc. v. U.S. Army Corps of Eng'rs* (3d Cir.1986) 787 F.2d 875, 889 & fn. 11 ["This claim of right for the President to *declare* statutes unconstitutional and to declare his refusal to execute them, as distinguished from his undisputed right to veto, criticize, or even refuse to defend in court, statutes which he regards as unconstitutional, is dubious at best."])

official personally believes violates the Constitution. In our view, this contention clearly lacks merit.

As Justice Mosk explained in his concurring and dissenting opinion in *Southern Pacific*, a public official "faithfully upholds the Constitution by complying with the mandates of the Legislature, leaving to courts the decision whether those mandates are invalid." A public official does not honor his or her oath to defend the Constitution by taking action in contravention of the restrictions of his or her office or authority and justifying such action by reference to his or her personal constitutional views. For example, it is clear that a justice of this court or of an intermediate appellate court does not act in contravention of his or her oath of office when the justice follows a controlling constitutional decision of a higher court even though the justice personally believes that the controlling decision was wrongly decided and that the Constitution actually requires the opposite result. On the contrary, the oath to support and defend the Constitution requires a public official to act within the constraints of our constitutional system, not to disregard presumptively valid statutes and take action in violation of such statutes on the basis of the official's own determination of what the Constitution means. (See also *State v. State Board of Equalizers* (1922) 94 So. 681, 682–683 ["The contention that the oath of a public official requiring him to obey the Constitution places upon him the duty or obligation to determine whether an act is constitutional before he will obey it is ... without merit. The fallacy in it is that every act of the legislature is presumed constitutional until judicially declared otherwise, and the oath of office 'to obey the Constitution' means to obey the Constitution, not as the officer decides, but as judicially determined."].)

G

The city further contends that a general rule requiring an executive official to comply with an existing statute unless and until the statute has been judicially determined to be unconstitutional is impractical and would lead to intolerable circumstances. The city posits a hypothetical example of a public official faced with a statute that is identical in all respects to another statute that a court already has determined is unconstitutional, and suggests it would be absurd to require the official to apply the clearly invalid statute in that instance.

Whatever force this argument might have in a case in which a governing decision previously has found an identical statute unconstitutional or in which the invalidity of the statute is so patent or clearly established that no reasonable official could believe the statute is constitutional, the argument plainly is of no avail here. Although we have no occasion in this case to determine the constitutionality of the current California marriage statutes, we can say with confidence that the asserted invalidity of those statutes certainly is not so patent or clearly established that no reasonable official could believe that the current California marriage statutes are valid. Indeed, the city cannot point to any judicial decision that has held a statute limiting marriage to a man and a woman unconstitutional under the California or federal Constitution. Instead, the city relies on state court decisions from Massachusetts, Vermont, and Hawaii, that, in interpreting their own state constitutions, assertedly have found similar statutory restrictions to violate provisions of their state's own constitution. A significant number of other state and federal courts, however, have reached a contrary conclusion and have upheld the constitutional validity of such a restriction on marriage under both the federal Constitution and other state constitutions. Although the state court decisions from Massachusetts, Vermont, and Hawaii relied upon by the city surely would be of interest to a California court faced with the question whether the current California marriage statutes violate the California Constitution, a California court would be equally interested in the decisions of the courts that have reached a contrary conclusion (and in the reasoning of the minority opinions in the state court decisions relied upon by the city). In light of the absence of any California authority directly on point and the sharp division of judicial views expressed in the out-of-state decisions that have considered similar constitutional challenges, this plainly is not an instance in which the invalidity of the California marriage statutes is so patent or clearly established that no reasonable official could believe that the statutes are constitutional. Therefore, this case does not fall within any narrow exception that may apply to instances in which it would be absurd or unreasonable to require a public official to comply with a statute that any reasonable official would conclude is unconstitutional.

H

Accordingly, we conclude that, under California law, the city officials had no authority to refuse to perform their ministerial duty in conformity with the current California marriage statutes on the basis of their view that the statutory limitation of marriage to a couple comprised of a man and a woman is unconstitutional.

I

In addition to the California decisions reviewed above and the weight of judicial authority from other jurisdictions, consideration of the practical consequences of a contrary rule further demonstrates the unsoundness of the city's position.

To begin with, most local executive officials have no legal training and thus lack the relevant expertise to make constitutional determinations. Although every individual (lawyer or nonlawyer) is, of course, free to form his or her own opinion of what the Constitution means and how it should be interpreted and applied, a local executive official has no authority to impose his or her personal view on others by refusing to comply with a ministerial duty imposed by statute.

Second, if, as the city maintains, a local official were to possess the authority to act on the basis of his or her own constitutional determination, such an official generally would arrive at that determination without affording the affected individuals any due process safeguards and, in particular, without providing any opportunity for those supporting the constitutionality of the statutes to be heard. In its opposition to the initial petition filed in this case, the city urged this court not to immediately accept jurisdiction over the substantive question of the constitutionality of California's marriage laws at this time, because that question properly could be determined only after a full presentation of evidence before a trial court. The city officials themselves, however, made their own constitutional determination without conducting any such evidentiary hearing or taking other measures designed to protect the rights of those who maintain that the statute is constitutional. Thus, despite the settled rule that a duly enacted statute is presumed to be constitutional, under the city's proposed rule a local executive official would be free to determine that a statute is unconstitutional and refuse to enforce it, without providing even the most rudimentary of due process procedures—notice and an opportunity to be heard—to anyone directly affected by the official's action.

Third, there are thousands of elected and appointed public officials in California's 58 counties charged with the ministerial duty of enforcing thousands of state statutes. If each official were empowered to decide whether or not to carry out each ministerial act based upon the official's own personal judgment of the constitutionality of an underlying statute, the enforcement of statutes would become haphazard, leading to confusion and chaos and thwarting the uniform statewide treatment that state statutes generally are intended to provide. Although in the past the multiplicity of public officials performing similar ministerial acts under a single statute never has posed a problem in this regard, that is undoubtedly true only because most officials never imagined they had the authority to determine the constitutionality of a statute that they have a ministerial duty to enforce. Were we to hold that such officials possess this authority, it is not difficult to anticipate that private individuals who oppose enforcement of a statute and question its constitutionality would attempt to influence ministerial officials in various locales to exercise—on behalf of such opponents—the officials' newly recognized authority. The circumstance that many local officials have no legal training would only exacerbate the problem. As a consequence, the uneven enforcement of statutory mandates in different local jurisdictions likely would become a significant concern.

Fourth, the confused state of affairs arising from diverse actions by a multiplicity of local officials frequently would continue for a considerable period of time, because under the city's proposed rule a court generally could not order a public official to comply with the challenged statute until the court actually had determined that it was constitutional. In view of the many instances in which a constitutional challenge to a statute entails lengthy litigation, the lack of uniform treatment afforded to similarly situated citizens throughout the state often would be a long-term phenomenon.

These practical considerations simply confirm the soundness of the established rule that an executive official generally does not have the authority to refuse to comply with a ministerial duty imposed by statute on the basis of the official's opinion that the statute is unconstitutional.

The city further claims, however, that even if *California law* does not recognize the authority of a local official to refuse to comply with a statutorily mandated ministerial duty absent a judicial determination that the statute is unconstitutional, under the federal supremacy clause (U.S. Const., art. VI, §2) California lacks the power to require a public official to comply with a state statute that the official believes violates the federal Constitution. Although in the present case the mayor's initial letter to the county clerk relied solely upon the asserted unconstitutionality of the California marriage statutes under the *California* Constitution, the city, in the opposition filed in this court, for the first time advanced the position that the action taken by the city officials was based, at least in part, on their belief that the California statutes violate the *federal* Constitution, and the city now rests its supremacy clause claim on this newly asserted belief. Putting aside the question of the bona fides of this belatedly proffered rationale, we conclude that, in any event, the federal supremacy clause provides no support for the city's argument.

The city has not cited any case holding that the federal Constitution prohibits a state from defining the authority of a state's executive officials in a manner that requires such officials to comply with a clearly applicable statute unless and until such a statute is judicially determined to be unconstitutional, nor any case holding that the federal Constitution compels a state to permit every executive official, state or local, to refuse to enforce an applicable statutory provision whenever the official personally believes the statute violates the federal Constitution.

Furthermore, numerous pronouncements by the United States Supreme Court directly refute the city's contention that the supremacy clause or any other provision of the federal Constitution embodies such a principle. To begin with, the high court's position on the proper role of federal executive officials with regard to constitutional determinations is instructive. In *Davies Warehouse Co. v. Bowles* (1944) 321 U.S. 144, 152–153, for example, in response to the plaintiff's contention that under one proposed reading of the applicable statute "the federal Price Administrator [an executive official] would have to decide whether the state regulation is constitutional before he should recognize it," the United States Supreme Court stated: "We cannot give weight to this view of [the Price Administrator's] functions, which we think it unduly magnifies. *State statutes, like federal ones, are entitled to the presumption of constitutionality until their invalidity is judicially declared. Certainly no power to adjudicate constitutional issues is conferred on the Administrator.... We think the Administrator will not be remiss in his duties if he assumes the constitutionality of state regulatory statutes, under both state and federal constitutions, in the absence of a contrary judicial determination.*" (Italics added.) In light of the high court's repeated statements that federal executive officials generally lack authority to determine the constitutionality of statutes, the city's claim that the federal supremacy clause itself grants a state or local official the authority to refuse to enforce a statute that the official believes is unconstitutional is plainly untenable.

Furthermore, there are several earlier United States Supreme Court cases that even more directly refute the city's contention. *Smith v. Indiana* was a case, arising from the Indiana state courts, in which a county auditor had refused to grant a statutorily authorized exemption to a taxpayer because the auditor believed the exemption violated the federal Constitution. A mandate action was filed against the auditor, and the state courts permitted the auditor to raise and litigate the asserted unconstitutionality of the statute as a defense in the mandate action, ultimately determining that the exemption was constitutionally permissible and directing the auditor to grant the exemption. The auditor appealed the state court decision upholding the constitutionality of the state statute to the United States Supreme Court.

In its opinion in *Smith*, the high court observed that "there are many authorities to the effect that a ministerial officer, charged by law with the duty of enforcing a certain statute, cannot refuse to perform his plain duty thereunder upon the ground that in his opinion it is repugnant to the Constitution."

In light of the foregoing high court decisions, we conclude that the California rule set forth above does not conflict with any federal constitutional requirement

VII

Finally, we must determine the appropriate scope of the relief to be ordered. As a general matter, the nature of the relief warranted in a mandate action is dependent upon the circumstances of the particular case, and a court is not necessarily limited by the prayer sought in the mandate petition but may grant the relief it deems appropriate.

In the present case, we are faced with an unusual, perhaps unprecedented, set of circumstances. Here, local public officials have purported to authorize, perform, and register literally thousands of marriages in direct violation of explicit state statutes. The Attorney General, as well as a number of local taxpayers, have filed these original mandate proceedings in this court to halt the local officials' unauthorized conduct and to compel these officials to correct or undo the numerous unlawful actions they have taken in the immediate past. As explained above, we have determined that the city officials exceeded their authority in issuing marriage licenses to, solemnizing marriages of, and registering marriage certificates on behalf of, same-sex couples. Under these circumstances, we conclude that it is appropriate in this mandate proceeding not only to order the city officials to comply with the applicable statutes in the future, but also to direct the officials to take all necessary steps to remedy the continuing effect of their past unlawful actions, including correction of all relevant official records and notification of affected individuals of the invalidity of the officials' actions.

In light of the clear terms of Family Code section 300 *defining* marriage as a "personal relationship arising out of a civil contract between a man and a woman" and the legislative history of this provision demonstrating that the purpose of this limitation was to "prohibit persons of the same sex from entering lawful marriage," we believe it plainly follows that all same-sex marriages authorized, solemnized, or registered by the city officials must be considered void and of no legal effect from their inception. Although this precise issue has not previously been presented under California law, every court that has considered the question has determined that when state law limits marriage to a union between a man and a woman, a same-sex marriage performed in violation of state law is void and of no legal effect. The city has not cited any case in which a same-sex marriage, performed in contravention of a state statute that bans such marriages and that has not judicially been held unconstitutional, has been given any legal effect.

The city and amici curiae additionally contend that we cannot properly determine the validity or invalidity of the existing same-sex marriages in this proceeding because the parties to a marriage are indispensable parties to any legal action seeking to invalidate a marriage, and the thousands of same-sex couples whose marriages were authorized and registered by the local authorities are not formal parties to the present mandate proceeding. The city relies on cases involving actions that have been brought to annul a particular marriage on the basis of facts peculiar to that marriage, in which the courts have held the parties to the marriage to be indispensable parties. In the present instance, by contrast, the question of the validity or invalidity of a same-sex marriage does not depend upon any facts that are peculiar to any individual same-sex marriage, but rather is a purely legal question applicable to all existing same-sex marriages, and rests on the circumstance that the governing state statute limits marriage to a union between a man and a woman. Under ordinary principles of *stare decisis*, an appellate decision holding that, under current California statutes, a same-sex marriage performed in California is void from its inception effectively would resolve that legal issue with respect to all couples who had participated in same-sex marriages, even though such couples had not been parties to the original action. Because the validity or invalidity of same-sex marriages under current California law involves only a pure question of law, couples who are not formal parties to this action are in no different position than if this question of law had been presented and resolved in an action involving some other same-sex couple rather than in an action in which the legal arguments regarding the validity of such marriages have been vigorously asserted not only by the city officials who authorized and registered such marriages but also by various amici curiae representing similarly situated same-sex couples. Requiring a separate legal proceeding to be brought to invalidate each of the thousands of same-sex marriages, or requiring each of the thousands of same-sex couples to be named and served as parties in the present action, would add nothing of substance to this proceeding.

The city and *amici curiae* further contend that it would violate the due process rights of the same-sex couples who obtained marriage licenses and had their marriage certificates registered by the local officials for this court to determine the validity of same-sex marriages without giving the couples notice and an opportunity to be heard. To begin with, there may be some question whether an individual who, through the deliberate unauthorized conduct of a public official, obtains a license, permit, or other status that clearly is not authorized by state law, possesses a constitutionally protected property or liberty interest that gives rise to procedural due process guarantees. In any event, these same-sex couples have not been denied the right to meaningfully participate in these proceedings. Although we have not permitted them to intervene formally in these actions as parties, our order denying intervention to a number of such couples explicitly was without prejudice to participation as amicus curiae, and numerous amicus curiae briefs have been filed on behalf of such couples directly addressing the question of the validity of the existing same-sex marriages. Accordingly, the legal arguments of such couples with regard to the question of the validity of the existing same-sex marriages have been heard and fully considered. Furthermore, under the procedure we adopt below, before the city takes corrective action with regard to the record of any particular same-sex marriage license or same-sex marriage certificate, each affected couple will receive individual notice and an opportunity to show that the holding of the present opinion is not applicable to the couple.

Finally, the city urges this court to postpone the determination of the validity of the same-sex marriages that already have been performed and registered until a court rules on the substantive constitutional challenges to the California marriage statutes that are now pending in superior court. From a practical perspective, we believe it would not be prudent or wise to leave the validity of these marriages in limbo for what might be a substantial period of time given the potential confusion (for third parties, such as employers, insurers, or other governmental entities, as well as for the affected couples) that such an uncertain status inevitably would entail.

In any event, we believe such a delay in decision is unwarranted on more fundamental grounds. As we have explained, because Family Code section 300 clearly limits marriage in California to a marriage between a man and a woman and flatly prohibits persons of the same sex from lawfully marrying in California, the governing authorities establish that the same-sex marriages that already have been performed are void and of no legal effect *from their inception*. In view of this well-established rule, we do not believe it would be responsible or appropriate for this court to fail at this time to inform the parties to the same-sex marriages and other persons whose legal rights and responsibilities may depend upon the validity or invalidity of these marriages that these marriages are invalid, notwithstanding the pendency of numerous lawsuits challenging the constitutionality of California's marriage statutes. Withholding or delaying a ruling on the current validity of the existing same-sex marriages might lead numerous persons to make fundamental changes in their lives or otherwise proceed on the basis of erroneous expectations, creating potentially irreparable harm.

Although the city and the *amici curiae* representing same-sex couples suggest that these couples would prefer to live with uncertainty rather than be told at this point that the marriages are invalid, in light of the explicit terms of Family Code section 300 and the warning included in the same-sex marriage license applications provided by the city, these couples clearly were on notice that the validity of their marriages was dependent upon whether a court would find that the city officials had authority to allow same-sex marriages. Now that we have confirmed that the city officials lack this authority, we do not believe that these couples have a persuasive equitable claim to have the validity of the marriages left in doubt at this point in time, creating uncertainty and potential harm to others who may need to know whether the marriages are valid or not. Had the current constitutional challenges to the California marriage statutes followed the traditional and proper course, no same-sex marriage would have been conducted in California prior to a judicial determination that the current California marriage statutes are unconstitutional. Accordingly, as part of the remedy for the city officials' unauthorized and unlawful actions, we believe it is appropriate to make clear that the same-sex marriages that already have purportedly come into being must be considered void from their inception. Of course, should the current California statutes limiting marriage to a man and a woman ultimately be repealed or be held unconstitutional, the affected couples then would be free to obtain lawfully authorized marriage licenses, have their marriages lawfully solemnized, and lawfully register their marriage certificates.

Accordingly, to remedy the effects of the city officials' unauthorized actions, we shall direct the county clerk and the county recorder of the City and County of San Francisco to take the following corrective actions under the supervision of the California Director of Health Services, who, by statute, has general supervisory authority over the marriage license and marriage certificate process. The county clerk and the county recorder are directed to (1) identify all same-sex couples to whom the officials issued marriage licenses, solemnized marriage ceremonies, or registered marriage certificates, (2) notify these couples that this court has determined that same-sex marriages that have been performed in California are void from their inception and a legal nullity, and that these officials have been directed to correct their records to reflect the invalidity of these marriage licenses and marriages, (3) provide these couples an opportunity to demonstrate that their marriages are not same-sex marriages and thus that the official records of their marriage licenses and marriages should not be revised, (4) offer to refund, upon request, all marriage-related fees paid by or on behalf of same-sex couples, and (5) make appropriate corrections to all relevant records.

VIII

As anyone familiar with the docket of the United States Supreme Court, of this court, or of virtually any appellate court in this nation is aware, many statutes currently in force may give rise to constitutional challenges, and not infrequently the constitutional questions presented involve issues upon which reasonable persons, including reasonable jurists, may disagree. If every public official who is under a statutory duty to perform a ministerial act were free to refuse to perform that act based solely on the official's view that the underlying statute is unconstitutional, any semblance of a uniform rule of law quickly would disappear, and constant and widespread judicial intervention would be required to permit the ordinary mechanisms of government to function. This, of course, is not the system of law with which we are familiar. Under long established principles, a statute, once enacted, is presumed to be constitutional until it has been judicially determined to be unconstitutional.

An executive official, of course, is free to criticize existing statutes, to advocate their amendment or repeal, and to voice an opinion as to their constitutionality or unconstitutionality. As we have explained, however, an executive official who is charged with the ministerial duty of enforcing a statute generally has an obligation to execute that duty in the absence of a judicial determination that the statute is unconstitutional, regardless of the official's personal view of the constitutionality of the statute.

In this case, the city has suggested that a contrary rule—one under which a public official charged with a ministerial duty would be free to make up his or her own mind whether a statute is constitutional and whether it must be obeyed—is necessary to protect the rights of minorities. But history demonstrates that members of minority groups, as well as individuals who are unpopular or powerless, have the most to lose when the rule of law is abandoned—even for what appears, to the person departing from the law, to be a just end.[8] As observed at the outset of this opinion, granting every public official the authority to disregard a ministerial statutory duty on the basis of the official's opinion that the statute is unconstitutional would be fundamentally inconsistent with our political system's commitment to John Adams' vision of a government where official action is determined not by the opinion of an individual officeholder—but by the rule of law.

Notes and Questions

1. The Attorney General argued that the Court should resolve the substantive constitutional question since it presented "pure legal issues;" the City argued that extensive fact-finding in a trial court was necessary to resolve this question. What facts need to be established to resolve the issue? Why did the Court decline to rule on the substantive question of the constitutionality of the California statutes limiting marriage to a union between a man and a

---

8. The pronouncement of Sir Thomas More in the well known passage from Robert Bolt's *A Man For All Seasons* comes to mind:

> "Roper: So now you'd give the Devil benefit of law!
>
> "More: Yes. What would you do? Cut a great road through the law to get to the Devil?
>
> "Roper: I'd cut down every law in England to do that!
>
> "More: Oh? And when the last law was down, and the Devil turned round on you—where would you hide, Roper, the laws all being flat? This country's planted thick with laws from coast to coast—man's laws, not God's—and if you cut them down—and you're just the man to do it—d'you really think you could stand upright in the winds that would blow then? Yes, I'd give the Devil benefit of law, for my own safety's sake." (Bolt, *A Man for All Seasons* (1962) p. 66.)

woman? Wouldn't it be preferable to actually resolve the matter instead of perpetuating the controversy by deferring the decision to another day?

2. Procedurally, the case came before the court on petitions by the Attorney General and some San Francisco taxpayers for an original writ of mandate or other relief. A writ of mandate is an order by a court to compel performance of a ministerial duty. Under the California Code of Civil Procedure §1085, the writ may be issued by any court, including the Supreme Court. But under the Rule 56 of the California Rules of Court, if a petition for a writ of mandate could have been filed first in a lower court, it must explain why the reviewing court should issue the writ as an original matter. In other words, if the petitioner wants to leap-frog over the lower courts, it has to explain why. While there are no set criteria for the exceptional circumstances under which the Supreme Court may decide to entertain such an original petition, it has done so "where some emergency exists *or* the public welfare is involved." *Roma Macaroni Factory v. Giambastiani*, 27 P.2d 371 (Cal. 1933). This procedure is truly extraordinary in that the petitioners were able to obtain a hearing and relief in the California Supreme Court without following the normal procedure of filing the action in the superior court, appealing to the intermediate appellate court, and petitioning the Supreme Court for discretionary review. Does the *Lockyer* case present an emergency or public welfare issue that justifies this extraordinary exercise of original jurisdiction?

3. Our courts require that petitioners have "standing" to seek court relief. That means that the parties must have a real stake in the outcome of the case; a speculative or hypothetical injury is not sufficient. Does the Attorney General have standing in this case? Do the taxpayers?

4. Why does the Court consider marriage to be a state matter rather than a local matter? Can local governments impose additional requirements on access to marriage beyond those contained in the state statutes? For example, can county health departments require blood tests for sexually-transmitted diseases? Can county officials charge a fee for issuing a marriage license or registering a marriage certificate?

5. If the substantive question of the constitutionality of the California marriage statutes cannot be brought before the Court by the county recorder's challenge to the constitutionality of the statutes, how can the issue be raised and by whom?

6. California Constitution III Section 3.5 prohibits administrative agencies from declaring a state law unconstitutional in the absence of an appellate court determination that the statute is unconstitutional. This was the principle argument of the Attorney General in support of the petition. Is San Francisco

an "administrative agency"? Is the San Francisco County Clerk? Is Mayor Gavin Newsom? Does the court resolve this question?

7. The court states: "The city has not identified any provision in the California Constitution or in the applicable statutes that purports to grant the county clerk or the county recorder (or any other local official) the authority to determine the constitutionality of the statutes each public official has a ministerial duty to enforce." Does the court cite any provision in the California Constitution or in the applicable statutes that precludes the county clerk or county recorder (or any other local official) from determining the constitutionality of the statutes the public official has a ministerial duty to enforce? Are there any constitutional or statutory provisions resolving this question?

8. The Mayor and the county officials all took an oath of office to support and defend the state and federal Constitutions. Does the Court's decision require them to violate this oath by forcing them to enforce laws they believe are unconstitutional? If they comply with the Court's order, aren't they violating their oath by failing to support the Constitution? Say, for example, they violated a state statute requiring segregation in public schools because they believed it to be unconstitutional? Or issued a marriage license in violation of a statute prohibiting interracial marriage? How can officials comply with their conflicting duties to support the Constitution and to faithfully execute the statutory law?

9. In concluding that the California statutes are unconstitutional, the Mayor relied on court decisions in other states. Are those decisions binding on the California Supreme Court? Are they persuasive? Are they relevant?

10. The City presented a hypothetical question to the Court arguing that it would be absurd to require a city official to comply with a statute where an identical statute had previously been declared unconstitutional. Why did the Court reject this argument?

11. Why did the City initially rely on the California Constitution and then add an argument based on the United States Constitution? Which would be the controlling authority? Is the current United States Supreme Court likely to find state laws limiting marriage to heterosexual couples unconstitutional?

12. In addition to legal arguments supporting its conclusion, the court also cites "practical consequences." What are the practical consequences? How persuasive is this argument?

13. In considering the scope of relief to be ordered, the Court noted that it was not necessarily limited to that requested in the mandate petition and declared the 4000 same-sex marriages void, even though it had denied the same-sex couples the opportunity to appear in the proceedings. On the other hand, the Court found that one of the problems with allowing local officials to determine the constitutionality of a state statute was that the parties would

not have "even the most rudimentary of due process procedures—notice and an opportunity to be heard—to anyone directly affected by the official's actions." Did the Court violate its own due process standards by voiding the marriages without giving the couples notice and an opportunity to be heard?

WERDEGAR, J., concurring and dissenting:

I agree with the majority that San Francisco officials violated the Family Code by licensing marriages between persons of the same sex. Accordingly, I concur in the decision to order those officials to comply with the existing marriage statutes unless and until they are determined to be unconstitutional. Because constitutional challenges are pending in the lower courts, to order city officials not to license additional same-sex marriages in the meantime is an appropriate way to preserve the status quo pending the outcome of that litigation. That, however, is the extent of my agreement with the majority.

I.

I do not join in the majority's decision to address the validity of the marriages already performed and to declare them void. My concern here is not for the future of same-sex marriage. That question is not before us and, like the majority, I intimate no view on it. My concern, rather, is for basic fairness in judicial process. The superior court is presently considering whether the state statutes that limit marriage to "a man and a woman" violate the state and federal Constitutions. The same-sex couples challenging those statutes claim the state has, without sufficient justification, denied the fundamental right to marry to a class of persons defined by gender or sexual orientation. Should the relevant statutes be held unconstitutional, the relief to which the purportedly married couples would be entitled would normally include recognition of their marriages. By analogy, interracial marriages that were void under antimiscegeny statutes at the time they were solemnized were nevertheless recognized as valid after the high court rejected those laws in *Loving v. Virginia*. By postponing a ruling on this issue, we could preserve the status quo pending the outcome of the constitutional litigation. Instead, by declaring the marriages "void and of no legal effect from their inception," the majority permanently deprives future courts of the ability to award full relief in the event the existing statutes are held unconstitutional. This premature decision can in no sense be thought to represent fair judicial process.

The majority's decision to declare the existing marriages void is unfair for the additional reason that the affected couples have not been joined as parties or given notice and an opportunity to appear. On March 12, 2004, we denied all petitions to intervene filed by affected couples. That ruling made sense at the time it was announced because our prior order of March 11, 2004, which specified the issues to be briefed and argued, did not identify the validity of the existing marriages as an issue. Only on April 14, 2004, *after* having denied the petitions to intervene, did the court identify and solicit briefing on the issue of the marriages' validity. To declare marriages void after denying requests by the purported spouses to appear in court as parties and be heard on the matter is hard to justify, to say the least.

The majority counters that "the legal arguments of such couples with regard to the question of the validity of the existing same-sex marriages have been heard and fully considered." But this is a claim a court may not in good conscience make unless it has given, to the persons whose rights it is purporting to adjudicate, notice and the opportunity to appear. This is the irreducible minimum of due process, even in cases involving numerous parties. Amicus curiae briefs, which any member of the public may ask to file and which the court has no obligation to read, cannot seriously be thought to satisfy these requirements. The majority writes that "requiring each of the thousands of same-sex couples to be named and served as parties in the present action, would add nothing of substance to this proceeding." Of course, the same argument can be made in many class actions with respect to the absent members of the class, but due process still gives each class member the right to notice and the opportunity to appear. Here, notice has been given to none of the 4,000 affected couples; and even the 11 same-sex couples who affirmatively sought to intervene were denied the opportunity to appear. What the majority has done, in effect, is to give petitioners the benefit of an action against a defendant class of same-sex couples free of the burden of procedural due process. If the majority truly desired to hear the views of the same-sex couples whose rights it is adjudicating, it would not proceed in absentia.

II.

I also do not join in the majority's unnecessary, wide-ranging comments on the respective powers of the judicial and executive branches of government.

The ostensible occasion for the majority's comments—a threat to the rule of law—seems an extravagant characterization of recent events. On March 11, 2004, when we assumed jurisdiction and issued an interim order directing San Francisco officials to cease licensing same-sex marriages, those officials immediately stopped. Apparently the only reason they had not stopped earlier is that the lower courts had denied similar applications for interim relief. While city officials evidently understood their oaths of office as commanding obedience to the Constitution rather than to the marriage statutes they believed to be unconstitutional, those officials never so much as hinted that they would not respect the authority of the courts to decide the matter. Indeed, not only did our interim order meet with immediate, unreserved compliance by city officials, but the same order apparently sufficed to recall to duty any other public officials who might privately have been thinking to follow San Francisco's lead. In the meantime, not one of California's 58 counties or over 400 municipalities has licensed a same-sex marriage.

Under these circumstances, I see no justification for asserting a broad claim of power over the executive branch. Make no mistake, the majority does assert such a claim by holding that executive officers must follow statutory rather than constitutional law until a court gives them permission in advance to do otherwise. For the judiciary to assert such power over the executive branch is fundamentally misguided. As the [United States Supreme Court] has explained, "[i]n the performance of assigned constitutional duties *each branch of the Government must initially interpret the Constitution*, and the interpretation of its powers by any branch is due great respect from the others." To recognize that an executive officer has the practical freedom to act based on an interpretation of the Constitution that may ultimately prove to be wrong does not mean the rule of law has collapsed. So long as the courts remain open to hear legal challenges to executive conduct, so long as the courts have power to enjoin such conduct pending final determination of its legality, and so long as the other branches acknowledge the courts' role as " 'ultimate interpreter of the Constitution' " in matters properly within their jurisdiction, no genuine threat to the rule of law exists. San Francisco's compliance with our interim order eloquently demonstrates this.

Furthermore, a rule requiring an executive officer to seek a court's permission before declining to comply with an apparently unconstitutional statute is fundamentally at odds with the separation of powers and, in many cases, unenforceable. The executive branch is necessarily active, managing events as they occur. The judicial branch is necessarily reactive, waiting until invited to serve as neutral referee. The executive branch does not await the courts' pleasure. A rule to the contrary, though perhaps enforceable against local officials in some cases, will be impossible to enforce against executive officers who exercise a greater share of the state's power, such as a Governor or an Attorney General. By happy tradition in this country, executive officers have generally acquiesced in the judicial branch's traditional claim of final authority to resolve constitutional disputes. (*Marbury v. Madison* (1803) 5 U.S. 137, 176.) But a court can never afford to forget that the judiciary "may truly be said to have neither Force nor Will, but merely judgment; and must ultimately depend upon the aid of the executive arm even for the efficacy of its judgments." (Hamilton, The Federalist No. 78 (Willis ed. 1982) p. 394.) Accordingly, we are ill advised to announce categorical rules that will not stand the test of harder cases.

The majority acknowledges that "legislators and executive officials may take into account constitutional considerations in making discretionary decisions within their authorized sphere of action—such as whether to enact or veto proposed legislation or exercise prosecutorial discretion." But the majority views executive officers exercising "ministerial" functions as statutory automatons, denied even the scope to obey their oaths of office to follow the Constitution. Contrary to the majority, I do not find the purported distinction between discretionary and ministerial functions helpful in this context. Were not state officials performing ministerial functions when, strictly enforcing state segregation laws in the years following *Brown v. Board of Education* (1954) 347 U.S. 483, they refused to admit African-American pupils to all-White schools until the courts had applied *Brown*'s decision about a Kansas school system to each state's law? We formerly believed that school officials' oaths of office to obey the Constitution had sufficient gravity in such cases to permit them to obey the higher law, even *before* the courts had spoken state by state. So, too, did the United States Supreme Court. Today, in contrast, the majority equivocates on this point and writes that "a public official 'faithfully upholds the Constitution by complying with the mandates of the Legislature, leaving to courts the decision whether those mandates are invalid.' " But as history demonstrates, however convenient the majority's view may be in dealing with subordinate officers within a governmental hierarchy, that view is not entirely correct.

The majority's strong view of judicial power over the executive branch leads it to suggest, albeit without actually so holding, that a state may properly condition on advance judicial approval its executive officers' duty to obey even the *federal* Constitution. The majority writes, for example, that "[t]he city has not cited any case holding that the federal Constitution prohibits a state from defining the authority of a state's executive officials in a manner that requires such officials to comply with a clearly applicable statute unless and until such a statute is judicially determined to be unconstitutional" and that " 'the power of a public officer to question the constitutionality of a statute as an excuse for refusing to enforce it … *is a purely local question*'—that is, purely a question of state (not federal) law."

Given that respondent city officials have complied with our interim order to cease issuing same-sex marriage licenses, and that the constitutionality of the existing marriage statutes is presently under review, I consider the majority's determination to speculate about the limits of a state official's duty to obey the federal Constitution unnecessary and regrettable. A court should not trifle with the doctrine invoked by recalcitrant state officials, in the years following *Brown v. Board of Education,* to rationalize their delay in complying with the Fourteenth Amendment. The high court definitively repudiated this erroneous doctrine: "No state legislator or executive or judicial officer can war against the Constitution without violating his undertaking to support it." The United States Constitution, itself, immediately commands the unqualified obedience of state officials in article VI, section 3, which declares that "all executive and judicial officers, both of the United States *and of the several states,* shall be bound by oath or affirmation, to support this Constitution."

We, as a court, should not claim more power than we need to do our job effectively. In particular, strong claims of judicial power over the executive branch are best left unmade and, if they must be made, are best reserved for cases presenting a real threat to the separation of powers—a threat that provides manifest necessity for the claim, a genuine test of the claim's validity, and a suitable incentive for caution in its articulation. None of these conditions, all of which are necessary to ensure sound decisions in hard cases, is present here.

III.

In conclusion, I agree with the majority's decision to order city officials not to license additional same-sex marriages pending resolution of the constitutional challenges to the existing marriage statutes. To say more at this time is neither necessary nor wise.

Notes and Questions

1. Although Justice Werdegar agrees that the city's officials violated the Family Code and that they should be ordered to comply, she does not agree that the marriages that they illegally performed should be declared void. Is this a consistent position? Can there be an illegally performed marriage that is not void?

2. Is her position explained by the fact that the affected couples were not represented and not allowed to participate in the proceedings. In other words is Due Process the basis of her dissent? Do you agree with the majority or Justice Werdegar on this issue?

3. Justice Werdegar also disagrees with the majority's view that local officials must execute laws they believe to be unconstitutional until a judicial determination proclaims them unconstitutional. She minimizes the practical consequences of allowing officials to make this determination individually before the judicial branch has decided the matter. Is the majority correct in concluding that this would violate the fundamental notion of the rule of law and lead to chaos? Or is Justice Werdegar correct in concluding that the majority is exaggerating the practical consequences and essentially making a judicial power-grab by intruding on the executive branch?

4. Assuming that the San Francisco officials concluded that the California marriage statutes violated the Equal Protection Clause of the United States Constitution, can the California Supreme Court order local officials to enforce a law they believe violates the United States Constitution?

5. Consider how the constitutionality of same-sex marriage will be resolved in our federal system. Under the Supremacy Clause, if the denial of the right to marry is found to violate the Equal Protection Clause of the United States Constitution, then state bans on same-sex marriage will be held unconstitutional and all states will be required to adopt laws providing for same sex marriage. On the other hand, if bans on same-sex marriages do not violate the Equal Protection Clause of the United States Constitution, states will be free to ban or allow same-sex marriages under their state constitutions and state statutes. Currently, thirty-nine states bar same-sex marriage, eighteen of them by state constitutional provisions.[9] The issue is further complicated by a number of state statutes providing for domestic partnerships granting certain legal protections to same-sex couples and state civil rights statutes preventing discrimination on the basis of sexual orientation. Is this body of conflicting law a healthy reflection of a dynamic federal system? Or is there a need for national uniformity on these questions?

Same-Sex Marriage Controversy in California

As the *Lockyer* opinion and the **Note** following the majority pointed out, the California Supreme Court did "not determine the constitutionality of the California marriage statutes" at that time. But, a lot has happened since. Placed in context with *Lockyer*, here is a time-line of the major developments up to our publication date:

- February 10, 2004—San Francisco Mayor Gavin Newsom requests the San Francisco County Clerk "determine what changes should be made to the forms and documents used to apply for and issue marriage licenses in order to provide marriage licenses on a non-discriminatory basis, without regard to gender or sexual orientation"
- February 12, 2004—the county clerk begins issuing marriage licenses to same-sex couples
- February 13, 2004—two separate actions filed in San Francisco Superior Court seeking to halt the issuance of same-sex marriage licenses and marriages and a stay of the City's actions; stay denied

---

9. Wyatt Buchanan, *Profound Issues in Seattle Lawsuit*, S. F. Chron., Jan. 3, 2006, at A8.

- February 27, 2004—California Attorney General (Lockyer) filed petition for original writ of mandate, prohibition, certiorari, and/or other relief and request for immediate stay in the California Supreme Court
- August 12, 2004—California Supreme Court decides *Lockyer v. City and County of San Francisco*

Post-*Lockyer* Developments

- May 15, 2008—deciding a series of cases launched in the wake of *Lockyer*, the California Supreme Court, in a 4-3 decision, rules the existing "California legislative and initiative measures limiting marriage to opposite-sex couples violate the state constitutional rights of same-sex couples and may not be used to preclude same-sex couples from marrying" *In re Marriage Cases* (2008) 43 Cal.4th 757 [76 Cal. Rptr.3d 683, 183 P.3d 384]
- June 2, 2008—Voter initiative, later known as Proposition 8, qualifies for the November 2008 ballot; would add new section 7.5 to Article I of the California Constitution to read: "Only marriage between a man and a woman is valid or recognized in California." The change would restrict the definition of marriage to opposite-sex couples, and eliminate same-sex couples' right to marry
- July 16, 2008—California Supreme Court denies petition calling for the removal of Proposition 8 from the November ballot on the ground it was a constitutional revision that only the Legislature or a constitutional convention could place before voters
- November 4, 2008—Proposition 8 passes with 52.24% of the vote
- May 26, 2009—California Supreme Court upholds Proposition 8 against a challenge that it was a revision of the California constitution. The court also declared that the same-sex marriages performed prior to the passing of Prop 8 would remain valid, *Strauss v. Horton*, 46 Cal. 4th 364.

Federal Court Litigation Relying on the United States Constitution

- May 23, 2009 [three days before *Strauss* was decided]—Lawsuits filed in federal court (*Perry v. Schwarzenegger*, Northern District of California) challenging California's ban on same-sex marriages under the 14th Amendment to the United States Constitution.
- Issues in *Perry v. Schwarzenegger*
  - Judge Walker ordered a trial set for January 11, 2010. The trial was to address issues including "how having same-sex parents affects children and if gay unions undermine male-female marriages," the "his-

tory of discrimination against gay people," and the "effects on gay people of prejudice."

- Plaintiffs sought prove that marriage is a fundamental right; that depriving gays and lesbians the right to marry hurts them and hurts their children; and there was no reason, no societal benefit in not allowing them to get married
- Defendants argued only that the people have the "right to vote on what is best."

• August 4, 2010—Judge Walker rules in favor of Plaintiffs, overturning Proposition 8 based on both the Due Process and Equal Protection clauses of the 14th Amendment, and
Concludes that California has no rational basis or vested interest in denying gays or lesbians marriage licenses
The court's opinion includes 80 findings of fact

• August 4, 2010—Defendant intervenors filed notice of appeal to the Ninth Circuit Court of Appeals; Attorney General Jerry Brown and Governor Schwarzenegger had refused to defend the lawsuit; in November 2010, Jerry Brown was elected Governor and Kamela Harris Attorney General; both continued to decline the defense of Proposition 8 in court; Governor Brown took office January 3, 2011

• Imperial County, denied right to intervene as Defendant, appealed that denial and the decision

• August 12, 2010—Defendant-Intervenors filed "emergency motion" in 9th Circuit for stay of the court's decision pending appeal; granted August 16, 2010; ordered expedited briefing; August 17, 2010 expedited briefing ordered on Imperial County appeal

• December 6, 2010—Ninth Circuit panel of Judges Stephen Reinhardt, Sidney Hawkins, and N. Randy Smith heard oral argument; motion to disqualify Reinhardt denied

• January 4, 2011—Ninth Circuit certified the question of whether initiative backers had sufficient interest to defend the law to the California Supreme Court; stayed appeal pending response from California Supreme Court; dismissed Imperial County appeal for lack of standing

• February 16, 2011—California Supreme Court agreed to address the request and hear argument September 6, 2011

• Judge Vaughn Walker retired February 2011, and revealed his same-sex relationship with a male doctor for the past10 years

• April 25, 2011—supporters of Proposition 8 moved to vacate the decision for Judge Walker's failure to disclose the relationship and "direct personal interest in the outcome of the case"

- Motion to vacate heard by United States District Court Judge James Ware on June 13, 2011; the motion was denied June 14, 2011 ("Requiring recusal because a court issued an injunction that could provide some speculative future benefit to the presiding judge solely on the basis of the fact that the judge belongs to the class against whom the unconstitutional law was directed would lead to a Section 455(b)(4) standard that required recusal of minority judges in most, if not all, civil rights cases. Congress could not have intended such an unworkable recusal statute.")
- November 17, 2011—The California Supreme Court holds that the non-governmental proponents of Proposition 8 have legal standing to defend the Proposition as a matter of California state law, *Perry v. Brown*, 134 Cal. Rptr. 3d 499 (2011) [case name changed with Brown's inauguration as Governor]
- February 7, 2012—the Ninth Circuit, in a 2–1 opinion by Judge Reinhardt, holds:
  - The official sponsors of Proposition 8 were entitled to appeal Judge Walker's decision given the elected officials' refusal to do so;
  - The denial of the sponsors' request to vacate the decision due to Judge Walker's relationship with his same-sex partner is affirmed
  - Proposition 8, by using the initiative power of California to target a minority group and withdraw the right to marry to that group, violates the Equal Protection Clause of the 14th Amendment; Judge Smith concurred in part (on standing and affirming the denial of the vacation request) and dissented in part (from the finding that Proposition 8 is unconstitutional)
- February 21, 2012—Proposition 8 proponents seek *en banc* review by the entire Ninth Circuit (in this circuit alone, *en banc* review is done by a panel of 11 of the 29 judges)
- June 5, 2012—Ninth Circuit denies request to hear appeal *en banc*

Glossary

Note to our Students: Over the years our students have suggested that a glossary would be very helpful because legal jargon can be a barrier to understanding. It can be frustrating, confusing, and downright intimidating. Conscientious students try to look words up in a comprehensive legal dictionary only to be stymied by the extensive and arcane definitions. We have hesitated to provide a glossary for fear of misleading students into thinking that there is a fixed meaning for every legal term. In fact, as with language generally, legal words and usage are hard to pin down definitively. Many words have multiple and specialized meanings. Sometimes we use words precisely, and sometimes we use them loosely. In truth, the language of the law cannot be learned by studying a set of definitions. We learn this language over time and in context. Despite our misgivings, we offer this simple glossary to help you begin to build a useful professional vocabulary.

Ad Hoc: "For this;" for this special purpose.

ADR: Alternative dispute resolution. ADR is the collective term used to describe processes to resolve disputes outside of formal litigation including mediation, arbitration, and early neutral evaluation.

A Fortiori: "All the more so;" a term of logic, long ago drafted into legal service to bolster the obvious. Regarding this term, one dictionary says: "let it die." But it's fun to say.

Answer: The written pleading filed by a defendant in a lawsuit that responds to the plaintiff's allegations of wrongdoing and sets out the defendant's affirmative defenses (reasons why the plaintiff's claims are legally invalid).

American Bar Association (ABA): A voluntary association of lawyers dedicated to improving the administration of justice, the standards of the profession, and legal education.

Amicus Curiae (amici): "Friend of the court;" someone not a party to the lawsuit, but usually favoring one of the parties, who is permitted to make an argument to the court (the judge, not the jury). The argument is usually in writing in a brief filed with an appellate court.

Association of American Law Schools (AALS): An organization of reputable law schools that comply with a set of national standards for legal education.

Bill of Attainder: A legislative act that inflicts punishment on named persons or a group of persons without a judicial trial. Historically, an English bill of attainder applied to capital offenses. The United States Constitution prohibits bills of attainder.

Binding Authority: Legal authority that a court is obligated to follow. For example, a trial court is required to follow the statutes and decisions of higher courts within its jurisdiction.

Blackstone: *Blackstone's Commentaries on the Common Law* is an 18th century treatise composed of Blackstone's Oxford lectures; Blackstone is regarded as one of the most influential authorities on the common law.

Brief: (1) A written argument prepared by one side in a lawsuit to explain its position to the judge or judges hearing the case; (2) a summary of a judicial opinion composed by a law student to analyze the case, prepare for class, and study for examinations.

Cause of Action: A set of facts sufficient to support a valid lawsuit; the legal theory on which a lawsuit is based. To survive an early attempt by the defendant to have the court dismiss a lawsuit, the complaint (a pleading filed in court) must state a cause of action.

Certiorari: A writ (order) issued by the United States Supreme Court when it determines that it will exercise its discretionary authority to review a decision by a federal appellate court or state court on a question of federal law.

Choice of law: When the law of more than one jurisdiction is arguably applicable to the resolution of a legal question, the court is required to chose which law to apply. This issue is referred to as a "choice of law" question.

Class Action: Generally, a suit by (sometimes against) a representative of a class: a large number of people "similarly situated" as to a claim that affects them all. The courts will permit class actions where it would be a great burden to have each individual prosecute a separate lawsuit.

Code: A compilation of legislative enactments (statutes) arranged by subject matter. For example, in most states there is a vehicle code, a code of civil procedure, a criminal code, a family law code, etc.

Common law: The legal system developed in England beginning in the middle ages wherein judges developed legal doctrines and applied them to cases. In the common law system, the courts carefully consider the facts of the case to be decided and apply the doctrines that have been developed to resolve cases having similar facts.

Complaint: The first pleading filed in a lawsuit by a plaintiff stating the facts showing that the defendant has committed a wrong or inflicted a harm and requesting specific relief or a remedy from the court.

Conflict of laws: In many instances the laws of more than one jurisdiction may apply to an issue and may produce different result. This area of legal disputes is covered by the legal rules governing conflicts of law.

Demurrer: A written statement filed court which admits for the sake of argument that the facts alleged in the complaint (plaintiff) or a defense (defendant) are true, but that they still do not constitute, respectively, a cause of action or a defense. Simply put, a response to a pleading that says, "Sure, that's all true. But, so what? You'll still don't have any legal rights to assert against me." To file a demurrer is to demur.

De Novo: Completely new from the start. Where appropriate, often because of procedural irregularities in the first trial, a court may order a trial de novo, meaning that a completely new trial will take place. When an appellate court reviews a case, sometimes the review is de novo (from the beginning) and sometimes great deference is given to the lower court. The nature of the review depends on the procedural posture of the case.

Deposition: The testimony of a witness under oath taken upon oral questions or written interrogatories, not in open court, but in pretrial proceedings authorized by the rules of procedure; a pretrial discovery device by which one party (through a lawyer) asks questions of the other party or of a witness.

Discretionary duty: A discretionary duty is one where the government official exercises his or her discretion in discharging official duties. See ministerial duty.

Disposition: The resolution of a matter; a judge's ruling is commonly referred to as the disposition, regardless of level of resolution.

Ejusdem Generis: A canon of statutory construction providing that the interpretation of a catch-all general description should be limited to the class of things which are specifically described.

En banc review: Three-judge panels initially decide appeals in the federal court system. If other members of the bench wish to have a case decided by all the members of the court, they may decide to review the three-judge decision "en banc" (by the entire bench).

Equity: A term with multiple meanings: (1) fairness; (2) the name for a system of courts that originated with the English courts of chancery which addressed problems that the existing laws did not fairly resolve. Equity courts administer a distinctive bundle of powers, procedures, and remedies different from the courts of law. In the United States, courts of law and courts of equity have been unified but procedural and remedial distinctions remain.

Estoppel: A bar against doing something or claiming something that arises in the interest of fairness to the other side. For example, when a person makes a representation on which another relies, the first person may be estopped from denying the truth of the representation.

Ex Post Facto: "From what is done afterwards;" a law making criminal what was innocent when done, or retroactively changing the punishment or manner of proof of a criminal act to the detriment of the accused.

Expressio Unius Est Exclusio Alterius: "Expression of the one is exclusion of the other;" When something but not everything of the same category has been expressed, one may infer that omissions are deliberate.

Federalism: The division of power between the federal and state governments. Under our Constitution, power not specifically granted to the federal government is reserved to the states or the people. The proper scope of federal authority has both historical and contemporary significance.

Federal Jurisdiction: Federal courts have limited jurisdiction. They can only resolve cases where the controversy involves a federal question or diversity of citizenship. Federal question jurisdiction arises where the dispute involves an issue of federal constitutional, statutory or common law. Diversity jurisdiction arises where the parties reside in different states or different countries.

Impeachment: A formal accusation by a designated public body charging high public officials or judges with misconduct in office.

Information: A formal written statement in which a prosecutor charges a named person with commission of a specific crime. The information is the charge made by the prosecutor, without the intervention of a grand jury.

Insolvent (antonym of solvent): Unable to pay debts as they become due; often used in tort law to describe a defendant who is unable to pay an awarded judgment.

Invitee: One invited onto property concerning the occupier's business; a status which may be decisive or a factor in determining the standards of liability of an occupier of land to those who are injured on the property; not a social visitor or trespasser.

Judgment Notwithstanding the Verdict (JNOV): A judgment given in favor of the side that has lost by verdict; a determination by the judge that despite the jury's conclusion to the contrary the other side should have prevailed as a matter of law.

Judicial review: Judicial review has two meanings: (1) it refers to the role of appellate courts in reviewing lower court decisions for errors of law; and (2) it refers to the role of the courts in determining whether statutes adopted by the legislature are constitutional.

Jurisdiction: The right and power of a court to hear and determine cases and to administer a system of justice; the authorized power of a court over the persons in court or over the subject matter of the case; the geographical area within which a court has the power to operate.

Justiciable: Capable of being resolved in a court of law or equity; a justiciable controversy is one that can be heard under our constitutional system and that is reserved for the courts.

Law: A word with multiple meanings: (1) practices and remedies included in law; (2) a legislative enactment (statute); (3) used in opposition to "fact," the term refers to legal questions for the court to decide as opposed to factual questions for the jury to decide; (4) used in opposition to "equity," the term refers to a court with jurisdiction to hear cases at law and provide legal remedies, specifically money damages.

Litigate; litigation: To litigate is to participate as a party to legal proceedings in court. Litigation means lawsuit.

Loan Repayment Assistance Program (LRAP): A number of law schools have adopted loan repayment assistance programs to ease the law school debt burden of graduates going into public interest and public service careers.

Ministerial duty: A ministerial duty is one where the government official is required to perform in a prescribed manner in accordance with legal authority regardless of his or her own judgment of the propriety or wisdom of the action.

Multiple Jurisdictional Practice: While admission to practice law has traditionally been granted on a state-by-state basis, a number of jurisidictions have developed rules and procedures permitting lawyers admitted in one state to practice in a sister state.

Nonsuit: Judgment against a plaintiff who fails to go forward with a case, or whose evidence at trial is insufficient as a matter of law to require presentation of a defense.

Noscitur a sociis: A canon of statutory construction which provides that the meaning of a word should be construed in context.

Ombudsman: An official or semi-official office or person to which people may come with grievances connected with the government. The ombudsman stands between, and represents, the citizen before the government.

Persuasive authority: A legal authority which a court is not legally obligated to follow, but which it may be persuaded to follow. For example, if there is no decision on point in a state, it may be persuaded to follow the decisions of sister states.

Pleading: A written document filed in court which sets forth a cause of action, defense, or part of either.

Precedent: A prior judicial decision involving similar factual and legal issues. Under the doctrine of *stare decisis*, courts follow precedents to ensure stability, predictability and fairness.

Preemption: When Congress has adopted a statute that is intended to foreclose any state regulation of the subject, additional regulation by the states is "preempted."

Probate: The gamut of procedures of judicial supervision over the administration of decedents' estates and of adjudication connected with decedents' estates; the proving and interpretation of wills.

Pro Bono: "For the public good;" serving for no fee or a reduced fee.

Pro hac vice: When a lawyer from a sister state has a special need to represent a client in another state, he or she may be permitted to practice in that state on that legal matter only.

Pro se: "In one's own behalf;" one is acting pro se in a lawsuit when proceeding without a lawyer.

Proximate Cause: A vague label for a sufficient causal and legal connection between conduct and harm to impose liability for the conduct; widely used throughout the law, especially in tort law and criminal law. You'll spend weeks on this concept in your first-year classes.

Removal: If a plaintiff files an action in state court, the defendant may have it removed to federal court provided that federal jurisdiction exists (i.e., the case involves a federal question or diversity of citizenship).

Rescission: The act of rescinding, which is to undo, as distinguished from ending, canceling, or terminating. For example, the court may rescind a contract which was signed based on fraudulent misrepresentations.

Separation of powers: Under the United States Constitution, each branch of government is given specific powers and checks on other branches. If one branch exceeds its proper authority, it has violated the separation of powers.

Sine Qua Non: "Without which not;" that without which the thing cannot be; an indispensable requisite or condition.

Sovereign: Having supreme political power within a particular area and over the relations of that area and its people with others beyond that area, as a sovereign nation. The quality of having that power is described as sovereignty.

Stare decisis: The doctrine which requires courts to follow prior decisions on an issue of law (precedent).

Statute: A validly adopted law originating in the legislature. Legislation begins when bills are introduced; when a bill is formally enacted it becomes a statute.

Sua Sponte: "Of one's own accord, spontaneously;" on its own initiative; said of a judge raising a legal point at a hearing without prompting from the litigants (and often resented by the litigants).

Summary Judgment: Judgment without a trial, upon the judge's determination that pleadings and affidavits show there is not a "genuine" issue of fact to be tried; a determination that reasonable people cannot reach different conclusions with respect to the facts and that therefore the matter may be resolved as a question of law.

Syllogism: A deductive scheme of formal argument including a major premise, a minor premise, and a conclusion.

Tort: A civil wrong actionable in court and remedied by money damages. Examples include assault, battery, trespass, and defamation.

Venue: The proper place of trial (geographically).

Writ: A court's written order.

Writ of Mandate (or writ of mandamus): An order to a lower court, or to an individual, a corporation, or a unit of government, directing performance of a public duty. A writ of mandate is issued when no other remedy is realistically available.

Index